iPhoto® '11

PORTABLE GENIUS

iPhoto® '11
PORTABLE GENIUS

by Brad Miser

Wiley Publishing, Inc.

iPhoto® '11 Portable Genius

Published by
Wiley Publishing, Inc.
10475 Crosspoint Blvd.
Indianapolis, IN 46256
www.wiley.com

Copyright © 2011 by Wiley Publishing, Inc., Indianapolis, Indiana

Published simultaneously in Canada

ISBN: 978-0-470-64202-3

Manufactured in the United States of America

10 9 8 7 6 5 4 3 2 1

For general information on our other products and services or to obtain technical support, please contact our Customer Care Department within the U.S. at (877) 762-2974, outside the U.S. at (317) 572-3993 or fax (317) 572-4002.

Wiley also publishes its books in a variety of electronic formats. Some content that appears in print may not be available in electronic books.

Library of Congress Control Number: 2010943538

WILEY

About the Author

Brad Miser has written more than 40 books on technology with the goal of helping people learn to get the most out of that technology as easily and quickly as possible. In addition to *iPhoto '11 Portable Genius*, Brad has written *MacBook Pro Portable Genius (2nd Edition)*, *My iPhone (4th Edition)*, *Teach Yourself Visually MacBook Air*, *Teach Yourself Visually MacBook*, *MacBook Portable Genius (2nd Edition)*, *My iPod touch (2nd Edition)*, and *Special Edition Using Mac OS X Leopard*. He also has been a coauthor, development editor, or technical editor on more than 50 other titles.

Brad has been a solutions consultant, the director of product and customer services, and the manager of education and support services for several software development companies. Previously, he was the lead proposal specialist for an aircraft engine manufacturer, a development editor for a computer book publisher, and a civilian aviation test officer/engineer for the U.S. Army. Brad holds a Bachelor of Science degree in mechanical engineering from California Polytechnic State University at San Luis Obispo and has received advanced education in maintainability engineering, business, and other topics.

In addition to his passion for silicon-based technology, Brad enjoys his steel-based technology, a.k.a. his motorcycle, whenever and wherever possible. Originally from California, Brad now lives in Indiana with his wife Amy; their three daughters, Jill, Emily, and Grace; and a rabbit.

Brad would love to hear about your experiences with this book (the good, the bad, and the ugly). You can write to him at bradmacosx@me.com.

Credits

Senior Acquisitions Editor
Stephanie McComb

Project Editor
Kristin Vorce

Technical Editor
Paul Sihvonen-Binder

Senior Copy Editor
Kim Heusel

Editorial Director
Robyn Siesky

Editorial Manager
Rosemarie Graham

Vice President and Group Executive Publisher
Richard Swadley

Vice President and Executive Publisher
Barry Pruett

Business Manager
Amy Knies

Senior Marketing Manager
Sandy Smith

Project Coordinator
Sheree Montgomery

Graphics and Production Specialists
Jennifer Henry
Andrea Hornberger

Quality Control Technician
John Greenough

Proofreading
Linda Seifert

Indexing
Rebecca R. Plunkett

The probability that we may fall in the struggle ought not to deter us from the support of a cause we believe to be just; it shall not deter me.

—Abraham Lincoln

Acknowledgments

While my name is on the cover, it takes many people to build a book like this one. Thanks to Stephanie McComb, with whom this project had its genesis and who allowed me to be involved. Kristin Vorce deserves lots of credit for keeping the project on track and on target; I'm sure working with me was a challenge at times. Paul Sihvonen-Binder did a great job of keeping me on my toes to make sure this book contains fewer technical gaffs than it would have. Kim Heusel transformed my stumbling, bumbling text into something people can read and understand. Lastly, thanks to all the people on the Wiley team who handle the other, and equally important, parts of the process, such as production, sales, proofreading, and indexing.

On my personal team, I'd like to thank my wife Amy for her tolerance of the author lifestyle, which is both odd and challenging. My delightful daughters, Jill, Emily, and Grace, are always a source of joy and inspiration for all that I do, and for which I'm ever grateful.

Contents

chapter 7

How Else Can I Find My Photos?   108

chapter 8

What Can I Do to Improve
My Photos?   118

chapter 11

How Can I Use Facebook to Share Photos? 178

chapter 12

How Can I Use Flickr to Share Photos? 194

chapter 13

What Can I Do with the Slideshow Feature?   210

chapter 14

How Can I Create Photo Books?   240

chapter 16

chapter 15

chapter 17

What Else Can I Do with Photos? 306

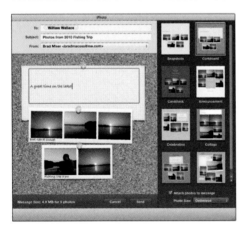

chapter 18

What Can I Do to Protect
My Photos? 324

Introduction

Technology is at its best when it enables you to focus more on what you are doing rather than how you are doing it. iPhoto is definitely technology at its best. It does so many things that it takes a whole book to describe them to you — this book, in fact. *iPhoto '11 Portable Genius* is your companion: It helps you get going with iPhoto and quickly improve your skills so that you'll be doing things with photos that will amaze and delight you.

iPhoto is built on its library, which is where you collect, label (tag), and organize your photos. Some of the coolest tag features are Faces, which identifies the people in your photos and helps you find photos with specific people in them, and Places, which serves a similar purpose for the locations associated with your pictures. You can add photos to your library from a digital camera, an iPhone, an iPod touch, from the Web, and many other sources. Of course, you can improve your photos by editing them. You can view your photos in collections iPhoto creates for you automatically or in slideshows or photo albums that you create. And speaking of projects, you can do all kinds of creative things with your photos, such as building photo books, designing cards, and creating calendars personalized with your photos. You can put amazing slideshows of your photos on DVD. And you can share your photos online many ways, including through MobileMe, Facebook, iWeb, and Flickr. All this photographic power is delivered in an intuitive interface, so it's easy to become an iPhoto pro in no time.

iPhoto definitely plays well with the other iLife applications, too. For example, you can use your photos to create Web pages in iWeb or to create slideshows in iDVD. And you can access your photos in the other applications, such as adding them to iMovie projects.

As you read through this book, you get information about the many tricks in iPhoto's bag. To help you find the ones that interest you most, this book is organized by common questions. Take a look at the Table of Contents to see which chapters address the questions you have. For in-depth answers, flip to specific chapters and get started. While the book explains the concepts you need to know, it focuses more on leading you through tasks step by step. I recommend keeping the book next to your trusty Mac so you experience iPhoto as you read about it.

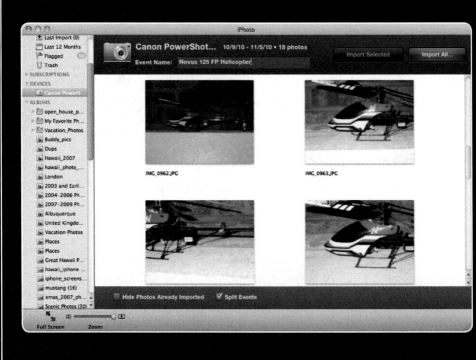

iPhoto empowers you to do amazing things with the photos and other images you store in your iPhoto library. Of course, to do those amazing things, you have to first stock your library with pictures and other images. You can do this a number of ways. The most obvious method is importing photos from a digital camera, but you can also import photos from an iPhone, an iPod touch, an iPad, DVDs, email, and other places on your computer. You should also configure fundamental iPhoto preferences, make sure you are using the current version, and learn about iPhoto's modes.

Adding Photos and Other Images to Your Photo Library

You store all the contents you manipulate with iPhoto's tools in the iPhoto library. It almost goes without saying (but I'll say it anyway) that you can import photos from a digital camera into your library, but that is just one source for images. You can also import photos, images saved from emails, and screenshots using an iPhone, iPod touch, or iPad (current versions of iPads don't have cameras, but you can still import the latter two types of images from one). If you have images on a DVD, you can import them from that into iPhoto as well. Email is a common way people share photos; when you receive images attached to emails, you can add them to your library. Last, and probably least known but very useful, you can import image files from your Mac's desktop into the library.

Importing photos from a camera or an Apple mobile device

Most digital cameras are compatible with iPhoto, meaning that iPhoto recognizes the camera and moves photos you take from it into your iPhoto library.

Apple's iPhone and iPod touch (fourth generation and later) include a digital camera and an associated application that you can use to snap photos. Of course, iPhones and iPod touches are compatible with iPhoto, so if you are using one of these devices to take photos, you don't need to worry about its compatibility. You import photos from those devices into iPhoto just like you import photos from a camera. You can also import images you save from emails and screenshots you capture on these devices, as well as on an iPad, just as easily.

Before you start moving photos into your library, take a moment to make sure iPhoto is configured for easy importing.

Configuring iPhoto to open when you connect a device

Because iPhoto is the tool you'll use for importing images from your camera or other devices, ensure that it is the application your Mac opens and uses whenever you connect a camera or Apple mobile device to it. Choose iPhoto ⇨ Preferences, and click the General tab. On the Connecting camera opens pop-up menu, choose iPhoto. Close the Preferences window.

Each time you connect your camera or other device (such as an iPhone) with photos ready to import to your Mac, iPhoto opens (or becomes active if it is open in the background) and mounts the device so its images are ready to import.

Camera Shopping?

If you already have a camera, you can tell if it is compatible with iPhoto by trying to import photos from it. If you are able to import photos, you're good to go. If you are shopping for a new camera, make sure it is compatible with iPhoto. The good news is that any camera that is compatible with the Picture Transfer Protocol (PTP) is, and most modern cameras are PTP compatible.

You can find information about specific camera models on Web sites such as www. apple.com, Amazon.com, or the camera manufacturer's Web site. In addition to the technical specifications about the cameras, reading reviews by current owners is often enlightening, particularly those from users who report problems using a camera with a Mac and iPhoto. If you can't find information about a specific model you are considering, but do find information about an earlier version of a model of the same line that is compatible with iPhoto, the later version is very likely to be compatible as well.

Be wary when buying an older camera or one that is exceptionally inexpensive because it might use some proprietary or outdated formats that aren't compatible with iPhoto.

Note   Your Mac detects when you connect an iPhone, iPod touch, or iPad that has photos stored on it that you haven't imported into iPhoto yet. iPhoto opens and you move into Import mode automatically. When you connect one of these devices that doesn't have images ready to import, iPhoto remains in its current state, such as closed (if it isn't open) or in the background (if it is running).

Defining an event

Events are groups of photos captured within a specific time period (you learn much more about using events in Chapter 2). When you import photos from a camera, by default, iPhoto automatically organizes the photos you import by grouping them into events. By default, an event is defined as all the photos captured on the same day. You can change this definition to better suit your purposes:

1. **Press ⌘+, (comma).** The iPhoto Preferences dialog opens.

2. **Click the General tab.**

3. **On the Autosplit into Events pop-up menu, select the length of time within which photos should be grouped into an event, as shown in Figure 1.1.** The options are One event per day (default), One event per week, Two-hour gaps, or Eight-hour gaps.

4. **Close the Preferences dialog.**

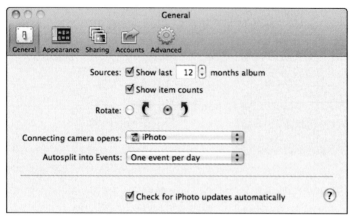

1.1 Use the Autosplit into Events pop-up menu to determine how long an event is.

Importing all or selected photos from a device

To import photos from a camera or an Apple mobile device into your library, perform the following steps:

1. **Connect the camera or other device to your Mac (if the device isn't on already, power it up).** iPhoto opens, the camera or other device is mounted, and you see it selected on the Source pane. In the Browsing pane, you see the photos on the device along with the import tools, as shown in Figure 1.2.

Note If the camera doesn't appear on the Source pane, make sure it is in Playback mode.

2. **In the Event Name box, type a name for the event for which you are importing photos.** When you name an event, that name is applied only to the oldest event being imported. All other events come in as untitled events, which you can rename at a later time (you learn how in Chapter 2). For example, if you took some photos today, yesterday, and three days ago, the event name is only applied to the photos you took three days ago; the rest are collected in untitled events.

Note iTunes also opens automatically when you connect an iPhone, iPod, or iPad to your Mac. The sync process starts in iTunes; sometimes, this takes place before you can import photos from the device into iPhoto. Just wait a few moments and iPhoto becomes ready to start the import.

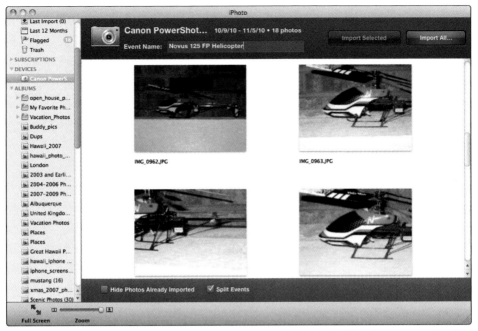

1.2 When you select a camera or other device on the Source pane, you see the photos it contains along with the import tools.

3. **If you don't want events to be created for photos based on when they were cap-tured, deselect the Split Events check box.** The most appropriate time to deselect this check box is when the photos you are importing are for an event that occurred over a longer period of time than you have currently defined as an event, and you want to col-lect these photos into a single group, such as a collection of pictures you've taken during a vacation. When the check box is selected, the imported photos are split into events based on when you took the photos. In most cases, you should leave this check box selected; you can reorganize the events iPhoto creates at any time, but automatic event creation gives you a good start.

4. **If the device has photos you've already imported that you don't want to see, select the Hide Photos Already Imported check box.** This happens when you don't delete photos from a device after importing them. If those photos are hidden, they are ignored during the import process. If you show those photos, you can select them and import them again, or if you import all photos, you are prompted to deal with the duplicates. If the device doesn't have any photos that were imported previously, this check box is deselected automatically.

5. **To import images do one of the following:**

 - To import all the images on the camera or iPhone, click Import All.

 - To import only specific images, select the images you want to import and click Import Selected. (Hold down the ⌘ key while you click images to select multiple images at once.)

The images are imported from the camera or other device into the library. As they are imported, you see a preview of each image. When the process is complete, you are prompted to keep the photos on the device or to erase them.

6. **To delete the photos you've imported from the device, click Delete Photos; to leave the photos on the device, click Keep Photos.** If you delete the photos, the photos you imported are deleted from the device's memory. If you elect to keep the photos, they are hidden automatically the next time you import photos from the device (or you can show them, in which case, you have to deal with duplicates, as I explain in the next section). When you complete the import process, the Last Import source is selected on the Source pane, and you see the photos you imported in the Browsing pane, as shown in Figure 1.3. The photos are now included in your iPhoto library and are ready for you to view and use.

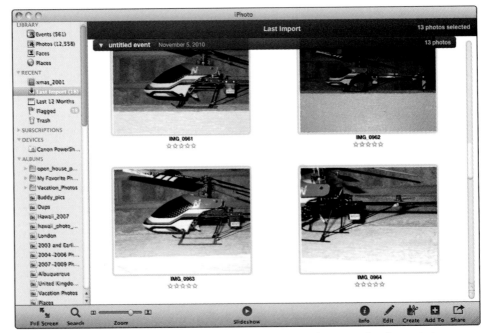

1.3 When the import process is complete, the Last Import source shows you the photos that are now part of your library.

If your Mac has a Secure Digital (SD) card slot, you can import photos directly from a device's memory card by inserting that card into the Mac's SD slot. This has the benefit that you don't need a cable; just take the card out of the camera (if it uses a card of a different kind, you need to place the card into an SD adapter first) and insert it into your Mac. The card is mounted in iPhoto and you can import its images using the same process as for a camera or other device.

Dealing with duplicates during import

If you try to import photos that are already in your library, iPhoto warns you with a Duplicate Photo dialog, as shown in Figure 1.4. The duplicate photo on the device appears on the left and the photo stored in your iPhoto library appears on the right. If you want to import the photo again, click Import; this creates a duplicate of the photo in your library. To ignore the photo (not import it again), click Don't Import. If you want the same decision applied to all the duplicate photos on the device, select the Apply to all duplicates check box. If you don't select this box, you're prompted to make a decision about each duplicate photo individually.

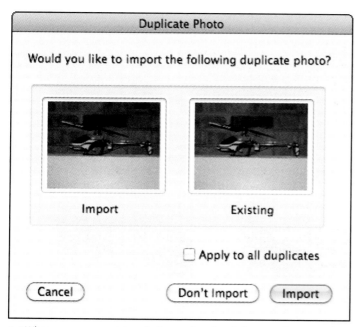

1.4 When a camera contains photos you've already imported, you see the Duplicate Photo dialog.

Date, Time, and Location

All digital cameras time and date stamp the photos they capture automatically, which is useful for organizing and finding photos. iPhoto uses this date and time information when you import photos to organize them into events. (Recall that the default definition of an event is all the photos taken on the same day.) As you learn in Chapter 2, you can use events to view, tag, and search for photos you want to work with.

iPhoto also can associate photos with locations, called Places. This is another really useful way to organize photos because it gives you a logical way to group photos for specific purposes. For example, when you take photos while you are traveling, iPhoto can group the photos you take by the places you take them. You can use a map to find photos you are interested in.

Some cameras tag the photos you take with their location, similarly to how they tag photos with time and date information. The camera on Apple's iPhone uses its built-in GPS to accomplish this. When you import photos from an iPhone, they are associated with locations automatically. If you shop for a new camera, look for this capability. While you can tag photos with location information manually, it's easier if the camera does it for you automatically.

Importing photos from a DVD

A DVD is a great way to store photos for viewing and protection. You can import photos from a DVD to your iPhoto library; how you do this depends on the specific kind of DVD you are working with. In the following sections, you learn how to import photos from a data DVD, a DVD created in iPhoto, and a DVD created with iDVD.

Importing photos from a data DVD

A data DVD is one on which photos are stored as files, just as you would store any file on a DVD using the Finder's Burn command. Depending on how the images were created, they might or might not have information iPhoto stores with photos, such as time and date, location, and so on, but you can import the images on a disc and add that information later. To import photos from a data DVD, do the following:

1. **Insert the DVD into your Mac's drive.**
2. **In iPhoto, choose File ⇨ Import to Library.** The Import Photos dialog appears.
3. **Select the DVD.**

4. **Select the photos on the DVD that you want to import, as shown in Figure 1.5.**

5. **Click Import.** The photos you selected are imported to your library, the Last Import source is selected, and you see the photos you've added.

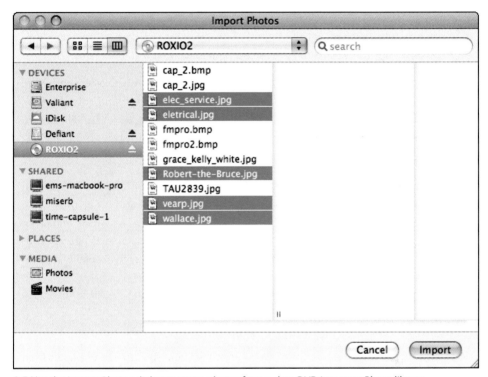

1.5 Use the Import Photos dialog to move photos from a data DVD into your Photo library.

Importing photos from an iPhoto DVD

You learn later in this book that you can use iPhoto to burn photos in its library to a DVD. When you do this, the structure and attributes applied by iPhoto in the library are maintained; this means when you import these photos, iPhoto recognizes them and maintains the same attributes. To import photos from a DVD created with iPhoto, perform the following steps:

1. **Insert the DVD into your Mac's drive.** The DVD is recognized as an iPhoto DVD, is mounted in the SHARED section on the Source pane in iPhoto, and is selected.

2. **Click the disc's expansion triangle.** You see all the contents on the disc, such as its library sources (Events, Places, Last 12 Months, and so on), photo albums, and folders.

3. **Select the source containing the photos you want to add to the library.** You see the photos in the selected source in the Browsing pane.

11

4. **Select and drag the photos you want to import from the Browsing pane onto the Photos source in your library, as shown in Figure 1.6.** As you drag, the number of photos you are moving appears next to the pointer. When the Photos source is high-lighted, release the mouse button. The photos you selected are imported to your library. If there are duplicates in the photos you select, you're prompted to deal with them just as you are when you import images from a device. When the process is complete, the Last Import source is selected and you see the photos you added to the library.

5. **Click the DVD's Eject button to eject it.**

1.6 Drag photos from an iPhoto DVD onto your library to import them.

Importing photos from an iDVD DVD

iDVD enables you to create DVDs with slideshows you can watch similarly to how you view movie DVDs you create. When you create an iDVD slideshow using photos stored in iPhoto, you can set iDVD to also add the individual image files from the slideshow to the disc along with the slideshow itself. In such a case, you can then import the image files from the iDVD disc to your iPhoto library. Here's how:

1. **Insert the DVD into your Mac's drive.** The DVD Player application opens and you see the disc's main menu as it starts to play.

2. **Quit DVD Player.**

3. **In iPhoto, choose File ⇨ Import to Library.** The Import Photos dialog appears.

4. **Select the DVD.**

5. **Open the folder called** *discname* **DVD DVD-ROM Contents, where** *discname* **is the name of the iDVD disc.**

6. **Select the Slideshows folder, then select the slideshow that contains images you want to import.**

7. **Select the Originals folder within that folder, as shown in Figure 1.7.**

8. **Select the images you want to import and click Import.** The photos you selected are imported to your library. (If some of the images are already in your library, you're prompted to deal with the duplicates.) When the process is complete, the Last Import source is selected and you see the photos you added to your library.

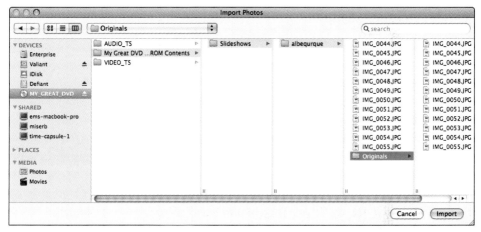

1.7 You have to drill down within an iDVD disc to get the photos you want to import to your library.

Importing photos attached to email

Email is a great way to share photos with others (in Chapter 17, you learn how you can email photos from directly within iPhoto). When you receive an email with photos attached, you can add them to your library. How you do this depends on how the photos are attached.

If the photos are attached as individual files and you use Mac OS X's Mail application, add them to iPhoto as follows:

1. **Open the email containing the photos.** In the body of the message, you see the photos that are attached to it.

2. **Click Save and on the resulting menu, select Add to iPhoto, as shown in Figure 1.8.** The photos are imported and added to your library.

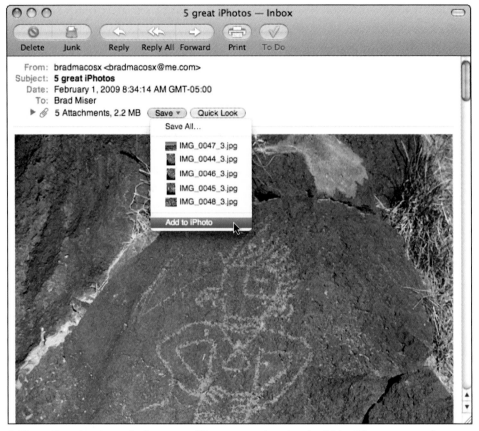

1.8 Importing photos attached to an email is as easy as choosing the Add to iPhoto command.

If the photos are attached as a single, compressed file (such as a ZIP file) and you use the Mail application, use these steps:

1. **Open the email containing the compressed file.**

2. **Click Save.** The compressed file is saved to your Downloads folder.

3. **Move to the compressed file and double-click it.** The file expands and you see a folder containing the photos that were in the compressed file.

4. **Import the files from the desktop to your library (see the steps in the next section for details).**

If you don't use the Mail application, the steps you use to import photos attached to messages are similar to the previous steps, but the details might be slightly different. First, save the attached images to your desktop. Second, import the images from the desktop to your library.

Importing files from the desktop

Because the word photo is in its name, you might think iPhoto is designed to work mostly with photographs, and it is. However, you can add many kinds of image files to your library, where you can then use the same tools on those images that you use on your photos. For example, if you take screenshots of your desktop, you might want to crop those images, make improvements to them, or just keep your desktop images organized. You can add these images to your library where you can act on them just like photos you take with a camera. Likewise, you can add images you've downloaded from the Web to your library.

iPhoto fully supports these file types:

- **JPEG (Joint Photographic Experts Group).** Most cameras use the JPEG format to create photo files, and many photos you encounter on the Web and in other places are in this format.

- **TIFF (Tagged Interchange File Format).** TIFF files are useful for many kinds of images. For example, screenshots you take of your desktop are often TIFF files.

- **RAW.** RAW image files are not compressed as JPEG files are and, therefore, do not require additional processing before they display correctly. The benefit to this file type is that it contains more information than compressed file types. You can work with RAW files in iPhoto. Some high-end cameras capture images in this format.

You can import files of other types, such as GIF (Graphics Interchange Format), but they might or might not work correctly. You don't lose anything if you try to import a specific file of another type. If the file doesn't work correctly, just delete it from your library.

One thing to keep in mind when you work with images of other types that you import from the desktop is the resolution of those images along with their default size. Images you capture with a camera or later-generation iPhone are likely to have a relatively high resolution, so they look good and are useable at many sizes in many formats (on-screen, prints, and so on). However, images you import from the desktop can be various resolutions; low-resolution images are of lower quality and might not be useable for the purpose you have in mind. Many of the images you download from the Web are a lower resolution than those you typically capture with a camera or iPhone.

You can check out the type, resolution, and dimensions of an image on your desktop by performing the following steps:

1. **Open a Finder window in Columns view.**

2. **Move to and select the file.** A preview of the file appears along with information about its type, size, and dimensions, as shown in Figure 1.9.

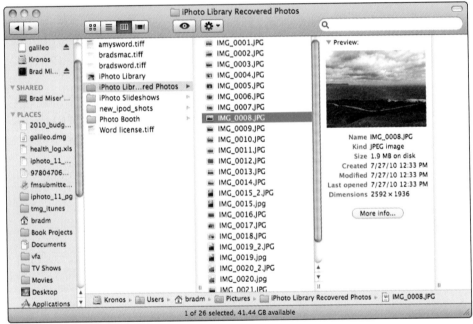

1.9 You can view information about an image file, such as its type and size, using the Preview column of a Finder window.

In many cases, you'll see file size and dimension information when you download images from the Web. For example, when you hover over an image in Google Images, you see information about the image, as shown in Figure 1.10. Use this information to gauge if the image is worth downloading.

In general, you get better results with larger files; image files that are 100K or less are probably of too low a resolution unless you are going to use them at a small size.

1.10 When you hover over images on Google Images pages, you see file type and size information for the images you can download.

You can move files from your desktop into iPhoto with the following steps:

1. **Locate and prepare the files you want to import on your desktop.** If you are working with a compressed file, expand it and then preview the images it contains to identify those you want to add to your library.

2. **In iPhoto, choose File ⇨ Import to Library.** The Import Photos dialog appears.

3. **Select the images you want to add and click Import, as shown in Figure 1.11.** These photos are imported to your library. When the process is complete, the Last Import source is selected and you see the photos you added to the library.

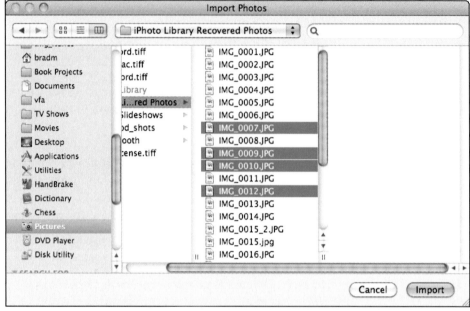

1.11 Use the Import Photos dialog to import images stored on your desktop.

Understanding image quality

Understanding what makes up the quality of images is important because you need images of a certain quality for specific kinds of projects. For example, you want relatively high-quality images if you are printing them at a large size in a photo book.

The quality of images depends on their resolution, their file type and amount of compression, and the size at which they're used and what they're used for.

Resolution is a measure of the amount of information in an image file. Resolutions are typically measured as the number of pixels vertically by number of pixels horizontally, such as 1600×1200 or 1024×768. (*Pixel* is an abbreviation of picture element and represents one "dot" of the image.) You can get the total number of pixels in an image by multiplying the pixel values. For example, a 1600×1200 image has 1,920,000 pixels or 1.92 megapixels. This image would typically be called a 2-megapixel image, or even more commonly, a 2 meg image. (By the way, this is how the resolution of cameras is defined: A 2-megapixel camera can capture 1600×1200-pixel images.) Higher resolutions mean more information in an image, and thus higher quality.

File type determines how the image's information is stored digitally. Most image file types, such as JPEG, use some level of compression, which means that information is processed so that the images can be stored in smaller files. Within these file types, more or less compression can be used. The more compression that is used, the less information the resulting image has, so the lower its quality is. For example, when you email photos from within iPhoto, you choose a relative compression level for the files that you attach to a message. There is almost always a trade-off between file size and image quality.

And last, but not least, an image's quality is also affected by where and how that image is used. An image that has a low resolution that can be used successfully at a small size for on-screen display might be acceptable when printed in an 8×10 format.

Remember that an image has a fixed amount of information in it that is determined by the number of pixels it contains and its level of compression. When you resize an image for a project, you are spreading its pixels across the space where you place it. When you make it larger, you are spreading the same number of pixels over more area. If the image doesn't have "enough" pixels, its quality can degrade. This usually results in *pixilation*, where the individual pixels of the image become so large that you can see them and the image appears to be blocky.

Typically, you should store the highest quality image you can in your iPhoto library because that gives you the maximum flexibility of how and where you use that image. Most cameras have settings that determine the quality (resolution) of the images you capture. Higher-resolution images are better, but take up more space so you can store fewer of them on the camera's memory card. Likewise, when you download images from the Web, you want to get the highest resolution version available.

Configuring iPhoto

There are a number of ways to configure iPhoto that affect how the application works and determine how images in the iPhoto window appear. It's a good idea to set your preferences when you start working with iPhoto, and to check them as you get more comfortable with iPhoto because they might need to be changed as you become an iPhoto pro.

Configuring General iPhoto preferences

Open the General tab of the iPhoto Preferences dialog and set the following options, as shown in Figure 1.12:

- **Show last.** This check box and number box determine if the last *X* months' album appears on the Source pane and if it does appear, how long *X* is. To show this source, select the Show last *X* months album check box and then type the number of months' worth of photos that should be contained in this source. By default, this source is enabled and shows the last 12 months' worth of photos.

19

● **Show item counts.** When you select this check box, the number of photos those sources contain appears next to some of the sources on the Source pane, such as the Photos source (under LIBRARY) and your photo albums.

● **Rotate.** These radio buttons determine the default direction that the Rotate tool uses when you click it. You should select the option that best matches the direction your camera captures portrait-oriented photos. For example, if these are oriented on the camera so the right side is at the bottom of the camera's preview screen, you want the default rotate direction to be counterclockwise.

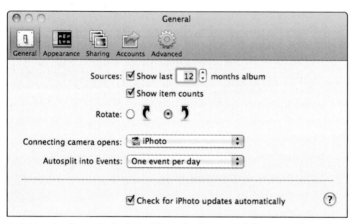

1.12 Use the General tab of the iPhoto Preferences dialog to configure iPhoto to suit your preferences.

The other pop-up menu options on the General tab were explained earlier in this chapter; the bottom check box is covered later.

Configuring the appearance of the iPhoto window

When you click the Appearance tab of the iPhoto Preferences dialog, you can set various options that primarily relate to the iPhoto window's appearance, as shown in Figure 1.13:

● **Photo Border.** Selecting the Outline check box places a thin border around the images shown in the Browsing pane. Selecting the Drop shadow check box places a subtle drop shadow around thumbnails. Both are purely aesthetic settings, and their impact on the window's appearance also depends on how large your thumbnails are and what color the background is.

- **Background.** Use this slider to set the brightness of the background of the Browsing pane. I find that a white background makes photos the easiest to work with because of the contrast between the photos and background, but it is a matter of personal preference. Note that this setting doesn't control the background in all cases; for example, when you view Events, the background is always dark.

- **Events.** If you select the Show reflections check box, when you browse events, a subtle reflection of the event's key photo (more on that in Chapter 2) is shown under the event's thumbnail. If the check box is not selected, you don't see this reflection.

- **Organize View.** If you select the Show informational overlays check box, when you browse photos using the Events or Photos sources, you see a window that provides information about what you are browsing, such as the month and year with which an event is associated.

- **Source Text.** This pop-up menu determines the relative size of text identifying items on the Source pane. The options are Small or Large.

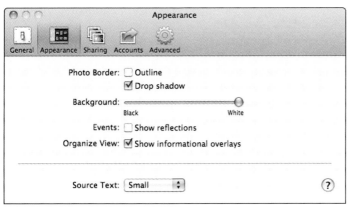

1.13 The settings on the Appearance tab are aptly named for the ways they affect the iPhoto window.

Updating iPhoto

Apple periodically releases updates to iPhoto to fix bugs, make features work better, and add new features. You can update iPhoto manually, or configure Mac OS X to keep the application updated automatically.

To update iPhoto manually, choose iPhoto ➪ Check for Updates. If an update is available, you are prompted to download and install it. If you are using the current version, a dialog informs you.

To set iPhoto to check for updates automatically, click the General tab of the iPhoto Preferences dialog and select the Check for iPhoto updates automatically check box. Whenever iPhoto finds an update, you're prompted to download and install it.

Note

Updates to iPhoto are included when you use the Mac OS X's Software Update tool to check for updates (manually or automatically).

Understanding iPhoto's Modes

iPhoto can operate in two basic modes: Standard and Full Screen. The differences in these modes are in both appearance and function. In most cases, you can perform tasks while in either mode, though some tasks can be done in only one mode (such as importing photos, which can only be done in Standard mode).

Using iPhoto in Standard mode

In Standard mode, as shown in Figure 1.14, the iPhoto window appears as a distinct window on your desktop. Like other windows, you can move it around, resize it, and so on.

Along the left side of the window is the Source pane, where you see the various categories of photos in your library and devices that are connected to your Mac (when they are connected, of course). This pane is organized in sections, such as LIBRARY, RECENT, ALBUMS, PROJECTS, and so on. You can expand or collapse each section; when you make a selection, its contents appear in the right pane of the window, which is the Browsing pane. You also use the Browsing pane to work with projects.

Along the bottom of the window, you see the iPhoto toolbar, which has various commands and menus. You learn about these throughout this book.

The primary benefit of using iPhoto in this mode is that it doesn't take over an entire screen, making it easier to use iPhoto and other applications at the same time. Also, you may find that accessing various sources in your library is easier because you can see the Source pane. The downside of this mode is that it doesn't maximize the use of your display's space.

1.14 In Standard mode, you see the Source pane along the left edge, the Browsing pane filling the right side, and the toolbar at the bottom of the iPhoto window.

Using iPhoto in Full Screen mode

In Full Screen mode, iPhoto uses all the display space available; all other windows move to the background and iPhoto fills the screen, as shown in Figure 1.15. Along the bottom of the screen, you see the iPhoto toolbar. In addition to commands and menus, you see sources of content, such as Events, Faces, Places, and so on. The contents of the selected source (highlighted in blue) appear above the toolbar. You can browse the contents of the selected source, navigate into the source (such as moving into an album), and so on. When you drill down into a source, navigation tools appear at the top of the window to enable you to move around your library (not shown in Figure 1.15).

Note   When you close iPhoto and open another application, iPhoto switches back to Standard mode. When you move back into Full Screen mode, Events is selected even if you previously selected another option.

1.15 In Full Screen mode, iPhoto takes advantage of all the display room it can.

The benefit of Full Screen mode is that it gives you the most room to view and work with content, which is important when you are dealing with images. The downside is that you may find navigation between sources a bit more cumbersome.

Because you can move into or out of Full Screen mode at any time (just click the Full Screen button located in the lower-left corner of the window), you can easily work around its navigation challenges. You can jump into Standard mode to move to the content with which you want to work and then click the Full Screen button to accomplish your task.

Note

If your Mac has multiple displays, you can move the iPhoto window onto one display and put it in Full Screen mode. It fills that display. Unfortunately (at least with the version that was current when I wrote this), if you make another application active on a different display, iPhoto drops into Standard mode so this doesn't really make using Full Screen mode with multiple displays more productive. Hopefully, this behavior will be addressed in a future update.

Many of the details for tasks in this book are for iPhoto in Full Screen mode, but you can accomplish the same tasks in Standard mode with some small differences in the details. Some tasks are better done or can only be done in Standard mode. If you experiment with both modes, you may develop a preference for one or the other, or you may find ways to use both of them efficiently. If your preference is the Standard mode, understanding how to accomplish a task in Full Screen mode also enables you to know how to do it in Standard mode.

How Can Events Help Me with My Photos?

Events are very useful to organize your photos in groups. You can use events to find photos to view in the iPhoto window and slideshows or to use in your projects. As you learn in Chapter 1, when you import photos, iPhoto can automatically group them into events based on the time frame when the photos were taken or you can choose to group all the photos in a single event. You can use iPhoto's default event settings to organize your photos, and you can configure events to group your photos by other criteria.

Understanding Events

Events are one of the ways in iPhoto to group photos and images in your library to keep them organized; events also help you find photos to view or use in projects. When you choose the Events source, you see the events in your library. You can browse your events to find photos in which you are interested, and then double-click an event to view and work with the photos it contains. Events also have information associated with them to help keep them organized and to enable you to find specific events and photos more easily and quickly.

Events can be created in several ways. When you import photos, you can choose to have iPhoto organize (called *auto-splitting*) the images you are importing into events based on the time frame in which those photos were captured. By default, all the photos associated with the same day are placed in the same event, but as you see in Chapter 1, you can change the definition of an event to be a different time frame, such as grouping all photos from the same week in an event. However, you can choose to combine photos into events for other reasons (such as the subject matter of those photos) or to group photos for time frames different then the default. How your photos are organized into events is completely up to you, which is one of the reasons events are so powerful.

Once you organize your photos into events, you can use those events to quickly move to and work with photos. For example, if you place all the photos from a recent trip into one event, you can easily move into that event to create a slideshow or to produce a photo book documenting your adventure.

Using Events to View Photos

Because events are created for you automatically when you import photos into your library, you can always use them to find and view photos. Because events are initially based upon the time frame with which the photos are associated, such as when they were taken, the device capturing the photo determines the date stamp, and, therefore, how photos are grouped into events. For example, when you take a photo with a digital camera or iPhone, that photo is identified with a time and date. When you import photos from the camera into iPhoto, it uses this information to gather the photos within specific time periods into events. Over time, you'll likely organize events based on other criteria, but this initial organization of events gets you off to a quick and organized start as you build your iPhoto library.

The Events source, in the LIBRARY section of iPhoto, is where all the events in your library are stored. You can browse your events and then move into events to view the photos they contain.

Browsing and viewing events

You can browse and view the events in your library a number of ways, and you can tailor how events are viewed to suit your preferences.

Browsing events

To browse your events, do one of the following:

- **Standard mode.** Click the Events icon in the Source pane.

- **Full Screen mode.** Click the Events button on the toolbar at the bottom of the screen.

Your events become visible in the iPhoto window, as shown in Figure 2.1 (Full Screen mode). Each event is represented with a thumbnail that has the event's title in the center of the bottom edge. By default, events are titled with the date on the images they contain, unless you provided a different title when you imported the event's images into iPhoto. Later in this chapter, you learn how to change the titles of events to be anything you want.

2.1 When you select Events as the source, you can browse the events in your iPhoto Library.

Within each event's thumbnail, you see the key photo of the event, which is designated automatically when the event is created; you can also set an event's key photo to be the image you prefer to use to identify that event.

You can browse your events by dragging the Scroll bar up or down or you can click the Up or Down arrows in the bottom-right corner of the window to browse them. As you move up and down the window, you can quickly scan your events. If you use a portable Mac, you can scroll by using gestures on its trackpad; you can do this with the Magic Mouse as well. (The exact gestures you use depend upon how you've configured the device.)

By default, as you scroll up and down the window using the Scroll bar, the date associated with the events that are generally in the center of the window appears in a pop-up window, giving you a sense of the event dates you are currently browsing. This information is useful for moving quickly to events in a certain time frame. When you release the Scroll bar to stop browsing, the date information disappears.

When you select an event, it is highlighted with a yellow box and you see additional information about the selected event under its thumbnail. This includes the date associated with the event's photos and the number of images the event contains.

Genius

Remember that you can show or hide the reflection under each event's thumbnail and determine if the time information appears when you scroll on the Appearance tab of the iPhoto Preferences dialog.

Setting the number of event thumbnails in the iPhoto window

The overall size of the iPhoto window (which is equal to the size of your Mac's display when you use Full Screen mode) and the size of the event thumbnails determine the number of event thumbnails you see in the window at one time.

Note

To set the size of the iPhoto window in Standard mode, drag its Resize handle. If you want the iPhoto window to be as large as possible, click the green Zoom button.

Drag the Zoom slider (located at the bottom of the window) to the left to make thumbnails smaller, so more events are displayed in the window, or to the right to make them larger, so that fewer are displayed in the window. Of course, this setting doesn't actually change the size of any photos in the events; it simply determines the size of the event thumbnails, and, therefore, the number of events you see in the window. The smaller the thumbnails, the more events you see in the window, but the smaller key photos might not be as easy to recognize. You want to choose a balance that enables you to see lots of events in the window without making the key photos for the events unrecognizable because they are too small.

Previewing events

You can preview the photos in an event to get a good sense of the photos that event contains.

When you move the cursor across an event's thumbnail, the key photo changes — in most cases it shrinks — so that you see the entire photo within the event's thumbnail. At the same time, the event's title information (located at the bottom of the event's thumbnail) expands so that you see the event's name, the date it is associated with, and the number of photos it contains, as shown in Figure 2.2.

2.2 Here you see six events; because I'm pointing to the event called "Cape Spear," you see its title, date, and the number of photos it contains.

Note The selected event (highlighted with a yellow box) also displays the additional information (title, date, and number of photos) so there can be two events showing this detail on the same screen, as is the case in Figure 2.2.

Move the pointer across an event's thumbnail to preview the images it contains. As you move the pointer across the event's thumbnail, you can flip through thumbnails of each image in the event by moving the pointer to the left or to the right. The faster you move the pointer, the faster you flip through the event's photos.

Previewing an event's images by dragging across its thumbnail is called *skimming*.

As you move the pointer outside the event's thumbnail, its detailed title information disappears and its key photo returns to its default size (in most cases, it zooms in so the image fills the thumbnail). When you move across the next thumbnail above, below, to the left, or to the right, that event goes into preview mode so you can scan its images.

Previewing events is a great way to quickly scan images in many events to find specific photos that you want to view in detail.

Viewing events individually

When you want to view the photos in one event, double-click the event's thumbnail. The photos in the event fill the iPhoto window, as shown in Figure 2.3 (Full Screen mode).

At the center of the top of the window, you see the title of the event and the date range of the photos it contains or a single date if all the photos are associated with one date. On the far right, you see the number of photos in the event and Forward/Back buttons. On the left side, you see the navigation arrow that takes you back to where you came from, such as the All Events button leading back to the Events browser. The thumbnail showing the key photo, the event's name, and the date or date range with which it is associated appears at the top center of the Browsing pane.

At the bottom of the window, you see the toolbar. You learn to use the tools you see here throughout this book.

When you view an event, you can do the following:

- **Scroll the window to see all the photos the event contains.** When you drag the Scroll bar, the date information for the photos currently near the center of the window appears in a pop-up window, just as it does when you are scrolling events (assuming you haven't deselected this option). Of course, if all the photos in the event are from the same date, this isn't so useful, but as you create or configure events to include photos from multiple dates, you can use this information to get to specific photos more quickly.

- **Use the Zoom slider to change the size of the thumbnails you see (which also determines how many you see in the window).** This doesn't affect the photos; it only changes the thumbnails you see in the window.

- **Click the Forward button (right-facing arrow next to the number of photos at the top of the screen) to move into the next event or the Back button (the left-facing arrow) to move to the previous event.**

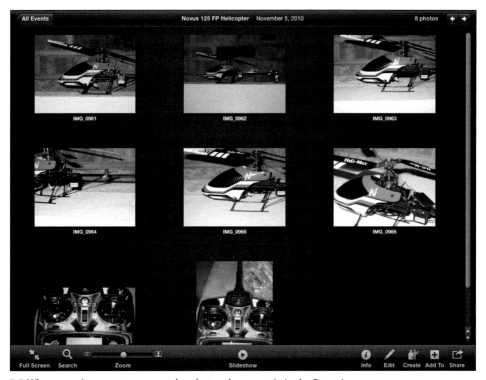

2.3 When you view events, you see the photos they contain in the Browsing pane.

◉ **Click the Info button on the toolbar.** The Info sidebar appears, as shown in Figure 2.4. At the top of the sidebar, you see the current key photo for the event, its title, the date range, the number of photos, and its description. Under this, you see the Faces and Keywords tools. At the bottom of the sidebar, you see the Places tool. (See the following note about these elements.) To close the sidebar, click the Info button again.

◉ **Select a photo.** When you click a photo, it is selected and is highlighted with a yellow box. You also see more information and tools you can use to tag the photo. If the Info sidebar is open when you do this, you see information about the photo rather than the event. You learn all the details of working with individual photos in Chapter 3.

Note   You learn about Faces in Chapter 4, Places in Chapter 5, and Keywords in Chapter 6. These really don't apply to an event unless all the photos in the event have the same information for each item. For example, if all the keywords for the photos in an event are the same, you can click the downward-facing arrow in the Keywords section to see those keywords. If not all the photos have the same keywords, this area is empty even if some of the photos do have keywords. These tools are much more applicable to individual photos than to events.

2.4 The Info sidebar displays information about the event you are viewing.

- **Configure the information displayed for photos.** Open the View menu, and choose Titles, Ratings, or Keywords to show or hide this information for each photo in the event.

- **View the photos at maximum size.** Double-click a photo you want to view. It displays at maximum size (see Figure 2.5). The Selector toolbar appears at the bottom of the window; this contains a thumbnail of each photo in the event with the thumbnail of the current photo highlighted in a yellow box. When you move the pointer over this toolbar, it expands so the thumbnails are larger and easier to see; a scroll bar appears at the bottom of the toolbar so you can scroll through the photos. To view another photo, click its thumbnail. When you move off the toolbar, it shrinks again. To return to viewing photo thumbnails, double-click the photo being displayed.

Genius

When you are viewing a photo at maximum size, the information at the top of the window is for that photo instead of the event. You can click the Return button, which is named with the name of the event you are viewing, to return to the event.

2.5 When you double-click a photo in an event, you see it at maximum size.

Viewing multiple events

You can select and view multiple events at the same time. Click the thumbnail of each event you want to view; hold down the ⌘ key to select noncontiguous events or hold down the Shift key to select contiguous events. Double-click one of the selected events; the photos in the selected events appear, as shown in Figure 2.6. At the top of the window, you see the number of events being displayed. Horizontal lines separate the photos in each event into sections.

At the top of an event's section, you see its name, dates associated with it, and the number of photos it contains. To collapse an event to show only this information, click the downward-facing triangle that appears before its name. To expand an event so that you see the photos it contains, click the right-facing arrow that appears before its name; the event expands so that you can view all the individual photos it contains.

You can browse and view the contents of multiple events in the same way you can a single event. For example, if you double-click a photo, it appears at maximum size; the Selector toolbar shows thumbnails of all the photos in the selected events.

Genius

When you view multiple events and open the Info sidebar, you see how many events you are viewing, the date ranges of those events, the number of photos, and the size of the associated files. This is especially useful when you are considering burning a collection of photos onto a DVD because you can easily see how much space you need to store all the photos in the selected events.

Click the All Events button located in the upper-left corner of the window to return to browsing your events.

2.6 You can view multiple events at the same time.

Sorting events in the iPhoto window

By default, events in the iPhoto window are sorted by their dates, with the earliest event appearing in the top-left corner of the window and moving toward the right and then down with later dates. However, you can change how events are sorted. You can have events sorted automatically, or you can sort them manually.

Determining how iPhoto sorts events automatically

To configure iPhoto to sort events automatically, choose View ⇨ Sort Events. On the resulting menu, choose one of the following options:

- **By Date.** Events are sorted by their dates.
- **By Title.** Events sorted by their titles.

Once you make a selection, choose View ⇨ Sort Events and then choose Ascending to sort the window so events are in ascending order (for example, the earliest dated events appear at the top of the window) or Descending to reverse that order (the most recent events appear at the top of the window).

Sorting events manually

You can also sort events manually. To sort the events, drag them up, down, left, or right. As you drag one event between other events, they slide out of the way so you can place the event you are dragging between them. When you have the event in the desired position, release the mouse button.

Note You can move into Manual Sort mode by choosing View ⇨ Sort Events ⇨ Manually. However, if you just drag an event, you move into this mode automatically so there isn't a good reason to choose the command first.

Genius If you sort manually and then sort automatically, you can return to the most recent manual sort order by choosing View ⇨ Sort Events ⇨ Reset Manual Sort.

Using Events to Find Photos

Events are an especially useful way to find photos because all photos are associated with events automatically. This is because all photos have a date associated with them, and events are created based on those dates automatically. This provides a good start, but if you don't update and configure your events consistently, finding photos by event will be less useful than it could be.

For the most effective searching by events, you should ensure your photos are grouped logically and you have a reasonable number of events. For example, if you take photos on a trip, by default, the photos for each day of the trip are grouped as a separate event. If you search for a specific photo from that trip, and don't remember the day you took it, it's harder to locate because you have to search through each event. To make this particular event more useful, you might want to merge all its photos into a single event so all you have to do is browse the trip's event to find the photo you want. You learn how to configure your events to make your library as efficient as possible in the next section.

To use events to find photos, perform the following steps:

1. **Select the Events source.**
2. **Browse the events until you find the events containing the photos you want to find.**
3. **Open the events containing the photos you want to find.** You can select and work with the photos you want, doing things such as sharing them via Facebook.

Configuring Events

You can configure the events in your library to organize it so you can find photos more efficiently. You can configure the information by which you identify events, and you can also configure the contents and number of events by organizing photos in specific events. You can also create new events and split existing events into multiple events.

Viewing and changing an event's information

As you've seen, every event in your library has information associated with it. This includes the event's name, a date range for the photos it contains or a single date if all the included photos are associated with one date, a description of the event, a key photo, and the number of images it contains. This information is useful because it helps you identify the contents of the event so you can find photos or other images that you want view or use in projects.

You can view an event's information by browsing the Events source as you learned earlier in this chapter. You can also expose all of an event's information by opening the Info sidebar when you view an event.

Genius

You don't have to open an event to use the Info sidebar. If you select an event when you browse the Events source and click the Info button, the same Info sidebar appears. The benefit of this approach is that you can easily view information for many events because all you have to do is click an event of interest and the information in the sidebar updates immediately to reflect the currently selected event.

You can change an event's information to make it more accurate, such as after you change it contents, by performing the following steps:

1. **View an event.**

2. **Click the Info button.** The Info sidebar appears as shown in Figure 2.7.

3. **To rename the event, select its current name in the text field just below the key photo, and edit or type over it.**

4. **Select the current description in the text box below the date, and edit or type over it.**

Genius

You don't have to use the Info sidebar to change an event's key photo. While you browse your events, preview the event whose key photo you want to change until the image you want to be the key photo appears. Right-click and choose Make Key Photo on the contextual menu. That photo becomes the key photo for the event.

2.7 You should ensure the information for events is accurate and descriptive so you can use it to find photos for projects or viewing.

5. **Move the pointer across the event's key photo.** You see a preview of all the photos in the event.

6. **To set the event's key photo, move over the thumbnail until the photo you want to use is shown and click the mouse button.**

7. **If the same keywords apply to all the photos in the event, use the Keyword tool to apply them (this is explained in Chapter 6).** Keywords mostly apply at the photo level, but in some cases you might want all the photos in the event to have the same keyword.

8. **If all the photos are in the same location, use the Places tool to assign a place to those photos (this is covered in Chapter 5).**

Genius

If you want to change the time frame associated with the event, you change the time frames of the photos included in the event (the time frame for an event is the earliest date of any photo in the event to the latest date of any photo). You can do this by adding or removing photos (explained in the next section). Or, you can change the times and dates of the photos themselves (you learn how in Chapter 3).

Changing the contents of events

While iPhoto automatically creates events for you, that doesn't mean that the events it creates are the way you want to organize your photos. You might want to include photos from several days during a vacation in a single event instead of having each day's photos in a separate event, for example. You can change the contents of events a number of ways, including merging events, splitting them, and creating new events.

Merging events

You can merge one or more events to combine the images they contain in a single event. For example, you may capture a series of photos for an event that lasts more than one day; when you import those photos with the standard settings and Autosplit enabled, they get carved up into an event for each day. If you want them to be part of one event, you can merge the separate events like so:

1. **Select the events you want to merge.**

2. **Right-click one of the events and choose Merge Events, as shown in Figure 2.8.** The photos in the selected event are merged into a single event.

3. **Open the merged event's information in the Info sidebar and update it to reflect the merged event's contents as needed, such as giving it an appropriate title.**

Genius

You can also merge events by dragging one on top of another.

Splitting events

You can also split a single event into two events to separate the photos the event contains into separate events. Here's how:

1. **View the event you want to split.**

2. **Select the photo at which point you want the split to start.**

3. **Choose Events ⇨ Split Event.** Two events are created. The first event retains the title of the original event while the event you split out is untitled. You can update the new, untitled event's information to properly identify the photos it contains.

2.8 Merging events is especially useful for related photos you've taken over a period of time that were organized into separate events automatically.

Genius

To automatically split an event into events according to the current event definition, select the event you want to split and choose Events ⇨ Autosplit Selected Events. Based on the time and dates of the photos it contains, the original event is split into events for each time frame associated with the photos it contained (such as each event having the photos associated with one date).

Moving photos into events

You can manually move photos from one event to another:

1. **Select the event containing the photo you want to move and then select the event into which you want to move the photo.**

2. **Double-click the events to open them.** The photos in the events open and you can see the photos they contain.

You can also copy and paste photos between events.

3. **Drag the photo you want to move from one event to the other.** The photo is moved into the event and the event's date range is adjusted such that it spans the oldest and newest photos in the event.

Note A photo can be in only one event at a time. When you move it from its current event to a different one, it is removed from the first event.

Creating events

There may be times when you want to organize some of your photos into a custom event. Suppose you follow a local sports team and attend each of the home games where you take photos. Each time you import photos (assuming the default event definition), each game's photos would be placed into its own event (where they would be combined with other photos you took on the same day). You might want to have all the game photos in one event for each season to make finding those photos later easy. You can manually create events and then place photos in them to tag those photos with the event's information. You can also create events from flagged photos.

Creating a custom event

To create a new, empty event, perform these steps:

1. **Select Events and make sure no specific events are selected.** Remember that selected events are highlighted, so no events should be highlighted to ensure none is selected.

Note If you select photos before performing Step 2, those photos are added to the new event when it is created and you see information based on those photos as well as a key photo.

2. **Choose Events ⇨ Create Event.** (If you don't see this command, an event is selected. Deselect it and try again.) A new event is created. The name of the event is New Event and the date associated with the event is the date you created it. The key photo is a placeholder graphic.

3. **Configure the new event's information.**

4. **Move photos into the new event.** As you learned, you can drag photos into the event, or copy and paste them.

Using flags to create events

You can use the flag tag to create and change events. Here's how:

1. **Flag a photo by clicking the flag icon that appears in the upper left-hand corner of the photo's thumbnail when you select it.** The flag icon turns orange to indicate the photo is flagged.

Caution When you perform this action, all the flagged photos in your library are moved into the new event. This can cause unexpected results if you aren't careful. If you've flagged photos, but then forgotten that they were flagged, you may find photos from other events have been moved to the new event that you didn't intend to move.

2. **Choose Events ⇨ Create Event From Flagged Photos.**

3. **Click Create.** A new event containing the flagged photos is created.

4. **Configure the new event's information.**

Note You can also add flagged photos to an existing event. Flag the photos you want to add to an event. Select the event. Choose Events ⇨ Add Flagged Photos To Selected Event.

Caution You can delete an event by selecting it and choosing Photos ⇨ Move to Trash. However, unlike some of the other tools you learn about later, such as photo albums, when you delete an event, you delete all the photos it contains. This can have unintended consequences, such as you mistakenly deleting photos. Instead, move any photos you want to keep into a different event, and then delete any of the remaining photos. Once all the photos in an event are gone, the event itself disappears.

How Can I Work with My Photos Individually?

n this chapter, you learn to browse and sort photos. This starts by tagging your photos with the information you'll need to find them later to view or use in projects. While this might not be the most fun thing that you'll do in Photo, it could be the most important. If you consistently tag your photos, you'll have a much easier time finding the specific photos you want for projects, such as creating a photo book or calendar. After you've tagged photos, finding and viewing them is a fun task!

Understanding the Photos Source

Every image you store in iPhoto is included in the Photos source. While you can change several aspects of how you view this source, realize that within the Photos source, your photos aren't grouped by any category (unlike the Events, Places, or other sources). When you work with the Photos source, you see all your photos in a list, and a very large list it is if you have a lot of photos in your library. There are many times you'll want to use this source to find photos to work with. To make working with individual photos easier, you should understand and definitely use tags.

There are two ways to open the Photos source:

- **In Standard mode.** Select Photos in the LIBRARY section of the Source pane.

- **In Full Screen mode.** Select Albums on the toolbar at the bottom of the window, and then double-click the Photos album, which appears in the upper-left corner of the window.

Understanding Tags

Tags are simply information that is associated with the photos in your library. While they serve a number of purposes, the most important one is aiding your search for photos. This might sound basic, but if you have 10,000 photos in your library, finding a specific photo is akin to finding the proverbial needle in a haystack.

You also use tags to organize photos, such as sorting the window by title or rating.

Finally, tags present information about photos, such as their titles and descriptions. You can include this information on-screen and in projects you create, including photo books and slideshows.

If you read Chapter 1, you learned that some tags are automatically applied when you add photos to your library, such as the time and date stamp that comes with photos when you import them from a camera. You assign other tags to your photos, including keywords and ratings. And others are a combination of information iPhoto applies and updates you apply manually; photo titles are a good example of this type.

Configuring the tags for your photos consistently and logically goes a long way toward making you more effective with iPhoto. It also makes using the application more enjoyable because you don't spend so much time searching for photos, which can be quite a chore when you are looking for a specific photo for a project from among thousands in your library.

You are better off if you apply and configure tags each time you import a new set of photos to your library as opposed to waiting until you have a large number of photos there. With small batches of photos, applying tags doesn't take much time or effort. With large groups of photos, applying tags can be time consuming and certainly more laborious.

Some tags are grouped under a general category of information; some of these tags are created automatically while others you have to add manually. You can change some of the automatic tags to correct or improve them, too. These automatic tags include:

- **Title.** The title is text automatically associated with a photo when you add it to the library. When you import photos from a camera, the title is the name of the photo's file, which is often something like IMG_3380.jpg. While default titles typically aren't very meaningful, you can modify them so they become something useful. And titles can be displayed when you view photos and in your projects; for many tasks, the title is the photo's caption.

- **Date.** The date is the month, day, and year associated with the photo. Dates are applied automatically when you import photos into the library, such as the time stamp on photos when you capture them with a camera. In most cases, you won't change the date, but you can if needed. (An example of when you might do this is if the battery in your camera fails and the date is reset to an incorrect date without your realizing it; not that this has happened to me, you understand.)

- **Time.** The time is the time of day when the photo was captured. Like the date, time information is captured automatically when it is available, such as when you import a photo from a camera. Also, like the date, you usually don't need to change the time unless the camera you used applied the wrong time for some reason.

- **Description.** The description is a text field that you can use to, well, describe the photo. Descriptions are useful to tag photos with more text than you use in the title. Unlike the title, the description field is empty until you add something to it.

- **Size.** Size measures two things about a photo. The resolution indicates how many *pixels* (short for picture elements) make up the picture and is indicated by the number of pixels in the horizontal direction multiplied by the number of pixels in the vertical direction, such as 1600×1200. The more pixels an image has, the higher its resolution and the more detail it has. The other size dimension is the file size of the photo's file, typically measured in K or MB. Larger files have more information, which means a higher-quality image that you can use at larger sizes in your projects. You don't directly change the size information, but it can change when you edit a photo, such as when you crop it. More importantly, the resolution affects how you can use a photo in projects. For example, photos need to have a relatively high resolution to print with good quality in a photo book while an image published to Facebook is fine at a lower resolution.

- **Kind.** The kind information identifies the format of the digital image. The most common is JPEG Image, which is the type most cameras create. You may see other kind tags, especially when you import files that you download from the Web. Kind is created automatically, and you can't change it in iPhoto (and really shouldn't change it outside of iPhoto, either).

- **Other Technical Information.** This general catchall is for tags that provide technical information about the photo as it was captured by a specific device. Each kind of device you use to capture photos provides its own set of technical details for the photos you take. Examples are things like if a flash was used, the shutter speed, and so on. If you are into the technical details of digital images, you may enjoy reviewing this information. However, you can do very well in iPhoto without understanding all the ins and outs of these details. (And explaining them is certainly beyond the scope of this book.)

Other tags are strictly user defined, such as ratings and keywords. You learn about these in later sections of this chapter.

Viewing and Changing Photo Tags

iPhoto provides several ways to view the tags for your photos along with the tools you need to make changes to or apply tags so that you keep your photos organized.

Start by opening the Photos source. In the Browsing pane, you see all the photos in your library, as shown in Figure 3.1. Configure the Browsing pane to suit your viewing preferences by showing or hiding tags, setting the size of the thumbnails, and so on (you learn the details for this later in this chapter).

Note Later in this chapter, you learn how to configure the tags that appear in the Browsing pane. For now, you just need to know how tags appear in this pane.

Viewing photo information

There are two fundamental places in which you can view photo tags: the Browsing pane and the Info sidebar. Each location has its uses.

When you browse your photos, as you see me doing in Figure 3.1, you see various tags near the photo thumbnails, such as title, rating, and so on. You can configure which tags are shown using the commands on the View menu.

3.1 Here you see photos in the library, and under each photo you see its title and rating (only for photos with a rating).

You get a more detailed view of photo information by using the Info sidebar. To open it, click the Info button. The sidebar opens. Select the photo whose tags you want to see and you see its information in the sidebar, as shown in Figure 3.2.

You can view information for individual photos, or if you select a group of photos, you see information that pertains to the group rather than to the individual photos you've selected.

Note Title and description are prime examples of tags to update as soon as you add photos to your library. Because it can be a bit tedious, it is much better to do it for a small group of photos rather than waiting until you have hundreds of photos to update. You can configure tags for multiple photos at the same time, as you learn later in this chapter.

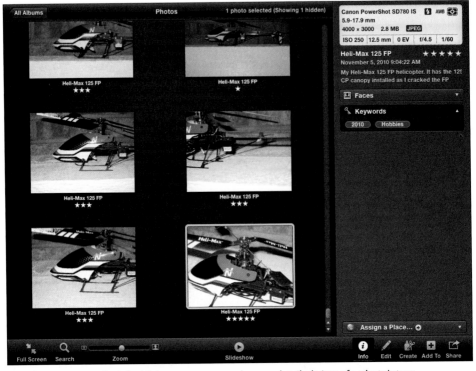

3.2 When you open the Info sidebar, you see a much more detailed view of a photo's tags.

Changing a photo's title in the Browsing pane

You can change a photo's title in the Browsing pane. Click the title you want to change; after a second, the title becomes highlighted indicating you can edit it. Change or type over the existing title and press Return. The new title is saved.

Genius

You can copy and paste text from title to title. So if one photo already has the title you want to use, or even one close to what you want to use, copy it and paste it over the title for the photo you want to rename.

Changing an individual photo's information using the Info sidebar

You can use the Info sidebar to configure a photo's information tags. Here's how:

1. **Select the first photo for which you want to configure tags.**

Note Most of the time, you'll update a photo's information tags, ratings, places, and so on, at the same time. For instructional purposes, I explain these as separate tasks just to make them clearer. After you understand how to configure each type of tag, you can develop your own efficient process to configure the tags you use.

2. **Click the Info button.** The Info sidebar opens (if it is already open, skip this step). The technical information about the photo appears at the top of the sidebar. Just below that you see the title, rating, date and time, and description.

3. **Select the current title and edit it or type a new title.** An example is shown in Figure 3.3.

4. **Select the default text "Add a description" (or whatever the current description is) and type a description of the photo.**

Note You can't change a photo's date or time in the Info sidebar, but you can do it using a command on the Photos menu.

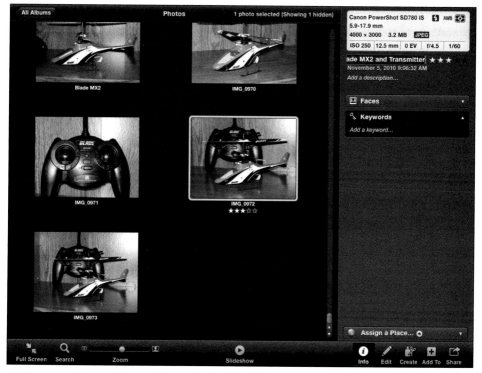

3.3 You can edit several of a photo's tags in the Info sidebar.

5. **Select the next photo whose tags you want to update.**

6. **Repeat Steps 3 and 4.**

7. **Continue updating information tags until you finish, and then click the Info button.**
   The Info sidebar closes.

Genius

To be consistent about updating tags for your photos, tag them immediately after you import them by selecting the Last Import item on the Source pane. This displays the most recent group of photos you've added to the library. Open the first photo's Info dialog, update it, and move through each imported photo until you've tagged them all.

Changing a photo's time and date stamp

Unlike the other tags, you usually only change a photo's time and date stamp when there is an error due to a camera malfunction or some other issue. Because you may occasionally need to do this, here's how to go about it:

1. **Select the first photo whose time and date stamp you want to change.**

Note

When iPhoto is in Full Screen mode, you can view its menu so you can choose commands by pointing to the top of the screen; the iPhoto menu bar appears and you can make a selection from it.

2. **Choose Photos ➪ Adjust Date and Time.** The adjust sheet appears, as shown in Figure 3.4.

3.4 Use this sheet to change a photo's date and time stamp.

3. **Use the Adjusted tools to configure the photo's new time and date stamp.**

4. **If you want the new time and date to be recorded on the photo's file in the Finder, select the Modify original files check box.** If you leave this deselected, the time and date you set is used in iPhoto, but the file on your desktop retains its previous time and date stamp.

5. **Click Adjust.** The new time and date stamp is applied.

Changing information for multiple photos at the same time

Sometimes, it's useful to configure the same tags for a group of photos. For example, you might want to use the same title for a series of photos with the same subject. You can do this with the Batch Change command as follows:

1. **Select the group of photos whose tags you want to set.**

2. **Choose Photos ⇨ Batch Change.** The tag change sheet appears.

Genius

The keyboard shortcut for the Batch Change command is Shift+⌘+B.

3. **On the Set pop-up menu, choose Title to apply a title to the photos.** The sheet is configured to allow you to input the title you want to use.

4. **On the to pop-up menu, choose the type of title you want to apply.** The options are: Text, where you type a text title; Empty, which causes the title to be empty; Event Name, which sets the title to be the same as the event's name in which the photo is grouped; Filename, which sets the title to be the name of the photo's file on the desktop; and Date/Time, which allows you to configure a date and time to use as the photo's title.

5. **Configure the rest of the sheet based on the option you selected in Step 4.** An example of setting text titles is shown in Figure 3.5. In this example, because the check box is selected, a sequential number is added to each title; if it's not selected, the same title is applied to each photo.

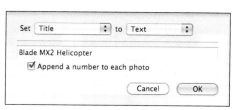

3.5 Setting the title for a group of photos

6. **Click OK.** The sheet closes and the tag you configured is applied to each photo that is selected.

7. **Using similar steps, configure the Date and Description tags you want to apply to the photos.** First, select the tag you want to configure on the Set menu and use the sheet to configure it. Click OK to apply the new tag.

Note

In the version of iPhoto available at the time I wrote this, you could only set one tag at a time. Only the tag that is visible on the sheet when you click OK is applied. You have to reopen the sheet each time you want to configure a different tag.

Genius

The Adjust Date and Time tool works on multiple photos, too. Just select the photos whose dates and times you want to change and configure the sheet, as described in the earlier task.

Applying flags to Photos

Flags are temporary tags that you apply to photos to mark them for a later action. Suppose you just imported a large collection of photos and want to post the best ones to your Facebook page. As you review the newly imported photos, you mark them with a flag. When you finish, you can use the flags to quickly find the specific photos you want to post. You can also create events based on flags or add photos to events based on flags.

To flag photos, do the following:

1. **Select a source of photos, such as the Photos source.** The photos in that source appear in the Browsing pane.

2. **Browse and view the photos.**

3. **Select the photos you want to flag.**

4. **Flag the selected photos by doing one of the following:**

   - Choose Photos ➪ Flag Photos.
   - Press ⌘+. (period).

The photos are marked with the orange flag icon in the upper-left corner of their thumbnails.

You can flag a single photo by moving the pointer over it and clicking the Flag icon that appears in the upper-left corner of the photo's thumbnail.

Genius

The number of photos currently flagged always appears next to the Flagged category on the Source pane and under the Flagged album's thumbnail in Full Screen mode.

You can unflag photos by selecting the photos with flags you want to remove and doing one of the following:

- Choose Photos ⇨ Unflag Photos.
- Press ⌘+. (period).

The flag is removed from the selected photos, and they disappear from the flagged album.

You can unflag a single photo by click the orange flag icon in the upper-left corner of its thumbnail.

Note

After you complete a task for which you flagged photos, you should clear the flags so you don't unintentionally include them in a project. The easiest way to do this is to select the Flagged source, select all the photos it contains, and press ⌘+. (period).

Tagging photos with keywords

Keywords are words or phrases that you associate with photos so you can find them later. You can associate combinations of the same keyword to an image, such as a general word *Holiday*, for example, with a more specific word, such as *Brad*. Then you could search for photos of Brad related to holidays by searching for photos with the keywords *Brad* and *Holiday*.

iPhoto includes a number of default keywords you can use, but you can also create your own so they are specific to you.

Configuring keywords

To configure your keywords, perform the following steps:

1. **Choose Window ⇨ Manage My Keywords or press ⌘+K.** The Keywords window appears with the keywords currently available. You can place the keywords you use most frequently in the Quick Group area at the top of the window. These keywords are assigned a keyboard shortcut so you can apply them quickly and easily. In the lower pane of the window, you see the other keywords you can use.

2. **Click Edit Keywords.** The window moves into Edit mode.

3. **To add a keyword, click the Add button (+) at the bottom of the window, type the new keyword, and press Return.** The keyword is added to the list.

4. **To assign a keyboard shortcut to a keyword, select the keyword, click Shortcut, type the letter or number you want to use as the keyword's shortcut, and press Return.**

5. **To remove a keyword that you no longer use, select it and click the Remove button (–).** The keyword is deleted from the list (and is also removed from any photos to which it is assigned).

Genius To change a keyword, select it, click Rename, type a new name, and press Return. The keyword is changed on the list and on any photos to which it is currently assigned.

6. **Click OK.** You return to the Keywords window, as shown in Figure 3.6.

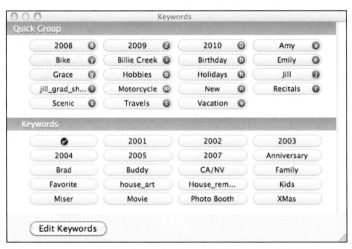

3.6 The Keywords window shows the keywords that are available to assign to your photos.

7. **To automatically assign a keyboard shortcut to a keyword, drag it from the lower pane to the upper pane.** The keyword moves to the top pane and a keyboard shortcut is assigned to it.

8. **To remove a keyboard shortcut from a keyword, drag it from the top pane to the bottom pane.**

9. **When you finish configuring keywords, close the window or press ⌘+K.**

Applying keywords to photos

After you configure keywords, you can assign them to your photos:

1. **Select the photos to which you want to assign keywords.**

2. **Press ⌘+K.** The Keywords window opens.

3. **Click the keywords you want to apply to the photos; if a keyword has a keyboard shortcut, you can press that key to apply the keyword.** Keywords that are applied to the selected photos are highlighted in blue, as shown in Figure 3.7. If a keyword is applied to some, but not all, of the photos, it is marked with a hyphen.

4. **To remove a keyword from the selected photos, click its button or press its keyboard shortcut.** If the keyword is applied to only some of the photos, you need to click its button twice to remove it (clicking it once applies it to all the photos).

5. **Select a different group of photos and continue applying keywords.**

6. **When you finish, press ⌘+K.** The Keywords window closes.

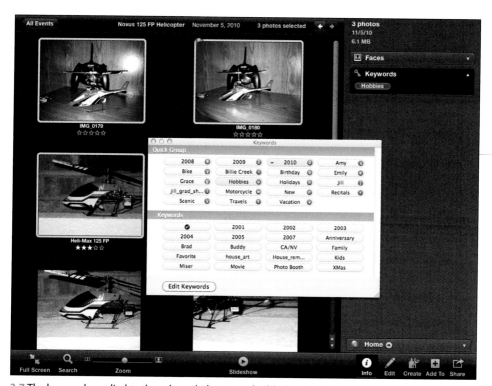

3.7 The keywords applied to the selected photos are highlighted in blue.

57

Genius

The check mark keyword is a temporary marker, which is similar to flagging a photo.

Note

When you assign a keyword to an image, it appears briefly in white on the image. When you remove a keyword, it briefly appears in red and disappears in a puff of smoke.

Rating photos

Ratings are a very simple tag you can apply to photos. A rating consists of one to five stars, with five stars usually interpreted as very good (of course, if you are a contrarian, you might tag your best photos with one star). You can use ratings as you can other tags, such as searching, collecting photos in albums, and so on.

There are several ways to rate your photos:

- **With photos displayed in the Browsing pane, open the Info sidebar and select a photo you want to rate.** Click the number of stars in the Rating area to the left of the title to represent the number of stars you want to apply.

- **Move the pointer over a photo.** Click the number of stars under the date and time information to set the number of stars.

- **Right-click on a photo.** Choose the photo's rating on the resulting contextual menu by clicking the number of stars you want to give it.

Genius

To remove a photo's rating, click to the left of the stars under the photo in the Browsing pane.

Viewing Photos Individually

You can view the photos in the Photos source in many ways, and you can configure the information that is displayed for this source.

Browsing and viewing photos

Open the Photos source. In the Browsing pane, you see thumbnails of all the photos you have added to your Library. You see how the thumbnails in the pane are organized and what information is determined by various settings available on the View menu. Open the View menu and you see the following View options (options that are active are indicated by a check mark):

- **Titles.** Select this option to display titles for the photos you are viewing.

- **Rating.** Select this option to see each photo's rating.

- **Keywords.** Select this option to display the Keywords section on the Info sidebar. You can expand this section by clicking its downward-facing triangle to see the keywords applied to the selected photo.

- **Event titles.** Select this option to show photos grouped by event. You see each event's information and lines separating each in the window. (This view is similar to what happens when you view a group of events.)

- **Hidden photos.** When you choose the Hidden photos option, you see all photos in the window regardless of whether specific photos are hidden. Later in this section, you learn how to hide and unhide photos.

Choose the view options you prefer. The default setting is Event titles, but you should experiment with the other settings until you see the information that suits your preferences. For example, if you don't rate photos, there's no reason to display rating information in the window.

After you configure the window, you see the photos in your library displayed according to your selections, as shown in Figure 3.8.

Like events, you can browse the photos in the Photos source by dragging the Scroll bar up or down or by clicking the up and down arrows at the bottom of the Scroll bar. When you drag the Scroll bar, date information pops up on the screen so you get a sense of where you are in your photo library (unless you have disabled that preference).

Also similar to events, you can determine how many thumbnails appear in the window by resizing the iPhoto window (in Standard mode) and using the Zoom slider in the lower-left corner of the window. When you use the Standard mode, you should click the green Zoom button to make the iPhoto window as large as possible. Making more thumbnails visible in the same window makes each thumbnail smaller, but enables you to see more photos at the same time.

3.8 In this iPhoto window, you see the title and rating for each photo.

Viewing photos at maximum size

To view an individual photo, double-click it. It expands to be as large as possible within the iPhoto window so that you can see the entire image, as shown in Figure 3.9 (Full Screen mode). The Thumbnail viewer appears at the bottom of the window; if you move the pointer over this, it magnifies so you can see its thumbnails more clearly. The thumbnail of the photo currently being displayed is highlighted in a yellow box.

To change the photo you are viewing, do any of the following:

- **Move to the next photo.** Press the right-arrow key or click the Forward button at the top of the window.

- **Move to the previous photo.** Press the left-arrow key or click the Back button at the top of the window.

- **Click the thumbnail of the photo you want to view.** You can scroll the viewer to see all the thumbnails though if you have a large library, this would take a long time.

To move back to the Browsing window, press Esc or double-click the photo being displayed.

3.9 Viewing photos in Full Screen mode at maximum size shows off your photos.

Hiding and unhiding photos

When you don't want to view a photo, but you want to keep it in your library, you can hide it. Hidden photos don't appear when you browse or search, but they remain in your collection so that you can view and use them again at any time.

To hide one or more photos, select their thumbnails and choose Photos ⇨ Hide Photos or press ⌘+L. You can also right-click a photo and click the Hide button.

What happens next depends on the View options you have set. If Hidden Photos is not enabled, the photo disappears from view. If Hidden Photos is enabled, the photo remains but is marked with an orange X in the upper-right corner, which indicates a hidden photo, as shown in Figure 3.10.

Genius

To quickly toggle whether hidden photos are displayed or not, press Shift+⌘+H.

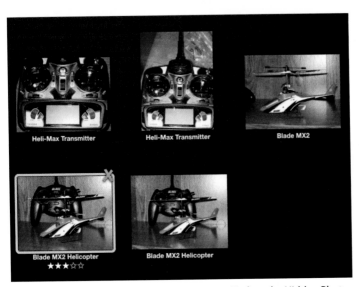

3.10 Hidden photos are marked with an orange X when the Hidden Photos view setting is enabled.

You can also hide a photo when you are viewing it in the iPhoto window or in Full Screen mode. If the Hidden Photos setting is active, you see hidden photos normally in these views.

When you search for photos, hidden photos are returned with the search, but they aren't displayed (unless you've enabled Hidden Photos using the View menu). In that case, you can perform a search and the event with which the hidden photo is associated might appear, but it could appear to be empty. To see the results, configure your view to show hidden photos.

Sorting photos

By default, photos are sorted in the window by date. Similar to events, you can choose how photos are sorted automatically or you can sort photos manually.

Configuring how photos are sorted automatically

To configure iPhoto to sort photos automatically, choose View ⇨ Sort Photos. On the resulting menu, choose one of the following options:

- By Date to have photos sorted by their dates
- By Keyword to sort photos by their keywords
- By Title to have photos sorted alphabetically by their titles
- By Rating to have photos sorted by their ratings

Once you make a selection, choose View ⇨ Sort Photos and then choose Ascending to sort the window so photos are in ascending order (for example, the earliest dated photos appear at the top of the window) or Descending to reverse that order (the most recent photos appear at the top of the window).

Sorting photos manually

When you are viewing photos in some sources, such as albums, you can also sort photos manually. Choose View ⇨ Sort Photos ⇨ Manually. Then drag photos around the window to sort the order in which they appear.

How Can Faces Help Me Organize and View My Photos?

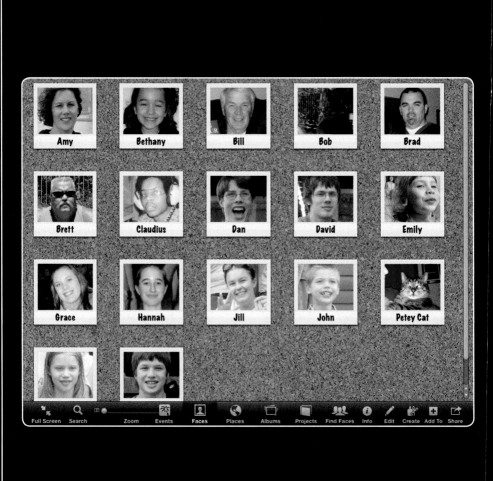

iPhoto includes a face recognition feature, cleverly called Faces, that identifies photos by the people in them. After you identify faces by associating them with names, iPhoto identifies photos with the faces it recognizes and collects them into groups for you automatically. This is a great way to be able to find photos to use in projects, and you can also discover photos that include specific people. Over time, you can train iPhoto to be better at recognizing certain faces so it is even more accurate at finding photos with specific people in them.

Understanding Faces

Faces is a great way to collect photos because it is based on the people in your photos, which is usually one of the most important considerations when you create projects or want to work with your photos for other purposes. Once you tag a face with a name, iPhoto searches for all the photos with that face in them and groups them under that person's snapshot on the Faces source (which is called the corkboard). When you want to find photos that include that person, you open the person's snapshot and view the photos it contains.

When you add new photos in which iPhoto recognizes the person's face, they are automatically added to the person's snapshot. Because of this, Faces is a dynamic way to tag photos, meaning that iPhoto automatically tags your photos with the faces it recognizes so the collections of photos by faces changes over time. For example, when you add new photos to your library, photos including people whose faces iPhoto recognizes are grouped without you having to do anything.

To use Faces, you need to identify the people whose faces appear in your photos. iPhoto then collects photos with those faces in them into snapshots; a snapshot contains all the photos associated with a specific individual. To make this process more accurate, you train iPhoto to better recognize specific faces.

Faces helps you find and view photos that include specific people because you can open a person's snapshot to work with photos in which that person appears.

Identifying Faces in Your Photos

For Faces to work, you tag faces in your photos with names so that iPhoto associates those names with faces. As it identifies the same faces in the photos in your library, it tags them with the appropriate names and collects them under the appropriate snapshots. You can help iPhoto's Faces tool recognize faces more easily over time if you confirm or deny faces it attempts to identify.

Note

Amazingly, iPhoto can identify the same face at different ages even if you only identify a person's face at one age or ages that are close to each other. For example, I tagged the face of someone in photos when she was between 16 and 19 years old, and iPhoto correctly identified her in pictures when she was a very young child.

There are two ways to access the Faces tools in iPhoto:

◉ In Standard mode, select Faces in the LIBRARY section of the Source pane.

◉ In Full Screen mode, select Faces on the toolbar at the bottom of the window.

Except for the first time you move into Faces (see the next section), you move to your corkboard where you see the snapshots in your library, as shown in Figure 4.1 (Standard mode).

4.1 The corkboard contains snapshots for the all faces you have tagged.

Finding faces

You can find faces in your library to identify people. There are two ways the process starts:

◉ When you click Faces for the first time, you are prompted to find people.

◉ After the first time you use Faces, move into the Faces tool and click the Find Faces button on the toolbar.

67

iPhoto presents snapshots with people it doesn't recognize to you. If iPhoto can't recognize the face in the snapshot, you see "unnamed" under it. If iPhoto has identified a potential match, you see the person's name with controls to confirm or reject the suggested match. For example, Figure 4.2 shows three snapshots. Two are of unnamed people, while the third has been matched with a person who has other photos in the library.

After you configure the names on the first screen, you can click Show More Faces to continue the process or click Continue To Faces to move into the Faces tool.

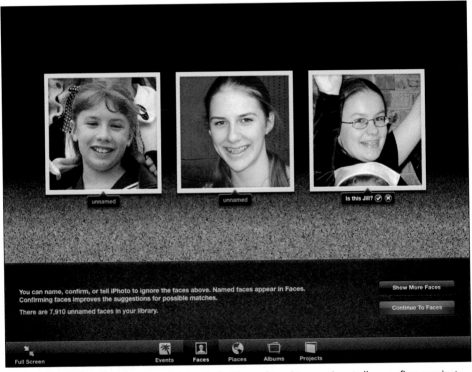

4.2 When you find faces, you can identify people iPhoto doesn't recognize at all or confirm or reject photos that are potential matches.

Genius

iPhoto Faces works with Facebook tags. You can associate a person's email address with a face. If you publish a photo with a face to Facebook, it becomes a tag in Facebook and if an email address has been associated with it, the person receives a notification. The process works in reverse, too; tagging in Facebook can associate faces with names in iPhoto. This link is covered in Chapter 11.

Identifying faces in photos

You can identify faces in photos by tagging those faces with names. Here's how:

1. **Browse photos until you find a photo with one or more faces you want iPhoto to recognize.** You can start this process from any source, such as Photos, Albums, and so on. It doesn't matter which source a photo is stored in.

2. **Click the Info button.** The Info sidebar appears.

3. **Click the downward-facing triangle in the Faces section to expand it.** In this section, you see the number of unnamed faces in the photo along with the names of people iPhoto recognizes. In Figure 4.3, iPhoto has recognized one person, but two others are unnamed (which means the face isn't recognized either because the person has never been named or the face recognition function has not identified it).

4.3 Expand the Faces section on the Info sidebar to work with faces in a photo.

4. **Identify each face in the photo based on one of the following situations:**

- If a face is unnamed, click the "unnamed" text and it becomes editable. Type the name associated with the face. As you type, iPhoto tries to match the name you are typing by presenting a list of existing names. If one of the matches is correct, click it to apply it to the face; if not, keep typing until you've entered the name and press Return.

- If a potential match has been identified, click the check mark to confirm it or click the "x" to reject it. If you reject the match, type a name to associate the face with it and press Return, or just press Return if you don't want to apply a name.

- If a face has been identified incorrectly, click the existing name to select it. It becomes editable. Configure the name just like unnamed faces.

- If a face hasn't been recognized as being a face (there's no tag under it), click Add a face in the Faces section on the Info sidebar. A new selection box appears on the photo. Drag the box onto the face and resize it so it includes only the face you want to identify. Click the text "click to name" and type a name as you do when a face is unnamed.

- If something has been recognized as a face that isn't a face, or at least not one you want to identify, click the close button "x" for its selection box. The selection box is deleted, and iPhoto no longer recognizes what was in the box as a face.

Note

In some cases, you can point to an unrecognized face and the face selection box appears. Click the mouse button to set the selection box and then name the face.

Genius

Try to identify people whose faces are in profile, too. This improves iPhoto's ability to recognize the face in all situations.

5. **To continue identifying faces, click the left- or right-facing arrow to move to the previous or next photo in the source you are working with, respectively.** iPhoto attempts to identify faces in the photo. When a potential match is found, iPhoto prompts you with a person's name.

Genius

Not surprisingly, iPhoto's face recognition doesn't recognize animal faces. However, you can manually identify animal faces just like people's faces, and iPhoto collects photos with those faces into snapshots for each animal. iPhoto won't automatically add photos containing those animals to the associated snapshots, but this can still be a useful way to collect photos of animals so you can organize and find them easily.

Improving iPhoto's automatic face recognition

You can train iPhoto's face recognition to become more accurate by doing the following:

1. **Move into the Faces source.**

2. **Select the snapshot for the person whose face you want to train iPhoto to better recognize.**

3. **Open the Info sidebar.** At the top of the sidebar, you see the snapshot. Just under that, you see the person's full name, email address, the date range of photos in which that person has been identified, the total number of photos in which she has been identified, and how many potential matches there are. At the bottom of the sidebar, you see a map showing the locations of photos in which the person has been identified, as shown in Figure 4.4.

4. **Add or edit the person's full name by replacing the "Add a full name" text or the existing full name.** You can associate a full name with a face if the name you've tagged the person's photos with isn't a full name. This is useful if you have multiple people in your library with the same first name, and you tag faces with first names only. You can use the full name to distinguish people during searches. The name you enter here is not the name that appears on the person's snapshot; that name is what you used to tag the person in photos.

4.4 When you select a snapshot, you see information about the person in the Info sidebar.

5. **Type an email address.** If you intend to publish photos to Facebook, the names you apply become Facebook tags. When you enter a person's email address, that person is notified when you publish photos in which he appears to your Facebook page. This is optional.

6. **Click the right-facing arrow next to the text "X unconfirmed matches," where X is the number of unconfirmed matches iPhoto has found.** You move to the confirmation screen, which shows thumbnails for all the photos associated with the person or that may be associated with the person. By default, this is in Faces mode, which focuses the photos down to the person's face. This screen has two sections. At the top you see the photos in which the person has been confirmed; these show the person's name in a green box. The lower section is labeled Unconfirmed Faces and shows the potential matches based on faces iPhoto thinks it recognizes.

Genius

You can also get to the Confirmation tool by opening a person's snapshot and clicking the Confirm Additional Faces button.

7. **Confirm or reject each photo by doing one of the following (see Figure 4.5):**

   ● If a photo is showing the person's face and is labeled "click to confirm" or "confirm," click it. The person's name appears in a green box indicating you have confirmed the face shown belongs to the person.

   ● If a different person's face appears in the photo and is labeled "click to confirm" or "confirm," Option+click it to reject it. The text "Not *name*," where *name* is the person's name, appears in a red box. The photo is no longer associated with the person.

   ● If a photo is labeled with the person's name, but it isn't the right face, click it. The text "Not *name*," where *name* is the person's name, appears in a red box. The photo is no longer associated with the person.

Genius

If you want to see the full photos instead of just the version focused on the person's face, slide the switch at the top of the window to Photos. To refocus the photos to be of the person's face only, slide it to Faces.

Genius

The fastest way to confirm photos is to drag the pointer through the photos containing the face you want to confirm. As you drag across photos, they are confirmed as including the person's face. If the selection included any that should have been rejected, go back to those and click them to reject them. You can also right-click a photo to choose Reject or Confirm from the contextual menu.

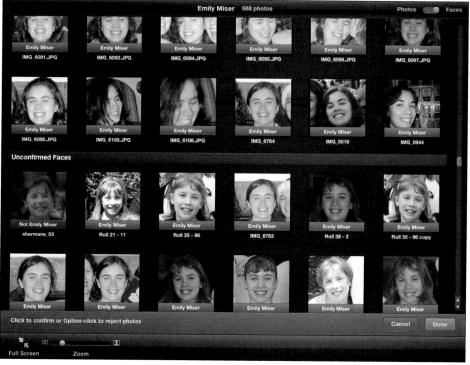

4.5 Training iPhoto by confirming or rejecting potential matches improves its ability to correctly recognize people.

8. **Continue rejecting or accepting names until you've addressed all of them or have run out of patience.** The more photos you confirm or reject, the better iPhoto becomes at recognizing that person.

9. **Click Done.** The changes that you made are saved and the photos are added or removed from the person's snapshot if you confirmed or rejected them, respectively.

Genius You should train iPhoto extensively on the people who appear most in your photos so that iPhoto accurately tags as many of your photos that contain those people as possible.

Configuring snapshots

As you have learned, the Faces source contains a snapshot for each person whose face you have named. As with events and other objects, you can configure and organize your snapshots.

Note One of the interesting things about Faces (to me at least), is how often it associates certain people in the same family with the same name, indicating more of a family resemblance than you might note just by looking at the related people. So don't be too surprised if iPhoto routinely incorrectly identifies people in the same family under the same name. As you train iPhoto, this occurs less frequently.

Setting information and a key photo for a snapshot

You can configure the information for a snapshot; for example, you might want to change the person's name or set the person's key photo. You change snapshots on the corkboard or using the Info sidebar.

To configure a snapshot on the corkboard, do the following:

1. **Move to the Faces source.**

2. **To rename a snapshot, click the name shown at the bottom of the snapshot and type the new name.**

3. **To change the key photo, move the pointer over the current photo to preview all the photos in the snapshot.** When you see the photo you want to be the key photo, right-click it and choose Make Key Photo on the contextual menu.

To configure a snapshot in the Info sidebar, select it and click the Info button. Use the Info sidebar to set a key photo, add or change the person's full name, or add or change the person's email address. To set the key photo, move the pointer over the snapshot's image until you see the image you want to use and click the mouse button. Configuring the full name and email address was covered earlier in this chapter.

Genius

If you end up with more than one snapshot for the same person on your corkboard (for example, in one snapshot, the person may be identified only by first name and in the other snapshot, the first and last names were used), you can merge them together to combine the two snapshots into one. Just drag one snapshot on top of the other one. Click Merge Faces. The photos associated with both snapshots are combined into one.

Organizing snapshots

You can organize the snapshots in the Faces source so that snapshots you use most often are in a convenient location. Perform the following steps:

1. **Select the Faces source.**

2. **Select and drag a snapshot you want to move from its current location and drop it in a new location.**

3. **Continue moving snapshots around until the Faces source is as organized as you want it to be.**

To sort the snapshots automatically, choose View ⇨ Sort Photos ⇨ By Name. The snapshots are sorted alphabetically from the top left to the bottom right.

Removing snapshots

If you decide you don't want a snapshot on your corkboard any more, select the snapshot and press ⌘+Delete. Click Delete Face. The person's name is removed from any photos to which it has been applied and the snapshot disappears. The photos in your library are not affected in any other way.

Using Faces to View Photos

To view the photos associated with a person, perform the following steps:

1. **Move into the Faces source.**

2. **Use the Zoom slider to adjust the size of the snapshots in the window.** Making the snapshots smaller allows you to see more of them without scrolling.

3. **Browse the snapshots, as shown in Figure 4.6.**

4. **To view the photos contained in a snapshot, double-click it.** You see all the photos in which the person's face is identified, as shown in Figure 4.7.

5. **Browse and view the person's photos.** This works like viewing photos in other categories, such as Photos. For example, double-click a photo to view it at maximum size.

4.6 When you select the Faces source, you see a snapshot for each person you identified in at least one photo.

Here are a few notes about viewing photos from a snapshot:

- You can edit the name of the snapshot by changing the text that appears next to the key photo at the top of the window.

- To reduce the thumbnails to show just the person's face, slide the switch at the top of the window to Faces.

- When you are viewing a photo, open the Info sidebar and expand the Faces section to see the name editing tools to identify more faces or change existing faces.

- To confirm the face in other photos, click the Confirm Additional Faces button.

- You can move into other snapshots by clicking the Forward or Back button.

- Click All Faces to return to your corkboard.

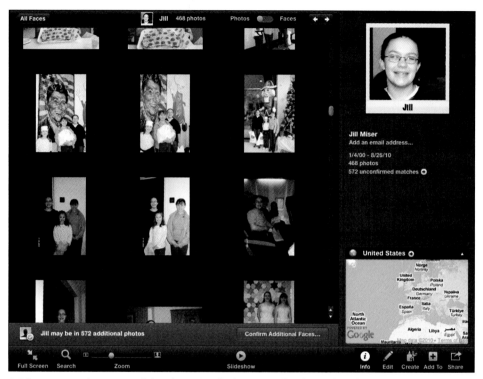

4.7 Open a snapshot to see all the photos in which a person has been identified.

How Can I Use Places to Organize and View My Photos?

You can associate your photos with geographic locations using iPhoto's Places tools. This is useful because you can then find photos based on their locations to quickly move to the photos you have related to specific places, and you can use maps to which your photos are connected in your projects. There are two ways to tag your photos with location information. When you take photos with a GPS-enabled device, such as an iPhone, the location information is captured for you automatically. Or you can manually add a location to any photos in your library.

Understanding Places

iPhoto can tag photos and events with locations. This tag enables some very cool things to happen because iPhoto automatically groups photos by the locations with which they are associated. You can then find and view photos using a map, making it easy to get to photos featuring places you've been, even if it has been a long time since you've been there. For example, in Figure 5.1, you see photos taken on a trip to the United Kingdom in my library.

5.1 The pushpins on this map show the locations in the UK where I have taken photos.

When your photos have location information, you can also add interesting elements to your projects. For example, you can add map pages to photo books and slide shows to make them more interesting to view.

Of course, to be able to use this feature, photos have to be tagged with locations. There are two ways to do this: automatic or manual.

When you capture photos with a camera that associates GPS (Global Positioning System) coordinates with pictures, those coordinates are imported along with the photos and iPhoto automatically assigns places to a photo based on its GPS coordinates. The iPhone is one example of a device that supports this functionality, and some cameras offer this capability as well.

You can also manually assign place tags for those photos or events that don't have location information. To make this easier, you can customize the places you associate with photos most frequently by configuring them in the My Places tool.

Using Places to Tag Photos

To be able to use Places, you need to tag your photos with location information. As mentioned, you can assign locations manually, or if you use a GPS-enabled device, it is done for you automatically when you import photos into your library.

As you use Places, you develop a My Places list. You can customize this list to make the places you assign to photos even more specific, down to individual street addresses if you want to. Using your My Places list makes manually assigning locations even easier.

Configuring automatic place lookups

Of course, automatic implies you don't have to do anything to have location information included with your photos, and that is true. However, you do need to make sure that iPhoto is set to use this information and that the device you use to take photos is configured to capture it.

Open the Preferences dialog and click the Advanced tab, as shown in Figure 5.2. Configure the following settings:

- **Choose Automatically on the Look up Places menu.** This causes iPhoto to look up the GPS coordinates with which photos are tagged and mark their location on a map. If you choose Never, this functionality is disabled.

- **Select the Include location information for published photos check box.** When this check box is selected and you publish photos to your MobileMe Web site or other locations, the location information goes along with the photos. This enables location-based features on such sites to work. If this check box isn't selected, location information is not published when the photos are.

How you enable your GPS-enabled camera to capture and store location information depends on the specific device you use. On an iPhone, enable Location Services through the Settings app and for the Camera app. This allows the camera to access the phone's GPS device so that it can identify the locations where photos are taken. Of course, for this to work, the iPhone must be able to access the GPS network, which means it can't be in Airplane mode, and if you are outside your normal service area, you may need to allow roaming.

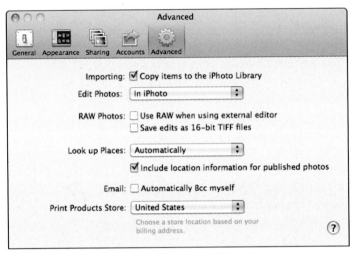

5.2 Configure iPhoto to take advantage of a GPS-enabled camera.

Note

When you launch the Camera app on an iPhone for the first time, you are prompted to allow it to use Location Services. If you tap Allow, photos you take are tagged with their GPS locations. If you don't allow it for some reason, you can reenable it by choosing Settings ⇨ General ⇨ Location Services and tapping OFF next to the Camera so its status becomes ON.

Assigning locations to photos or events manually

To assign place tags to photos or events, perform the following steps:

1. **Select the photos or events to which you want to assign a location.**

Genius

If you select an event and perform these steps, the location is assigned to all the photos in the event. The new location overrides any existing locations.

2. **Click the Info button.** The Info sidebar opens. It looks a bit different depending on whether you selected a photo, a group of photos, or an event, but the location tools appear at the bottom of the sidebar.

3. **Click Assign a Place.** The text disappears indicating you can type a location.

Note If you see a location and map at the bottom of the Info sidebar, a location has already been set. You can change that location, as you learn later in this chapter.

4. **Type the name of the location you want to associate with your selection.** As you type, iPhoto attempts to match what you type to a location, as shown in Figure 5.3. iPhoto uses Google Maps to find locations, so you can be as specific as you want, down to a street address, attraction, or place of business.

Note Because Places relies on Google Maps, your Mac must be connected to the Internet for this feature to work.

5.3 When you type a location, iPhoto attempts to match it.

5. **When you see the location you want to associate with your selection, click it.** The location is associated with each photo included in your selection, and you see the location's pin on the map, as shown in Figure 5.4.

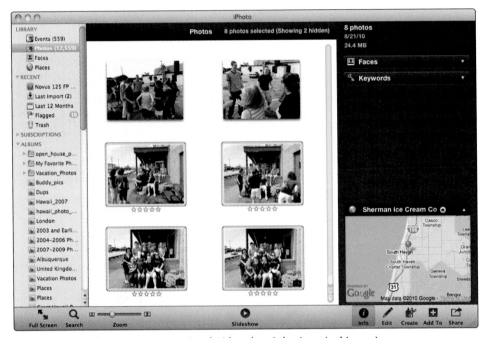

5.4 The selected photos are now associated with a place (a business in this case).

Genius You can copy a location from one photo to others. Select the photo with the location you want to copy and copy it. Select the photos to which you want to copy the location and choose Edit ⇨ Paste Location. The photos you selected will have the location you copied.

Genius The map shown in the Info sidebar is a fully featured Google map. When you move the pointer over it, the toolbar appears. You can use to zoom out, zoom in, center the location on the map, and choose the Terrain (map), Satellite, or Hybrid view. You can also drag around the map to change the part you see in the window. iPhoto saves your map settings from photo to photo so the next time you view the map for a photo, you see the previous configuration, including zoom, type, and so on.

84

Changing locations

You can change the location with which photos are selected using a similar process. Open the Map on the Info sidebar. You see the current location. Click in the text for the current location and then click the Clear (X) button. The current location is removed from the search bar. Search for and select the new location to replace the existing location with a different one.

Genius

You can expand or collapse the Map by clicking the Places header (the bar with the globe icon on it).

Defining your places

You can customize places you use frequently or that you want to personalize. For example, instead of marking a location with grandma's street address, you can personalize the location name by calling it "Grandma's House." As you customize names, you create a My Places list that you can use to further customize your places.

Personalizing locations

To create a personalized location, perform the following steps:

1. **Move to the map showing the location of a photo on the Info sidebar.**

2. **Click the location's pushpin.** The name of the location appears in an edit box along with the check mark and X buttons.

3. **Type the personalized name of the location and click the check mark button as shown in Figure 5.5.** The location is renamed with your personalized version and is also added to your My Places list.

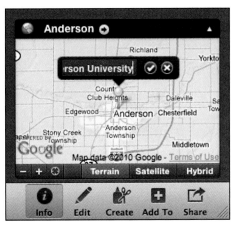

5.5 You can rename locations to make them more meaningful to you.

85

Note Any personalized places you create become available on the results list when you search for locations with which to associate a photo. If you do have a location called "Grandma's House," you can search for grandma's house to add that location to photos. Of course, you can still search for grandma's street address, too.

Configuring locations on your My Places list

To further customize places on your My Places list, perform these steps:

1. **Choose Window ⇨ Manage My Places.** The Manage My Places sheet appears. The My Places tab shows the locations that you've customized; think of these as your bookmarked or favorite locations that you can easily apply to photos.

2. **Select a location that you want to further customize.** The location is shown with a pushpin on the map, as in Figure 5.6. A circle is shown around the location to indicate how close another location has to be to be considered to be part of that location. For example, if you have a location for Lucas Oil Stadium in Indianapolis, you want the circle to be tightly around the stadium on the map so only photos in or very close to the stadium are grouped under that location while photos in the general Indianapolis vicinity are grouped under Indianapolis.

3. **To change the location, do any of the following:**

    -   To remove a location you no longer need, click its Remove button (–).
    -   To rename a location, click its name and edit it or type a new name; then press Return.
    -   To change the size of the area associated with a location, select it on the list and increase or decrease the size of the circle around its pin by dragging its Resize handles.

4. **When you finish customizing your places, click Done.** The sheet closes and the changes you made take effect.

Genius To define places really precisely, place the map in Satellite mode and zoom in so that you can see the actual features (such as buildings) of the area. Then size the location circle so that it includes the specific area you want to identify as a place.

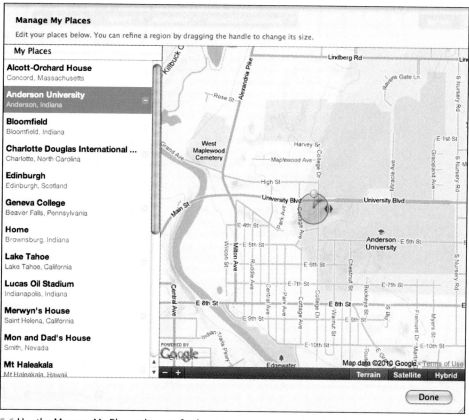

5.6 Use the Manage My Places sheet to further customize your custom locations.

Using Places to Find and View Photos

When your photos are associated with locations, you can use the Places tools to find and view photos for any of your locations. Here's how:

1. **Open the Places source by clicking Places on the Source pane (Standard mode) or click the Places button on the toolbar (Full Screen mode).** You see a map showing the locations of your photos with red pins (see Figure 5.7).

2. **Click the Style buttons in the upper-right corner of the window to set the map's style.** The options are Terrain, Satellite, and Hybrid. The map changes to the style you select.

5.7 Places is a very intuitive way to find and view your photos.

3. Focus on the location for which you want to see photos using any of the following techniques:

- Use the Zoom slider to zoom in and drag the map to move the area you are inter-ested in toward the center of the screen so it remains visible.

- Use the Countries, States, Cities, and Places menus to focus on specific locations. The options you choose on the higher-level menus limit the options you have on the other menus. For example, if you choose Canada on the Countries menu, you only see the provinces (on the States menu), cities, and places in Canada with which pho-tos are associated. You can jump to more specific locations by using the lower-level menus, such as Cities or Places. When you make a selection, the map refocuses on your selection, as shown in Figure 5.8.

5.8 Because I've selected Ottawa on the Cities menu, the map shows all the photos in my library associated with Ottawa.

- Use the scroll wheel or a gesture on a trackpad to zoom.

- Double-click on the map where you want to focus. Each time you do so, the map zooms in where you double-click.

4. **Point to a pushpin to see the location it points to.** The location name appears above the pushpin, as shown in Figure 5.9.

Genius

To see the photos for a group of locations, configure the map so those locations are shown and then click the Show Photos button on the toolbar. The resulting screen shows you all the photos from the selected locations along with the numbers of places the photos come from. The map on the Info sidebar places a pushpin at each individual location.

5.9 When you point to a pushpin on the map, you see the location with which the pin is associated.

5. **To view the photos associated with a location, click the right-facing arrow in the pin's label.** The photos associated with that location appear, as shown in Figure 5.10.

6. **View the photos.** You can view photos you've moved to via Places just like those you move to through Events, Faces, and so on.

7. **Click Map to return to the Map view.**

To zoom out so you see pins for all the locations in your library, click the Zoom All button.

Genius

You can change the locations with which photos are associated by relocating their pushpins on the map when you view the map in the Info pane. Click the pushpin (it turns yellow) and drag it to a new location.

Genius

90

5.10 Here, I'm viewing photos associated with the National Wallace Monument in Stirling, Scotland.

Can iPhoto Help Me Keep My Photos Organized?

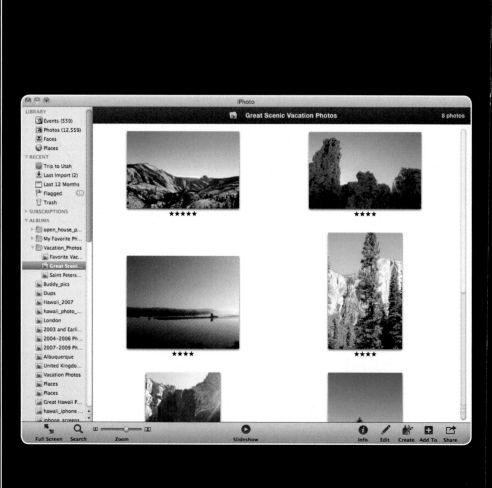

In a short time, you'll accumulate many photos in your library. It wastes time (and isn't much fun) to have to browse your photos when you want to view, or do something else, with them. Instead of browsing, use photo albums to collect and organize your photos for viewing or as the starting point for many kinds of projects. Over time, you manage your photo albums to keep them current and use those albums to quickly find and view photos. An important part of organizing is removing photos you don't want so they don't clutter your library.

Creating and Configuring Standard Photo Albums

Photo albums are a good way to create collections of photos for many purposes, including to view those photos and to use them in projects. A standard photo album is a collection of photos that you gather and arrange manually (contrasted with a Smart Album where photos are collected automatically based on criteria you specify). The benefit of a standard photo album is that you determine exactly which photos are included and how those photos are organized. The downside of a standard photo album is that it is a static entity; any changes you make to it have to be done directly.

Note You'll notice that most of the screenshots in this chapter show iPhoto in Standard mode while in the previous chapters, they were mostly in the Full Screen mode. That's because working with albums is an area where I think the Standard mode is much easier and more efficient to use than Full Screen mode. This is primarily because of the Source pane in the Standard mode, which makes working with albums much better than trying to manage albums in Full Screen mode. Like the other areas, you should try both modes to see which you prefer, but I suspect you'll end up with the same preference I have.

Creating a standard photo album

To create a standard photo album, perform the following steps:

1. **Select the photos you want to include in the new album.** You can do this by viewing and selecting photos in any source, even in other albums.

2. **Click the Add To button on the toolbar at the bottom of the window and choose Album on the resulting menu.** The Album sheet appears. On this sheet, you see your existing albums along with the New Album option.

3. **Click the New Album icon, as shown in Figure 6.1.** The photos you selected are placed in a new folder, which appears and is selected on the Source pane.

4. **Type the new album's name and press Return.** The new album is saved with the name you entered, and you see the photos that you selected. The album is ready to use, add more photos to, and so on.

Genius You can also create a new standard album by selecting photos and choosing File ➪ New ➪ Album or pressing ⌘+N.

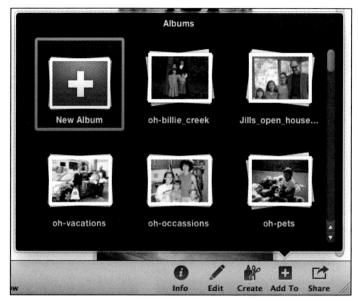

6.1 Click the New Album icon to create a new album containing selected photos.

Adding photos to a standard photo album

Adding photos to a standard album is a two-step process. First, find the photos you want to add. Second, add them to the album.

You can always find photos to add to a standard photo album by browsing various sources, such as Events or Photos. As you learn in Chapter 7, you can use more sophisticated ways to find photos. But regardless of the technique you use to find them, your photos always end up in the Browsing pane.

To add photos to an album, select the photos you want to move into an album. Each photo you select is highlighted with a yellow box. Drag the selected photos onto the album to which you want to add them. As you drag, the number of images you've selected appears in a red circle above the pointer; when the album icon is highlighted and the green circle containing a + appears, release the mouse button, as shown in Figure 6.2. The photos are placed into the album. That's all there is to it.

Genius

Another way to add photos to an album is to select the photos you want to add, click the Add To button, and on the album sheet, click the album in which you want to place the photos. The benefit of this approach is that you don't need to be able to see the folder on the Source pane so it is easier to find photos from other sources to add to a folder.

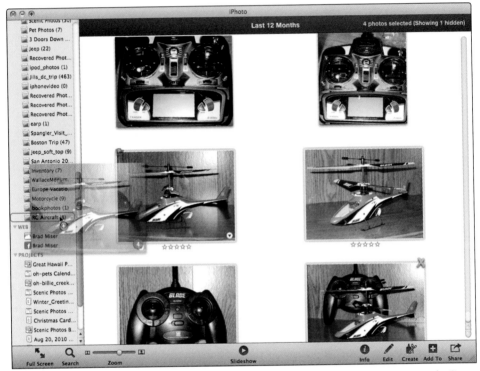

6.2 Add photos to a standard album by dragging their thumbnails onto the album's icon on the Source pane.

When you place a photo in an album, you aren't doing anything with the photo itself. Instead, a pointer is created to the photo from its location in the library. The pointer file acts just like the photo in the library, meaning you can view it, edit it, and so on. However, because a pointer is used instead of the file itself, you can include the same photo in as many albums and projects as you want. This also means that a change you make in one place affects all the others. For example, when you crop a photo in an album, each occurrence of that photo is cropped in the same way (because you are actually working with just one instance of the photo no matter how many times it appears in albums and projects).

To see the contents of an album, select it on the Source pane. That album's photos appear in the Browsing pane, as shown in Figure 6.3.

Genius

If the album in which you want to place photos isn't visible on the Source pane, just drag the photos toward the top or the bottom of the Source pane. It will scroll so that you can move to the album in which you want to place the photos.

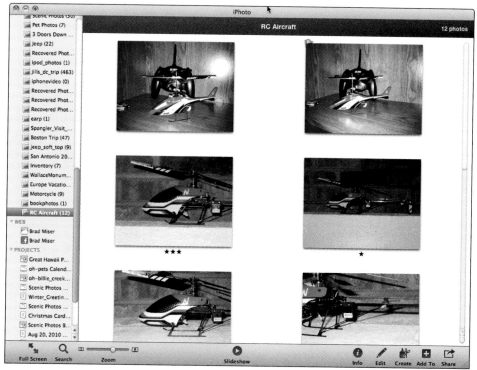

6.3 To view the contents of a photo album, select it on the Source pane.

Removing photos from a standard photo album

To remove photos from an album, perform the following steps:

1. **Select the album from which you want to remove photos.**

2. **Select the photos you want to remove.**

3. **Press Delete.** The selected photos no longer appear in the album.

Note Because albums only contain pointers to image files, deleting a photo from an album only removes the pointer from the album. The photo itself remains in your library.

Organizing photos in a standard photo album

You can determine the order in which photos in a standard photo album appear, as shown in Figure 6.4. The direction of photos starts at the top left and moves to the right until the end of the first row; the next photo in the sequence is the first photo in the second row. For example, when you view the photos in an album by playing a slideshow, they appear in the order they are shown in the album, starting from the top left and moving toward the bottom right. This is especially important when you create a project based on an album because the order of the photos in the project will initially be determined by the order of photos in the album.

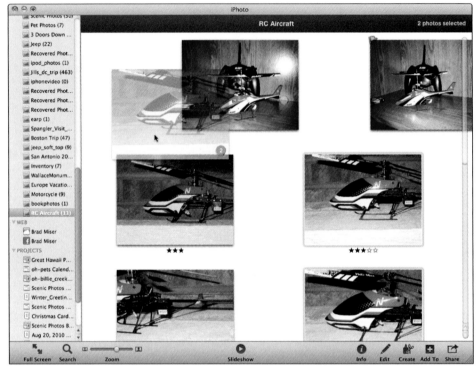

6.4 To change the order of photos in a standard album, drag them to be in the order in which you want them to appear.

To set the order of photos in a standard album, do the following:

1. **Select the album you want to organize.** Its photos appear.

2. **Drag photos within the window until they are in the order you want them to appear, working from the top-left corner toward the bottom-right one.** As you drag photos, the number you are dragging appears next to the cursor. As you move between photos, they slide apart to "make room" for the photos you are moving.

Creating and Configuring Smart Photo Albums

A smart photo album is smart because you tell it the kind of photos you want to collect (using criteria) and the Smart Album sorts through all the photos in your library, gathering those that meet your criteria. As time passes and you add more photos that meet these criteria, the Smart Album keeps up and adds the new photos to the collection. A smart photo album is dynamic in that it always contains the set of photos that currently meet your requirements.

Like standard photo albums, Smart Albums are useful for viewing photos, creating projects, sharing photos, and so on.

Tagging your photos is critical to being able to create Smart Albums because you use those tags to define the rules for a Smart Album. You learn about tagging photos in Chapters 2 through 5.

Creating a Smart Album

When you create a Smart Album, you create the basic container and then define the rules for the photos it should contain. Here's how:

1. **Click the Create button on the toolbar at the bottom of the window.** The Add sheet appears.

2. **Hold the Option key down and choose Smart Album.** The tools you use to define the Smart Album's rules appear on a sheet that drops down.

3. **Name the album.**

4. **Select the attribute of the first rule using the pop-up menu on the far left of the sheet, as shown in Figure 6.5.** The pop-up menus, boxes, and other tools in the rule definition area change so they are germane to the attribute you selected. For example, if you choose Keyword, you see a pop-up menu and a text box. Other choices might have fewer or more options.

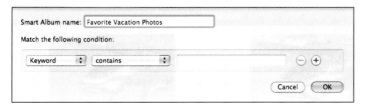

6.5 Here, I've selected Keyword for the first rule of this Smart Album.

5. **Use the condition pop-up menu (if one appears) to define how you are going to match the information you enter.** For example, choose *contains* if you are defining a text rule and want anything that contains the text to be included, while you should choose *is* to search for only an exact match.

6. **Type the data for the rule you are creating using the tools that appear; this involves making choices on pop-up menus, typing text, selecting dates, and so on.** Your specific entry depends on the attribute you select in Step 4.

7. **To add another rule, click the Add button (+) at the end of the rule's row.** A new, empty rule appears.

8. **Repeat Steps 4 through 6 to configure the new rule.** To remove a rule, click the Remove button (–) at the end of the rule's row.

9. **Repeat Steps 7 and 8 to add more rules.**

10. **On the Match pop-up menu, choose all if you want all the rules to be met for a photo to be included or any if only one of the rules has to be met for a photo to be included.**

11. **Click OK, as shown in Figure 6.6.** The sheet closes, the Smart Album is created, all the photos that meet its rules are collected within it, and you see the contents of the new Smart Album.

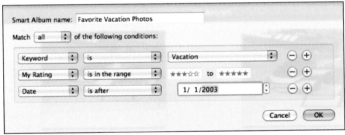

6.6 This Smart Album will contain photos that are tagged with the keyword "Vacation," are rated with three, four, or five stars, and have a date later than 1/1/2003.

Sorting a Smart Album

As with a standard photo album, the order in which photos appear in a Smart Album determines the order in which those photos appear when you view them, initially create projects, and so on. However, unlike standard photo albums, you don't change the order of photos in a Smart Album by dragging them around the window. Instead, you use the Sort command to choose a sort order for the photos within a Smart Album. Here's how to sort a Smart Album:

1. **Select the smart album you want to sort.**

2. **Choose View ⇨ Sort Photos.**

3. **Choose how you want the album to be sorted on the submenu that appears.** The options are by date, keyword, title, or rating. The photos in the Smart Album are sorted according to the selection you made.

4. **To reverse the order of the sort, choose View ⇨ Sort Photos and then choose Ascending or Descending (whichever isn't currently selected).**

Changing the photos in a Smart Album

To change the photos contained in a Smart Album, you change the rules on which the album is based.

1. **Select the smart photo album you want to change.**

2. **Right-click on the album's icon and choose Edit Smart Album.** The Smart Album's sheet appears and you see the album's current rules.

3. **Change the rules that are part of the Smart Album in the following ways:**

   - Add rules.

   - Remove rules.

   - Change the conditions in existing rules.

   - Change the setting in the Match pop-up menu to require all or any of the rules to be met.

4. **Click OK.** The photos contained in the Smart Album are changed so that only photos that match the current rules are included.

Using Folders to Organize Photo Albums

Photo albums (standard and Smart) are very useful, and over time you'll probably accumulate a lot of them. This can make working with the Source pane tough because you have to scroll a long distance up and down frequently. You can organize your albums into folders to reduce the clutter on your Source pane.

Genius

You can make the Source pane wider or narrower by pointing to the right edge of its border; when the pointer changes to be a vertical line with two horizontal lines coming out of it, drag the edge to the left or right.

To create a folder, follow these steps:

1. **Choose File ⇨ New ⇨ Folder or press Option+Shift+⌘+N.** A new folder appears on the Source pane.

2. **Type the folder's name and press Return.** The folder is ready for items you want to place within it.

To place items within a folder, simply drag them onto the folder's icon. When you release the mouse button, the items are placed within the folder. An expansion triangle appears next to the folder's icon; click this to expand or collapse the folder's contents.

You can also place folders within other folders to create a nested structure for more organizational flexibility, as shown in Figure 6.7. When you place one folder within another, it moves under the first folder's hierarchy. You can continue adding folders to create a "deep" structure for multiple levels of organization.

When you select a folder, you see all the photos it contains.

Finally, you can reorganize the items in a folder just by dragging them up or down the Source pane.

6.7 You can create nested folders to keep your photo albums and projects organized.

Managing Photo Albums

You can do the following to manage your photo albums:

- **Rename a photo album.** Select an album's name and press Return. Type a new name or edit the current one and then press Return to save your changes.

- **Change an album's information.** Select an album and click the Info button. On the Info sidebar, you see information about the album. This includes the key photo, title, date range, description, and map. You can configure an album's information just like configuring an event's information (which is explained in Chapter 2).

- **Update the photos in an album.** For a standard photo album, you can add or remove photos and reorganize photos. For a Smart Album, update the album's rules to change its contents and use the Sort tool to change how photos are organized.

- **Sort the order of albums on the Source pane.** Right-click on the Source pane and choose Sort Albums. Within the ALBUMS section, folders are grouped at the top, next are Smart Albums, and lowest on the list are standard albums. Each of these is sorted in alphabetical order among its respective types.

- **Delete photo albums.** To remove a photo album, select it and press Delete. You see a confirmation sheet; click Delete to remove the album. Only the album is removed; the photos remain in the library.

Genius

You can use folders to organize just about everything on your Source pane, including photo albums, slideshows, photo books, and so on. You can mix and match items within a folder, too. For example, you could create a folder for vacation photos and store an album, slideshow, and photo book containing those photos in the same folder.

Using Albums to Find Photos

Photo albums are very useful for finding photos. You can use photo albums a couple of ways when you search.

You can create a Smart Album for searches that you repeat. You can add many tags to a Smart Album's criteria to search by multiple tags at the same time (something you can't do with any other search technique), as shown in Figure 6.8. When you create the Smart Album, the photos that meet your search criteria are immediately added to that album. And, as you add photos to your library that are tagged with the search criteria, those photos are added to the album automatically. This means you can always see your current search results by selecting the Smart Album.

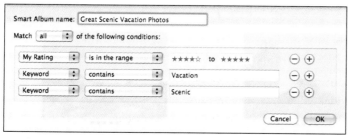

6.8 This Smart Album will always contain photos that are rated at four or five stars and associated with the keywords Vacation and Scenic.

You can create a Smart photo Album for a location by opening the map, clicking a location, and then clicking the Smart Album button. This creates a Smart Album whose name is the location name and whose search condition is Place is on map, with the location represented by the pin's location. The album will contain all the photos associated with that location, and you can add more conditions to it, such as the photos must have a specific star rating.

You can also use a standard photo album as a great holding area for search results, especially when you want to perform several different searches to find the photos you need. Here's how:

1. **Create a standard photo album to hold your search results.**

2. **Perform the first search.**

3. **Drag the photos that are of interest onto the standard photo album you created in Step 1.**

4. **Perform the next search.**

5. **Store its results in the photo album.**

You can repeat these steps as many times as you need while gathering the fruits of your searching efforts in the standard photo album and storing them there until you want to use them. In this way, a standard album is like a shopping cart you use at a retail Web site. It becomes a holding place to store the photos that turn up from your searches.

Using Albums to View Photos

You've already seen how you can use albums to view photos in Standard mode. When iPhoto is in the Standard mode, simply select the album whose photos you want to view on the Source pane and you see its photos in the right part of the window. You can use the browsing and viewing tools you learned about in earlier chapters to view those photos.

While working with albums is better in Standard mode, the Full Screen mode is useful for viewing photos in albums. In Full Screen mode, click the Albums button. You see all the albums in your library, as shown in Figure 6.9. In addition to the albums you've created, you see iPhoto's default albums, such as Photos, Last X Months, Import, and Flagged. You can browse your albums.

6.9 In Full Screen mode, you see a thumbnail for each of the albums in your library.

To view an album's photos, double-click its icon. You see the album's photos and can use the viewing tools you learned about in earlier chapters to view them, as shown in Figure 6.10.

6.10 Viewing photos in an album is one area where the Full Screen mode is better than the Standard mode.

Removing Photos from Your Library

Part of organizing your library is keeping the clutter down. In this case, clutter means photos or other images for which you have no use now or in the future. You should remove such photos so that they don't take up disk storage space and so that they don't make your library more cumbersome to use. iPhoto has its own Trash that is separate from the Trash on your desktop; iPhoto's Trash is located in the Recent section of the Source pane (don't ask me why).

As with working on the desktop, when you remove a photo by deleting it, it goes into the Trash. To remove a photo, select it in a Library source (such as Events, Photos, Faces, or Places) and press Delete. The photo is moved from the Library to the Trash, as shown in Figure 6.11.

Note

Remember that removing a photo from a photo album or project only removes that item from the specific album or project because the photos in those places are merely pointers to the actual photo stored in the library.

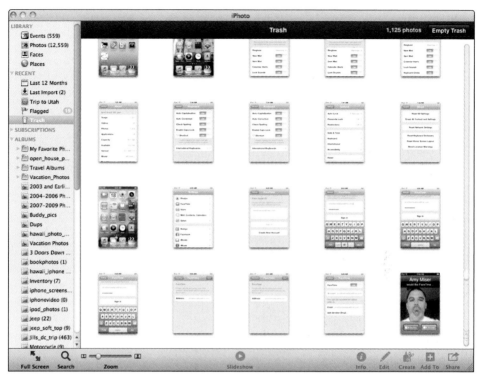

6.11 iPhoto's Trash contains your photo refuse, which you can recover at any time (until you empty it).

You can recover photos from the Trash by selecting the Trash and moving photos from the Trash back onto the Events or Photos source. The photo is restored in the source on which you dropped it. If you are sure that the Trash contains only photos or images you'll never need again, you can (and should) empty it. This recovers the disk space being used by your photographic rubbish so that you can put it to better use.

Select the Trash and browse its contents to make sure it doesn't contain anything you might need again. When you are ready to take out the digital trash, click the Empty Trash button. Click OK at the prompt. Once you empty iPhoto's Trash, its contents are gone for good so be careful before you use this command.

How Else Can I Find My Photos?

Being able to find photos is a fundamental iPhoto skill because it is the first step with almost everything you do with iPhoto, from viewing photos to building photo books. In Chapters 2 through 6, you learn how to use iPhoto's categorization, tagging, and organization tools to be able to find your photos. However, iPhoto has a couple more searching tricks up its digital sleeve: Recents and the Search tool. Learning to use these effectively rounds out your ability to find any photos in your library that you want to view or use.

Using Recents to Find Photos

Often, the photos you want to find are those that you've added to your iPhoto library recently. To that end, iPhoto offers the following sources in the RECENT section of the Source pane (shown in Figure 7.1 and listed here from the top of the RECENT section toward the bottom):

- **Last Event.** By default, last event is the event you most recently opened, which appears at the top of the RECENT section. This is a quick way to get back to an event that you had most recently viewed. You can select that event to see the photos it contains.

- **Last Import.** This source contains the photos you imported during your most recent import session from any source (camera, the desktop, and so on). This is particularly useful right after you import photos; select this source and apply the appropriate tags to them as the last step of the import process. Doing this consistently as part of the import process makes tagging new photos part of your routine so that you keep up with it.

- **Last _X_ Months.** By default, this source is called Last 12 Months because it contains the photos you've added to your library over the past 12 months. You can change the time period this recent tracks as you learn shortly.

- **Flagged.** This source contains all the photos you've tagged with the flag marker (see Chapter 3 to learn how to flag photos). This isn't really related to the concept of recent because flagged photos remain here until you remove their flags, but my guess is that the iPhoto developers decided it was the best place to provide this very useful source.

- **Trash.** Like the Flagged source, the Trash doesn't really relate to the concept of recent because photos you move to the Trash remain there until you empty it. But it is a convenient place to keep the Trash.

Note   You must open an event to see its photos before it appears as the Last Event; if you just browse an event, it won't appear here.

To configure how many months of photos are in the Last _X_ Months album, open the General pane of the iPhoto Preferences dialog. Enter the number of months for this album in the Show last field by clicking the Up or Down triangle or by typing a number.

Note   If you don't want the Last _X_ Months album displayed for some reason, deselect the Show last check box on the General pane of the Preferences dialog.

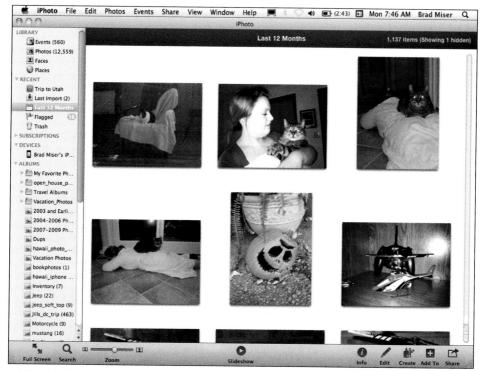

7.1 Use the albums in the RECENT section of the Source pane to locate photos you've imported or viewed recently.

You can use the Recents albums just like other sources you work with to view photos, select them for projects, and so on.

Genius

You can access the Recents albums in Full Screen mode, too. Click the Albums button. On the top row of your albums, you see the Last Import, Last X Months, and Flagged albums.

Using the Search Tool to Find Photos

The Search tool, located at the bottom of the iPhoto window, enables you to search photos by the various kinds of tags associated with them. These include all, date, keywords, and rating.

Searching by all

The All search tool, which is the Search tool's default mode, finds photos by searching all the text tags associated with photos. (The text tags are the title and description.) To search by all, perform the following steps:

1. **Select the source that you want to search.** For example, to search your entire library, click Photos or Events.

2. **Click the Search button on the toolbar.** The Search tool expands.

3. **Type the text for which you want to search in the Search tool.** As you type, iPhoto matches your search text with the photos in the selected source and shows those that match your search, as shown in Figure 7.2. To be included in the results, a photo's title or description must contain the text or numbers you type; the Search tool is not case sensitive. The more specific the search text or numbers, the more specific the search is.

7.2 If you just type text in the Search tool, iPhoto searches for photos with titles or descriptions containing the text you type.

Genius

To clear any search, click the Clear button (X) in the Search tool. The search criterion is cleared and you see all the photos in the selected source.

Searching by month

Using the date to search is a powerful way to find photos because all photos are tagged with dates automatically. You can be sure every photo in your library has a date associated with it so it is a very reliable tag for searching (unlike titles or descriptions, which are only as reliable for searching as you are disciplined about making sure you configure these tags on your photos). To search for photos associated with one or more months, perform the following steps:

1. **Select the source that you want to search.** For example, to search in a photo album, click it in the Source pane.

2. **Click the Search button on the toolbar.** The Search tool expands, as shown in Figure 7.3.

7.3 Use the Date search tool in month mode to search for photos associated with a month.

3. **Click the Magnifying Glass icon in the Search tool.**

4. **Click Date on the pop-up menu.** The Date search tool appears. This tool has two modes: search by month or search by date.

5. **Click the right-facing arrow at the top left of the tool to change modes until the tool is in the month mode.** When it is in month mode, you see the year at the top with the 12 months of the year below. The names of months that have photos are highlighted.

6. **Click the left- or right-facing arrow until the year you want to search appears at the top of the tool.**

7. **Select the months you want to search (hold down the ⌘ key while you click each month you want to search).** The photos associated with the months you selected appear.

You can search in the same year or in different months in different years at the same time by selecting the months in one year and then selecting the next year you want to search. As you hold down the ⌘ key, select the months in the second year you want to search. You can continue adding years to expand your search.

Searching by date

You can also search for photos associated with specific dates using the Date search tool by doing the following steps:

1. **Select the source that you want to search.**

2. **Click the Search button on the toolbar.** The Search tool expands.

3. **Click the Magnifying Glass icon in the Search tool.**

4. **Click Date on the pop-up menu.** The Date search tool appears.

5. **Click the right-facing arrow at the top left of the tool to change modes until the tool is in the date mode.** When it is in this mode, you see a month in the tool, as shown in Figure 7.4. The dates that have photos associated with them are highlighted.

Genius

You can combine month and date searches. Perform one type of search and click the Mode button at the top left of the tool to switch to the other mode. Add search criteria in the mode and the photos that meet both the date and month criteria appear.

Note

When you exit the Search tool, the date range of the photos currently being shown is displayed in the Search tool.

7.4 Use the Date search tool in date mode to search for photos associated with specific dates.

Searching by keywords

You can search by keyword easily by doing the following steps:

1. **Select the source that you want to search.**

2. **Click the Search button on the toolbar.** The Search tool expands.

3. **Click the Magnifying Glass icon in the Search tool.**

4. **Click Keyword on the pop-up menu.** The Keyword search tool appears, as shown in Figure 7.5. You see all the keywords you have configured.

Genius

Keywords are connected by "and" when you search by multiple keywords. This means all the keywords must apply to a photo for it to be found. You can exclude photos with a keyword from the results by holding down the Option key while you click the keyword you want to exclude.

115

7.5 You can select combinations of keywords to find photos that are tagged with all the keywords you have selected.

5. **Click the keywords for which you want to search.** As you click, the selected keywords are highlighted and the photos tagged with all of them appear.

Searching by rating

You can look for photos based on their rating by performing the following steps:

1. **Select the source that you want to search.**

2. **Click the Search button on the toolbar.** The Search tool expands.

3. **Click the Magnifying Glass icon in the Search tool.**

4. **Click Rating on the pop-up menu.** Stars appear in the Search tool.

5. **Click the star representing the number of stars you want photos to have as a minimum to be included in the results.** The photos that are rated at that number of stars or higher appear. For example, if you click the fourth star, you find all the photos that have a four- or five-star rating, as shown in Figure 7.6.

7.6 Searching by rating finds all the photos rated at the number of stars you select or higher.

Searching by names or places

You can also search for photos based on the places or names with which they are associated by performing the following steps:

1. **Select the source that you want to search.**

2. **Click the Search button on the toolbar.** The Search tool expands. (If you have previously selected a search type, choose All on the menu.)

3. **Type the name or place for which you want to search in the Search tool.** As you type, iPhoto matches your text with the photos in the selected source and shows the ones that are associated with the place you typed.

You can only search for one name or one place at a time.

Note

One of the best things about digital photographs is that you can edit them. iPhoto includes editing tools you can use to correct problems with or make enhancements to your photos. iPhoto editing is nondestructive, meaning that you can always restore a photo to its original condition should the changes you make not be what you want. If you prefer to use a different photo-editing application, you can configure iPhoto to automatically use that application when you edit photos.

Working with iPhoto's Editing Tools

When you edit photos, you select the photos you want to edit and then open iPhoto's Edit sidebar, on which you can access three tabs of editing tools (as shown in Figure 8.1), which are:

- **Quick Fixes.** The Quick Fixes tab provides editing tools that do most of the work for you. You usually either just click a button or select part of a photo to edit and then use simple tools to make changes.

- **Effects.** Using this tab, you can change the brightness and color and apply different effects to photos, such as Sepia or Antique.

- **Adjust.** On this tab, you see a series of sliders that enable you to adjust technical aspects of your photos, such as exposure and contrast.

8.1 You use the tools on the three tabs of the Edit sidebar to fix problems with or to make improvements to your photos.

Before you start making too many changes, you need to understand your editing options and how the edits you make in a photo can affect your iPhoto projects. You should also understand how to create duplicates in the event you want multiple versions of the same photo in your library. No matter how extensive the changes to a photo are, you can always go back to the original version because iPhoto edits are nondestructive; this means iPhoto retains the original versions of your photos as you imported them so you can always undo your editing work if needed.

Choosing a mode to edit in

You can edit photos using one of the following options:

- **Standard mode.** In Standard mode, you see three panes, as shown in Figure 8.2. The far left is the Source pane, the center pane is the editing area, and the far right is the Edit sidebar. Exposing the Source pane makes selecting photos easier, but you lose valuable screen space, and when you are editing, more room to work in is generally a good thing.

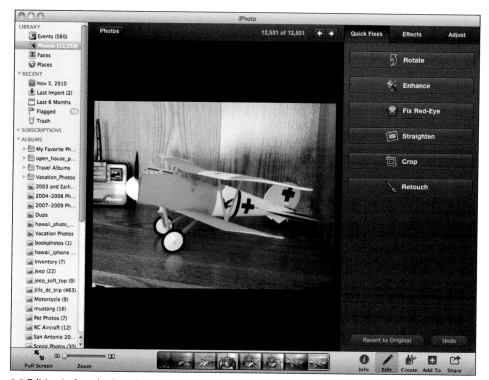

8.2 Editing in Standard mode makes choosing the photos you want to edit easier, but you lose valuable editing space that is taken up by the Source pane.

- **Full Screen mode.** This is similar to editing in Standard mode except you only see two panes, which gives you the maximum amount of room for the photo you are editing. In general, you should edit in Full Screen mode because having plenty of working space makes editing more efficient.

⦿ **Other applications.** If you have a different photo-editing application that you prefer, you can configure iPhoto to use that application instead of its own editing tools. (I explain this option in the last section of this chapter.)

With the first two options, the same set of iPhoto editing tools is available to you, so the steps you use to edit in both of them are the same. With the third option, the application you select provides the editing tools.

No matter which mode you use and what specific editing tasks you want to accomplish, you will do certain steps as part of every editing session. You need to know about these fundamental steps in the editing process, from selecting photos to edit to comparing photos.

Selecting and editing photos

The first part of the editing process is to select the set of photos you want to edit and enter Edit mode, as shown in Figure 8.3. You use iPhoto's editing tools to improve the photos you select. When you finish, you exit Edit mode.

8.3 The photo selected on the Selector tool is in focus and is ready to edit.

Following are the general steps for selecting and editing photos:

1. **Select the source containing the photos you want to edit on the Source pane.** You can edit photos in any source. Generally, you want to choose an event, album, or other subset of your library to make selecting the specific photo you want to edit easier.

2. **Click the Edit button.** The Edit sidebar appears. The photo appearing in the window is the one in focus, meaning it is the one you are editing. The editing tools appear on the three tabs on the right side of the window. At the bottom of the window is the Selector tool. Here, you see thumbnails for all the photos in the source you selected in Step 1.

3. **On the Selector tool, click the thumbnail for the photo you want to edit.** When you point to the tool, it zooms and expands so you can select specific photos more easily. You can scroll the tool using its scrollbar. You can also move from photo to photo by pressing the Right and Left arrow keys on your keyboard. The thumbnail of the photo you are editing is highlighted in a yellow box, as shown in Figure 8.4.

8.4 Use the Selector tool to choose the photo you want to edit.

If you select the photo you want to edit before you click the Edit button, that photo is in focus as soon as you click the button.

4. **Edit the photo.** Use iPhoto's editing tools to make changes to the image. I explain these tools throughout the rest of this chapter.

5. **When you finish editing a photo, use the Selector tool to move to the next photo you want to edit.**

6. **Repeat Steps 4 and 5 until you've edited all the photos in the selected group.**

7. **Click the Edit button.** You exit Edit mode.

Note

You don't need to save editing changes as you make them. iPhoto does that for you automatically.

Duplicating photos to edit

As you edit, it's important to understand that when you move a photo to a photo album, project (such as a calendar or photo book), or any other source, you aren't actually moving the photo there. Instead, iPhoto places a pointer to the photo's file in those locations. This is good because it keeps the disk space required to store your photos at a minimum; you are storing only one file per photo. (You see that's not exactly true when you learn how to restore the original, but I get to that shortly.)

In the context of editing, this is critical because when you edit a photo, you are editing the only version of that photo stored in your library. Suppose you have used the same photo in a calendar, card, and slideshow. When you edit the photo, the changes you make are reflected everywhere that photo is used. For example, if you crop the photo so you only see half of it, you only see half of it in all the projects it appears in.

This is good because a lot of edits you make, such as removing red eye, are appropriate any time you use a photo. You make this edit once, and it applies to the photo in every location you use it in.

It can be bad with other kinds of edits, such as applying effects, because you might not want that photo effect each time the photo appears in your projects. Suppose you use a photo in both a photo book and a slideshow. You create the slideshow first and place the photo in it. Sometime later, you create the photo book with the same photo in it. In the photo book, you want the photo to have a matte finish so you edit it and apply the Matte effect. The photo also gets the matte finish in the slideshow, which might not be what you want.

Note You can make some changes to photos in projects, such as photo books, calendars, and cards that affect the photo only in that project. You make these types of changes using the tools that appear in the Project mode. Any time you use the Edit mode's tools, the changes you make to a photo change it wherever it appears.

As you edit a photo, you need to determine if you want the changes you make to apply everywhere the photo is used. If you don't, you need to make a copy of the photo and then edit the copy.

To make a copy of a photo, do the following:

1. **Select the photo you want to copy.**

2. **Choose Photos ⇨ Duplicate or press ⌘+D.** The photo you selected is copied, and both versions are stored in your library. The duplicate version has "Version X," where X is a sequential number for each version you create, appended to its title, as shown in Figure 8.5.

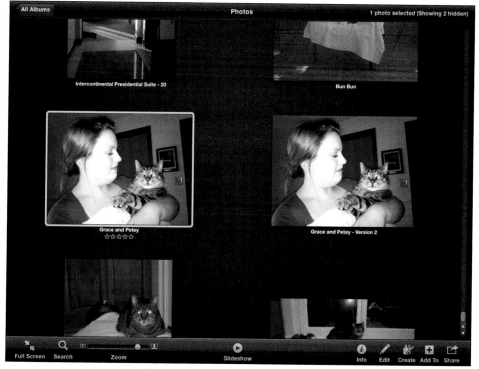

8.5 Make a copy of a photo when you want to have different versions of the photo for various projects.

3. **Update the information for the copy to distinguish it from the other version.** For example, if you create a copy for a specific project, edit the copy's title so it has the project name in it. This step is important because as time passes, you might forget why you made a copy and accidentally delete it thinking you don't need it anymore.

Choose photos to duplicate carefully. One reason is because each copy adds to the space required to store your photos. A more important one, however, is that the more photos you have, the more difficult it becomes to keep your library organized and you cannot work as efficiently. So only make a copy of a photo when you are really sure you need to have more than one version of it.

Zooming and navigating around a photo you are editing

Some editing tasks, such as removing red eye, are best done when you are zoomed in on the area of the photo that you want to edit. You can zoom in or out using the Zoom slider at the bottom of the window. When you zoom in such that not all of the photo can be displayed in the window, the Navigation tool appears, as shown in Figure 8.6.

8.6 When you zoom in a photo for close-up editing, use the Navigation tool to focus on a specific area to edit.

Genius

If the Navigation tool is in your way, you can close it. The zoom settings aren't affected. To open the box again, click to the left or right of the Zoom slider or drag the slider.

In this box, you see the entire photo shaded except for a smaller unshaded box that shows you the relative location of the part of the photo on which you are zoomed. You can move the zoomed area around the photo by dragging the Navigation tool until you see the part of the photo you want to work with both in the smaller box and on the screen. You can also drag the Navigation tool on the screen to position it where it is most convenient for you.

Seeing the impact of and undoing changes

As you edit, you might not always be sure a change you make improves a photo. You can see the impact of your most recent changes by pressing the Shift key. The version of the photo before your last change is displayed. When you release the Shift key, the version with the change you last made is shown. By flipping back and forth, you can decide if the change was an improvement or not. If not, you can undo it.

Here's how this part of the editing process works:

1. **Make an editing change, such as a crop, as shown in Figure 8.7.**

2. **Press the Shift key and hold it down.** The photo reverts to what it was before your most recent change, as shown in Figure 8.8.

3. **If you decide the change you made wasn't an improvement, choose Edit ⇨ Undo, press ⌘+Z, or click Undo at the bottom of the Edit sidebar.** The change that you made is undone and the photo moves back to what it was before you did the most recent edit action.

You should get in the habit of pressing Shift frequently as you edit so you can see the impact of the changes you are making. If you get too far into the process before you realize that the photo is headed in the wrong direction, you might have to start over.

Genius

If you want to undo an undo, choose Edit ⇨ Redo.

8.7 This photo has been cropped to focus on the plane.

8.8 Holding down the Shift key shows the photo as it was before the most recent change.

Restoring the previous versions of photos

iPhoto saves edited photos to your library when you close the Edit sidebar. If you decide your previous edits were better than your current ones, click Revert to Previous at the bottom of the Edit sidebar. The version of the photo as you previously edited it appears and you can restart your editing session.

Note

Restoring the original versions of photos

Occasionally, the edits you make take a photo in the wrong direction. While you are editing a photo, you can go back in time by repeating the Undo command (Edit ⇨ Undo or press ⌘+Z) as many times as needed to get back to the version of the photo you want to keep. Or, you can revert to the previous saved version of the photo. If you decide that you don't want to keep any of the editing you've done and you want start over so that the photo becomes as it was when you imported it, you can restore it. Here's how:

1. **Select an edited photo that you want to restore to its original (as imported) state.**

2. **Choose Photos ⇨ Revert to Original, or click Revert to Original at the bottom of the Edit sidebar.**

3. **Click Revert in the resulting confirmation dialog.** The version of the photo you imported to the library is restored in place of the edited photo. Any changes you've made to the photo are lost (which was the point after all).

Comparing or editing multiple photos simultaneously

Sometimes it's useful to be able to compare photos. They might be different shots of the same subject or different versions of the same photo you've created. Or you might want to edit a series of photos at the same time. To compare photos or edit more than one at a time, do the following:

1. **Hold down the ⌘ key while you select each photo on the Selector that you want to compare.** Each photo you select appears in the Editing area at the same time, as shown in Figure 8.9. As you add photos, the view of each photo gets smaller so they all fit on the screen. The photo you are currently editing is highlighted in a white box with a Close (X) button in the upper-left corner.

Genius

If you select multiple photos and then click Edit, each photo you select opens in the Edit mode.

Photos | Heli-Max 125 FP | 12,519 of 12,533 | Quick Fixes | Effects | Adjust

Rotate
Enhance
Fix Red-Eye
Straighten
Crop
Retouch

Navigation

Revert to Original | Undo

Full Screen | Zoom | Info | Edit | Create | Add To | Share

8.9 You can see photos at the same time to compare them.

2. **Compare the photos.**

3. **To edit one of the photos, select it.** It is surrounded with a white box to indicate it is the active photo that you can edit.

4. **Edit the selected photo.**

5. **To remove one of the photos, select it and click its Close button.** The photo closes and the remaining photos expand to fill the editing space.

6. **When you finish comparing or editing photos, exit Edit mode.**

Genius

You can zoom within each photo independently. For example, in Figure 8.9 you can see I've zoomed in on the photo on the far left and far right so I can compare the same area on both. The Navigation tool shows your location in the active photo.

Note In the following sections, you learn how to use each of iPhoto's editing tools. The explanations assume you've done, or are doing, the general steps described so far, such as selecting photos, checking an edit, and so on. Only information related to the specific tool is described.

Rotating Photos

While it is one of the simplest to use, the Rotate tool is also one of the most useful editing functions. As I'm sure you can guess, when you select a photo and activate the Rotate function, the photo rotates 90 degrees in the clockwise or counterclockwise direction. You can rotate an image four times, with the fourth time returning the photo to its original orientation. Here are some ways you can rotate a selected photo:

Genius You can set the default direction for the Rotate command. To do so, open the General pane of the Preferences dialog and select the Rotate radio button for the direction you want to be the default. Of course, you can still rotate in the opposite direction by holding the Option key down when you rotate a photo. The Rotate keyboard shortcuts assume the default direction is counterclockwise. If it is clockwise, the shortcuts are opposite of what is listed.

- Click the Rotate button to rotate the photo in the default direction.
- Hold the Option key down while you click Rotate to rotate the photo in the opposite direction.
- Choose Photos ⇨ Rotate Clockwise or Photos ⇨ Rotate Counterclockwise.
- Press Option+⌘+R to rotate a photo in the clockwise direction.
- Press ⌘+R to rotate a photo in the counterclockwise direction.

Genius The Rotate keyboard shortcuts and menu commands work at any time. So you can easily fix the orientation of photos when you view them without opening the Edit sidebar.

Enhancing Photos

The Enhance tool is useful when a photo is either too dark or too light overall. It changes the photo's exposure and contrast settings (which you can also do separately when you use the Adjust

131

tool). Using the Enhance tool is as simple as editing gets; just click the Enhance button. You see the impact of the tool on the photo.

Genius

Remember to press the Shift key to see the photo as it was before your most recent change. This is especially useful when you are enhancing photos.

Removing Red Eye from Photos

When you take photos of things with eyes while you are using flash, the dreaded red eye is inevitable. Fortunately, iPhoto includes a tool that helps you restore the appearance of your subjects' eyes to a more normal looking state. You can have iPhoto remove red eye automatically or you can remove it manually. Try the automatic approach first. If that doesn't work, try removing it manually.

Genius

As you edit, remember to use the Zoom slider to zoom in or out of the photo so you can see it at the appropriate level of detail. This is especially useful when removing red eye.

1. **Focus on eyes that have red-eye problems, as shown in Figure 8.10.**

2. **Click the Fix Red-Eye button.** The Red-eye tools appear. By default, the Auto-fix red-eye check box is selected and iPhoto fixes the red-eye issues in the photo, as shown in Figure 8.11.

3. **Review all the eyes in the photo; if the results are what you want, click Done.** The Red-eye tool closes.

If the automatic fix doesn't work the way you want, you can also manually remove red eye. Follow these steps:

1. **Focus on eyes that have red-eye problems.**

2. **Click the Fix Red-Eye button.** The Red-eye tools appear and iPhoto attempts to remove red eye automatically.

3. **Deselect the Auto-fix red-eye check box.** The red eyes return.

4. **Drag the Size slider until the red-eye pointer is the same size as the red area of the eye, as shown in Figure 8.12.**

8.10 This young woman is not actually possessed by demons; it just appears that way.

8.11 The Red-eye tool often removes red eye correctly automatically.

8.12 Set the size of the red-eye pointer (just to the left of the Done button in this figure) so it is about the size of the red in the eye that you want to fix.

5. **Move the pointer over a red eye, as shown in Figure 8.13, and click the mouse button.** The red within the circle is replaced with black.

6. **Take the appropriate action based on the results:**

   - If the eye looks good, move to the next red eye and repeat.

   - If you still see red, increase the size of the circle and try again.

   - If you see too much black, undo the red-eye removal, make the circle smaller, and try again.

7. **Repeat Steps 1 through 6 until you've removed all the red out of the eyes in the photo.**

8. **Click Done.** The Fix Red-Eye tool closes.

8.13 Position the red-eye pointer over the eye you want to fix and click the mouse button.

Straightening Photos

The Straighten tool enables you to rotate a photo within its frame as opposed to changing its orientation, which is what the Rotate tool does. Use the Straighten tool when a photo is a bit off kilter and you want to make it line up with a vertical or horizontal axis. Here's how to straighten a photo:

1. **Click the Straighten button.** A grid appears over the photo and the Straighten slider appears.

2. **Drag the slider to the left to rotate the image to the left, or to the right to rotate the image to the right, as shown in Figure 8.14.** As you drag the slider, the photo rotates within its frame and you see the degree of rotation at the right end of the slider. When the image is straight, stop moving the slider.

8.14 Use the Straighten tool to better align a photo with horizontal and vertical axes.

3. **Click Done.** The grid disappears.

If you rotate an image a lot, part of it might move out of the frame and you might start to see black at its edges. It's not unusual to have to crop a photo that you straighten. Also, the more you straighten an image, the more you distort it, so your goal should be to straighten it just enough that you don't notice it isn't straight anymore.

Cropping Photos

Cropping a photo ensures it is at its best by removing the parts that detract from the photo's overall effect. You can crop photos to remove parts you don't want to see and to focus specifically on the part you do want to see. To crop, do the following:

1. **Click the Crop button.** The crop box appears on the photo. The portion inside the crop box is the part of the photo that remains after a crop; anything outside the box is removed when you crop.

2. **To maintain a specific proportion when you crop, select the Constrain check box and choose the proportions you want to maintain on the pop-up menu.** There are many options, such as 3 × 5, 4 × 6, and so on. When you use the Constrain option, the crop box always maintains the proportions you select, no matter what size you make it.

3. **Drag the edges of the crop box so its size is the size you want the cropped photo to be, as shown in Figure 8.15.** As you drag, the box is filled with a grid; when you release the mouse button, the grid disappears. If the Constrain option is on, all the sides of the box move as you drag any part of it. If not, you can drag sides individually.

8.15 Cropping a photo is a good way to change its focus or remove unwanted content.

4. **Position the crop box by dragging the entire box so the part of the photo you want to keep is in the box.**

5. **Continue adjusting the size of the crop box and its location until the crop looks right.**

6. **Click Done.** The photo is cropped.

Genius

Click Reset to remove cropping.

Retouching Photos

The Retouch tool removes blemishes, such as scratches, from a photo by blurring the surrounding area over the blemish. You should only use the Retouch tool on small areas and apply the least amount of blurring you can to correct a problem. Because the tool actually smears or blurs the surrounding image, too much retouching can look worse than the original blemish.

To retouch, try these steps:

1. **Click the Retouch button.** The Retouch slider appears.

2. **Drag the Size slider toward the left to reduce the size of the circle to make the retouch pointer relatively small.** The size of the pointer is the area that will be blurred. You want the pointer to be slightly smaller than the size of the blemish on the photo. Start with a small size because you can make it bigger if you need to. As you drag the slider, you see the current size of the slider, as shown in Figure 8.16.

3. **Move the cursor over the area you want to retouch.** When you move the pointer over the image, you see the retouch pointer.

4. **Click and drag over the blemish.** As you drag, the area being retouched appears in brown, as shown in Figure 8.17.

5. **When you've covered the blemish, release the mouse button.** The area to which you applied the tool is retouched.

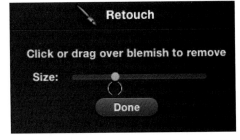

8.16 Keep the area you retouch (indicated by the size of the pointer, which is just above the Done button) relatively small so the blurring doesn't become a bigger problem than the problem you are fixing.

6. **Take the appropriate action based on the results:**

   - If the retouched area looks good, you're done.

   - If you notice the retouching more than you did the blemish, undo the retouch, make the circle smaller, and try again.

   - If the blemish is still too noticeable, undo the retouch, make the circle larger, and try again.

7. **When the blemish is fixed, click Done.**

You can also retouch a specific area by moving over it and clicking the mouse button one or more times.

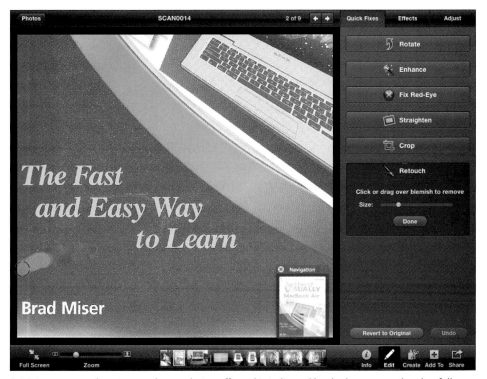

8.17 As you retouch an image, the part being affected is indicated by the brown smudge that follows the cursor as you move it.

Applying Effects to Photos

The Effects tool provides a number of special effects you can apply to your images. Examples include B & W, which converts an image to black and white; and Matte, which adds an adjustable border that you can use to frame the image. Applying effects to photos can be a lot of fun:

1. **Click the Effects tab.** The Effects pane appears and you see a button for each effect.

2. **Click the button for the first effect you want to apply.** It is applied to the photo. If there is only one level of the effect, you see ON at the bottom of the effect's button to indicate it is applied. If the effect has levels, you see the level of the effect currently applied instead.

3. **To change the level of the effect, click the left- or right-facing arrow at the bottom of the effect's button, as shown in Figure 8.18 (the arrows appear on the Matte effect in the figure).** The effect increases or decreases accordingly. For example, when you increase the Matte effect, the matte gets larger and you see less of the image.

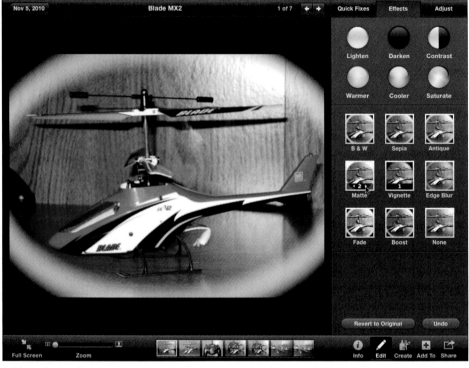

8.18 Applying effects to images is a good way to improve their visual impact.

4. **To remove an effect, click its button if it doesn't have a level or reduce the level below zero if it has a level.** To remove all effects from an image, click the Revert to Original or Revert to Previous button.

5. **Continue to apply and adjust effects until the photo appears as you want it to.**

Note

There are two basic types of effects. One type, B & W for example, is either ON or OFF. The other type, of which Matte is an example, has levels of the effect you can apply from 1-9. You can tell what type an effect is by clicking its button. When you click the type you can adjust, you see the level indicator and controls. When you click the other type, you see ON in its button. If an effect is not applied, you only see the effect's button.

Genius The six buttons at the top of the tab can be applied multiple times to increase their effect. Each mouse click applies more of the effect to the image. If you click one time too many, just click Undo.

Adjusting Technical Aspects of Photos

The changes you make with the Adjust tool are easy to do, but it's much harder to predict how each change will affect the photo. You probably need to experiment quite a bit with each option to see how it affects your photos in general and how it changes the specific image you are editing at any time. The tools on the Adjust pane definitely require the deftest touch and most of the options actually improve, not just change, a photo.

To use the Adjust tool, do the following:

1. **Click the Adjust tab.** The Adjust pane appears, as shown in Figure 8.19.

8.19 The Adjust pane enables you to change many aspects of a photo.

2. **Use the sliders and other controls to make changes to the image.** As you make changes, you see the impact of those changes on the photo in real time. The graphic representation on the pane changes and the number at the end of the slider, which is a relative measure of the change, updates.

The tools on the Adjust pane are

- **Levels.** This graph (at the top of the pane) is a visual representation of the properties that you can adjust. As you make changes, the graphed lines change. I'm not sure that the actual information here is that meaningful to anyone who doesn't happen to be a photographic expert or scientist, but you can get a general sense of what you are doing to a photo by watching the impact of your changes on this graph. You can also make changes to the black point, midtones, and white point of the image by dragging the three triangles (respectively) along the horizontal axis.

- **Exposure.** This slider sets the total amount of light in the photo.

- **Contrast.** This slider sets the contrast level between the light and dark parts of the image.

- **Saturation.** This slider controls the depth at which you perceive the color in the image.

- **Definition.** This slider sets the clarity of details in the image.

- **Highlights.** This slider controls how prominent various highlights in the photo are.

- **Shadows.** This slider brightens or darkens areas of shadow.

- **Sharpness.** This slider makes the edges of objects more or less distinct.

- **De-noise.** This slider removes random pixels that appear to be in the image.

- **Temperature.** This slider changes the balance between yellow and blue.

- **Tint.** This slider changes the balance between red and green.

- **Eyedropper tool.** This is used to correct the whites and grays in an image. Click the eyedropper and then click a white or gray area in the image that looks closest to how you think it should look.

To see what a specific tool does, move its slider to the far left and far right and look at the image in both extremes and as you move the slider. The impact of each slider can be somewhat different based on the particular image you are editing, so you'll have to try a control on several images to understand it better.

Each tool has an impact on the others. As you make a change to one control, you might have to compensate with others. Using the Adjust tool is a bit of a balancing act as you aim to achieve the best overall photo that you can.

Using a Different Application to Edit Photos

With plenty of editing power, and editing functions that are well integrated with the rest of its tools, iPhoto is a complete package. However, other editing applications are available. You can configure iPhoto so that you edit images in another application even though they are stored within iPhoto. First, configure iPhoto to use a different editing application. Then edit your photos with that application.

Configuring iPhoto to use a different application to edit photos

To configure iPhoto to use a different editing application, do the following:

1. **Press ⌘+, (comma) to open the Preferences dialog.**

2. **Click the Advanced tab.**

3. **On the Edit Photos menu, choose In application.** The Open dialog appears.

4. **Move to and select the editing application you want to use, then click Open.** That application is set as your editor. You return to the Advanced tab and see the application you selected on the Edit Photos menu.

5. **Close the Preferences dialog.**

Editing photos with a different application

To edit a photo in another application, do the following:

1. **Start the edit process as you normally would.** When you do so, the application you configured as your editing application opens and the photo you selected to edit is moved into it.

2. **Use the application's tools to edit the image.**

3. **Save your changes.** The saved photo is stored in iPhoto.

4. **When you finish editing, move back into iPhoto.** You see the edited image.

With iPhoto and a MobileMe account, you can publish photos and other images in your library to your MobileMe Gallery on the Web quickly and easily. From your Gallery, you and visitors to your site can view your photos using a Web browser running on any type of computer. You can allow viewers to download photos from your MobileMe photo pages, and can even allow them to upload images, making your Gallery pages interactive.

Getting Started with MobileMe

Apple's online service MobileMe provides you with the following capabilities:

- Information synchronization on Macs, Windows PCs, iPhones, iPod touches, and iPads

- File storage online using a virtual hard drive (called an iDisk in MobileMe lingo)

- Text, audio, and video chat

- Web site publishing

- Email using email applications on desktop computers or Apple mobile devices and via the MobileMe Web email application

- Contact management online via the MobileMe Web Contacts application

- Calendar viewing on the Web

To use MobileMe services, you need to have a MobileMe account and to configure your Mac to use it.

How to sign up for a MobileMe account is beyond the scope of this book, but to get started, visit www.apple.com/mobileme and click the Free Trial button. (You can use MobileMe for 60 days at no cost.) After you complete the online process, you will have a MobileMe member name and password.

Note

To get detailed information about MobileMe, see *MobileMe for Small Business Portable Genius* (Wiley), which is useful even if you don't have a small business.

Configure your Mac to access your MobileMe account as follows:

1. **Choose Apple menu ⇨ System Preferences.** The System Preferences application opens.

2. **Click the MobileMe icon.** The MobileMe pane appears.

3. **Type the member name and password for your MobileMe account.**

4. **Click Sign In.** When you log in to your account, you see information similar to what appears in Figure 9.1. Access to your account is now configured and various applications, including iPhoto, can use MobileMe transparently.

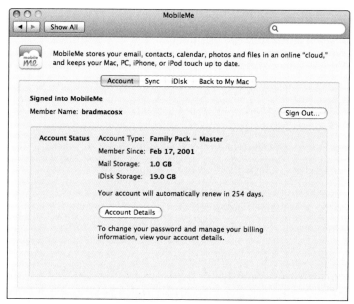

9.1 After you sign in to your MobileMe account on the MobileMe pane of the System Preferences application, you can access MobileMe services from within iPhoto and other applications.

To make sure iPhoto can access your MobileMe account, open the iPhoto Preferences dialog and click the Accounts tab. Select your MobileMe account on the list of accounts on the left side of the dialog. You see information about your account, such as its status (enabled) and the amount of disk space you are using.

If you don't see the MobileMe account on the list that you want to use to publish photos, add it by clicking the Add (+) button at the bottom of the Account list. Type the account's username (member name) and password. Then click Log In.

Sharing Photos via MobileMe

Using MobileMe to publish photos in your iPhoto library is straightforward. After you publish your photos, you can let people know where they can go to view them on the Web.

Publishing photos to MobileMe

You can publish photos in your library to the Web as follows:

1. **Select the photos you want to publish.** The best way to do this is to create a photo album containing the photos you want to publish and then select that album, but you can select photos in any source to publish them to the Web.

2. **With the album or photos selected, click the Share button on the toolbar and click MobileMe Gallery.** You see the albums currently published on your Gallery site along with the New Album option.

3. **To publish the photos to a new album, click New Album or to add the photos to an existing album, click the album to which you want to add the photos.** The rest of these steps are for a new album, you learn how to update published albums later in this chapter. The Publish sheet appears, as shown in Figure 9.2.

4. **Configure the album's name in the Album Name field.** If you started with an album, the default name is the name of the album, but you can name the album on your MobileMe site differently if you want.

5. **On the Album Viewable by pop-up menu, choose one of the following options:**

   - **Everyone.** This option makes the album available to everyone who visits your gallery's Web site.

   - **Only Me.** This option limits access to the album to you. (It won't appear on your gallery's Web site for other visitors.)

   - **Edit Names and Passwords.** This option lets you protect an album by requiring a username and password to view it. When you choose this option, use the resulting sheet to create usernames and passwords. After you create usernames and passwords, the usernames appear on the Album Viewable by pop-up menu.

   - **User name.** This option limits access to the album to a username you select. It only appears after you've configured at least one username and password using the previous option.

Note

You can limit access to published photos only to one username at a time. Of course, you can provide that single username and password to multiple people to allow more than one person to view your photos.

6. **To allow visitors to be able to download photos from the album, select the Downloading of photos or entire album check box.**

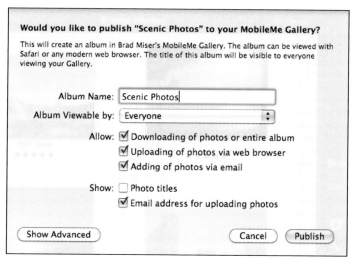

Would you like to publish "Scenic Photos" to your MobileMe Gallery?

This will create an album in Brad Miser's MobileMe Gallery. The album can be viewed with Safari or any modern web browser. The title of this album will be visible to everyone viewing your Gallery.

Album Name: Scenic Photos

Album Viewable by: Everyone

Allow: ☑ Downloading of photos or entire album
☑ Uploading of photos via web browser
☑ Adding of photos via email

Show: ☐ Photo titles
☑ Email address for uploading photos

(Show Advanced)   (Cancel) (Publish)

9.2 Use this sheet to publish an iPhoto photo album or selected photos to your MobileMe Gallery on the Web.

7. **To permit people to upload photos to the album via the Web, select the Uploading of photos via web browser check box.**

8. **To allow viewers to add photos to the album by sending them via email, select the Adding of photos via email check box.**

Genius

Allowing people to add images to an album (via the Web or email) is a great way to make your photo Web sites interactive. For example, you can allow people to add photos they've taken at an event to your Web page for that event.

9. **To display the titles for the photos in iPhoto on the gallery, select the Photo titles check box.**

10. **If you selected the check box in Step 8, select the Email address for uploading photos check box to display the email address on the Web page.**

11. **Click Show Advanced.** Additional advanced options appear.

12. **To hide the album on your gallery's Web site, select the Hide album on my Gallery page check box.** With this selected, the album is no longer visible to anyone visiting your main Gallery page. But visitors can still access that album if they type in or click on its unique URL.

13. **Use the Download quality pop-up menu to choose one of the following options:**

   - **Optimized.** This option provides faster uploading with photos that print at good quality up to 16 × 20 inches.

   - **Actual Size.** This option uploads images at their actual size, which means they will be at their maximum quality, but can take longer to upload.

14. **Click Publish.** iPhoto publishes the photos to the Web. In the WEB section of the Source pane, you see each MobileMe account and other online accounts that are configured in iPhoto. If you select the account you used to publish the photos, you see the albums that are published to that account. If you open a published album, you see the photos that have been published to it, as shown in Figure 9.3. At the top of the window, you see status information, such as the progress of the publish process while the album is being published. When the upload is complete, you see the number of photos included and the email address people can use to upload photos to the album's page if you allow it. While the photos are being uploaded, the process happens in the background so you can go about your business while it is being done. When the process finishes, the site becomes available on the Web.

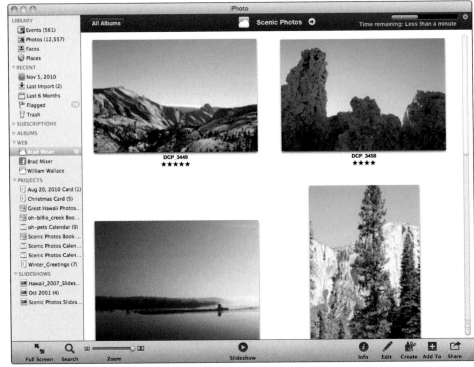

9.3 While photos are being published, you see progress information at the top of the iPhoto window when you view the album.

Note If you choose to publish individual photos instead of an album, iPhoto uses the name of one of the events with which the photos are associated as the name of the published Web site.

Inviting people to view published photos

After you publish an album, you'll want to make it available to people to view. Here's how:

1. **On the Source pane, select the MobileMe account through which the album was published.** You see all the albums that have been published through that account.

2. **Select the album you want to tell someone about.**

3. **Click the Info button.** The Info sidebar opens.

4. **Click the Tell a Friend button.** iPhoto creates a new email message and information about the album is pasted into the message, as shown in Figure 9.4. This includes the key image from the album along with the View Album button.

Note iPhoto uses the email accounts configured in it to send emails from within the application. To learn how to configure email accounts in iPhoto, see Chapter 17.

5. **Address the message, make changes to its default content, and send it.** Recipients can use the View Album button in the message to view the album's Web site.

Note If the album is protected by a username and password, visitors have to provide that information when prompted to do so before they can view an album. So don't forget to provide this information to the people you want to be able to access your photos.

Genius Like albums and other collections of photos, published albums have a key photo that is the image that fills the album's thumbnail, both in iPhoto and on the Web. You can change the key photo in the same way, too (move the pointer across the album's thumbnail in the Info sidebar and click when the photo you want to use appears). You have to refresh the published album for this change to take effect on the Web. That topic is covered later in this chapter.

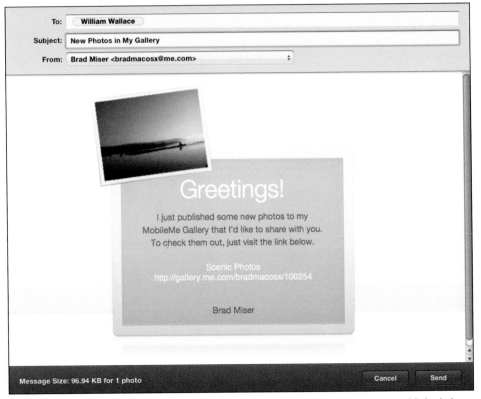

9.4 The Tell a Friend button creates an email message you can use to announce your published photos.

Viewing a published album

To view a published album with a Web browser, locate it in one of the following ways:

- Open the account through which the album is published on the iPhoto Source pane, open the published album, and click the right-facing arrow that appears next to the album's name at the top of the iPhoto window.

- Type the URL for the album (http://gallery.me.com/*membernamealbum#*, where *membername* is the member name of the account associated with the gallery and *album#* is the number of the album assigned by MobileMe). You have to visit the album first to see what the album number is by looking at the page's URL. But once you know the album number, you can save and use the album's URL just like any other Web page.

- Move to the account's gallery in which the album is stored by selecting that account on the Source pane and clicking the right-facing arrow next to the account's name at the top of the iPhoto window. Then click the thumbnail for the album you want to view.

- Click the View Album button in an email message announcing the album.

Whichever method you use, your default Web browser moves to the album's Web page, as shown in Figure 9.5.

At the top of the album's window, you see its title and the number of images it contains. Within the window, you see thumbnails of the images in the album.

Visitors can view and work with an album in a number of ways. (The following list includes all the possible options you can enable for an album. If a specific feature isn't enabled, such as download-ing images, you won't see the related button when you view that album.)

- To browse all the album's thumbnails, scroll in the window.
- To change the size of the thumbnails, use the slider in the lower-right corner of the window.
- To change the background color of the album, click one of the Color radio buttons next to the Size slider.

Note

The term color here is somewhat misleading. You really choose from among black, white, and two shades of gray.

- To download all the images in an album, click the Download button in the album tool-bar. You see the download sheet explaining that all the images in the album will be com-pressed into a Zip file. Click Download. The Zip file is downloaded to your computer. Uncompress the file and you can work with the downloaded images.

- To subscribe to the album so you are notified when its contents change, click the Subscribe button in the album's toolbar. A sheet containing the address you use to sub-scribe to the album appears. You can enter this into an RSS (Really Simple Syndication) reader application or in iPhoto.

- To add images to the album via the Web browser, click the Upload button. You see the Upload sheet. Provide your name and email address, and type the security code dis-played at the bottom of the sheet. Then click Choose Files and select the files you want to add to the album.

- To add images to the album via email, click the Send to Album button. You see a sheet containing the email address for uploads to the album. Click the address, and a new email message is created in your default email application. Attach the images you want to add to the album, and send the email.

- To tell other people about the album, click the Tell a Friend button. This works just like the Tell a Friend button in iPhoto.

9.5 Albums you publish can be viewed in any Web browser.

- To move to the gallery in which the album is stored, click My Gallery.

- To hide the album's toolbar, click Hide Options. To show the toolbar again, click Show Options.

- To view an image, click its thumbnail. The image appears in the window along with its title, as shown in Figure 9.6. When you move the cursor, a toolbar appears below the image. Click the Download button (downward-facing arrow) to download the image to your computer. Click the left or right arrow to move to the previous or the next image in the album. Click the Info button (i) to view information about the image. Click Back to Album to return to the image's album.

- To see thumbnails of photos organized in a grid, click Grid at the bottom of the window. This is the default view; you can browse the thumbnails or click a photo's thumbnail to view it in detail.

- To be able to see thumbnails of an album's images and a large view of a selected image, click the Mosaic button at the bottom of the window. Along the right side of the window, you see smaller thumbnails of the album's images. Select a thumbnail, and you see a large view of the image in the left side of the window.

9.6 When you click an image's thumbnail, it appears by itself in the album's window.

◉ To see images that you can flip through, click the Carousel button. You see thumbnails of images fanned out across the window. (This view is similar to the Cover Flow view in iTunes.) The image in focus appears larger at the center of the window. Scroll through the images by dragging the slider to the left or right or clicking on images that are to the left or the right of the image in focus. To scroll through the images automatically, click the Play button at the left end of the slider. To focus on an image, click its thumbnail.

◉ To view images in a slideshow, click the Slideshow button. A new, maximized window appears, and the album's images begin playing, as shown in Figure 9.7. When you move the cursor, the Slideshow toolbar appears at the bottom of the screen. To download the current image, click the Download button (downward-facing arrow) to download the image to your computer. Use the left- or right-facing arrow to move back or ahead in the slideshow. Use the Play/Pause button to start or stop the slideshow. Use the Return button (two arrows pointing to each other) to close the Slideshow window and return to the previous album view.

155

9.7 You can view the images in an album in a slideshow.

Viewing a gallery

Your MobileMe Gallery is the collection of all the albums that you've published to the Web. To view your gallery, move to its URL, which is http://gallery.me.com/*membername*, where *membername* is your MobileMe member name. You see the gallery in a Web browser window. Within the gallery's window, you see each of its visible albums. (Remember that albums can be hidden within a gallery.)

When you view a gallery, keep these things in mind (as shown in Figure 9.8):

⊙ For each album, you see its title, number of images, and key photo.

⊙ To preview the images in an album, move the pointer across its thumbnail.

⊙ If you don't see an album's key photo and it has the Lock icon, that album is protected with a username and password. When you click a protected album, you're prompted to type its username and password. You need to type it correctly to be able to view the album.

⊙ To view an album, click its thumbnail (see the previous section for information about viewing albums).

If you use an RSS reader, you can subscribe to a gallery so you are notified when its contents change. To do so, click the Subscribe to Updates link in the upper-right corner of the gallery window. You see a sheet containing the address you use to subscribe to the gallery.

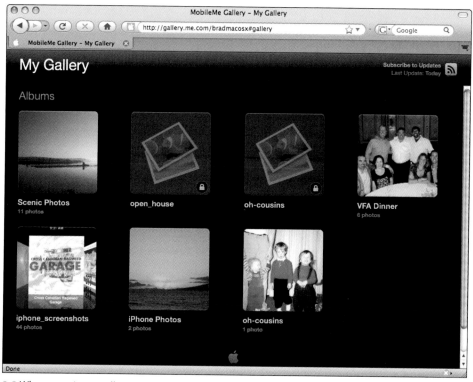

9.8 When you view a gallery, you see the albums it contains. (You don't see albums that are hidden.)

Updating Published Albums

You can update your published albums a couple of ways. You can change the content of your published albums and you can change the settings by which an album is published.

Updating the content of published albums

You can update the content of your published album in the following ways:

- **Add photos to a published album.** Select the photos you want to add, click the Share button on the toolbar, click the MobileMe account to which the album you want to change is published, and click the album to which you want to add the photos. The photos are uploaded to the published album and become available for viewing, downloading, and so on.

157

- **Remove photos from a published album.** Open the album (select the account through which it is published on the Source pane and then double-click the published album), then select the photos you want to remove, press the Delete key, and click the Delete button at the prompt. The photos you selected are removed from the published album.

- **Reorganize the published album.** Move the photos around in the iPhoto window.

- **Set the key photo for the album.** Open the Info sidebar, move the pointer across the album's thumbnail, and click the mouse button when the image you want to use appears.

Whenever you make changes to a published album, it is updated on the Web automatically. While the changes are being published, you see a progress bar in the upper-right corner of the iPhoto window when you are viewing the album's contents.

Genius

For published albums, the Info sidebar includes the Sharing section. Expand this to see information about the publish process (such as when the album was published) or to visit the site (by clicking the "Published to" text).

If you allow others to update your site via the Web or email, and someone adds a photo through either means, the next time you refresh the published album or launch iPhoto, the new content moves from the Web into the published album in iPhoto. However, the added photos are not automatically added to your library. If you want them to become part of your library, drag them from the published album onto the Photos or Events sources. The photos are imported into your library where they become available just like photos you import using other means.

Genius

You can update a published album at any time by opening it.

Updating a published album's settings

You can change how an album is published by updating its settings. For example, you might want to add password protection to a site or enable photos to be uploaded to it via email. To do so, perform the following steps:

1. **Select the MobileMe account through which the album is published and select the album whose settings you want to change.**

2. **Open the Info sidebar by clicking the Info button.**

3. **Click Change Settings.** The Publish sheet appears and you see the current settings for the album.

4. **Make changes to the published album.** The tools on the sheet work just as they do when you first publish a site.

5. **Click Publish.** The site is republished according to the new settings.

Unpublishing Albums

To unpublish an album, select the MobileMe account through which it is published, right-click its thumbnail, choose Delete Album, and click Delete in the warning sheet. The album is deleted from the Source pane and the published Web page is removed from your Gallery site.

Note If other people have added content to the published album that you want to keep, make sure you save that content to your library before deleting the album. Once you delete the album, the added content is deleted from iPhoto unless you've added it to your Library.

How Can I Use iWeb to Share Photos?

Photo is part of the iLife suite, which also includes iWeb. iWeb is an application that, especially when combined with a MobileMe account, makes creating and publishing your own Web sites simple. iWeb manages the complexities of site building and provides an interface that allows you to focus on the content and design of your pages rather than the mechanics of publishing a site. iPhoto's iWeb tool sends a group of photos to iWeb and starts the creation of photo pages. Once you complete a photo page, you can publish it to your Web site with a single mouse click.

Publishing Photos on an iWeb Web Site

Apple's iWeb application enables you to build Web sites by choosing a template for each page on your site and linking the pages together to create an integrated site. You also can add Web widgets, HTML snippets, and other features to your pages.

One benefit of iWeb is that it is very fast and easy to create a site that looks good, even if you aren't artistically or graphically inclined. Another benefit of iWeb is that MobileMe is integrated so you can publish sites to the Web just by clicking the Publish button. Lastly, iWeb requires less effort to maintain and update a site than some other tools do.

iPhoto is designed to work with iWeb so that you can easily publish photos in your library to your iWeb Web sites.

Note

This chapter assumes you are using MobileMe to publish your Web site, which requires a MobileMe account and a Mac configured to access it (see Chapter 9 for more information on this topic). You can publish a Web site that you build with iWeb using other hosting services, but doing so is beyond the scope of this chapter.

To publish a site, two steps are required and one step is optional:

1. **Create your Web site.**

2. **Publish the site via MobileMe.**

3. **Register and configure a personal domain (optional).**

For Steps 1 and 2, you will primarily use iWeb while adding content you have created in the other iLife applications; this chapter focuses on using iPhoto to publish photos to your Web site, but you can publish content you create in iMovie or other iLife applications just as easily.

Any Web site you publish under MobileMe has the default URL http://web.me.com/*membername*, where *membername* is your MobileMe member name. This URL works fine, but it may not be easily recognizable as yours. Optionally, you can register your MobileMe Web site under a personal domain so it's both easier to type and more obviously associated with you (such as bradmiser.com instead of web.me.com/bradmacosx).

Because this chapter focuses on publishing photos, you learn how to build and publish photo pages. You can create many other kinds of pages in iWeb, but once you understand how to create photo pages, you'll be able to quickly figure out how to add pages of other types.

Note Explaining the details of how to obtain and use a personal domain is beyond the scope of this chapter. The general steps are: register your domain name (there are many domain registration services on the Web you can use), configure your domain account to refer to your MobileMe Web site using the registration provider's Web site, and configure your MobileMe account with your personal domain using the Account management tools on your MobileMe Web site.

Starting a Web site

To get started building your Web site, perform the following steps:

1. **Launch iWeb.** The iWeb window opens, and if you haven't used iWeb before, you are prompted to select the theme and template for the first page in the site, as shown in Figure 10.1.

10.1 Each time you add a page to a Web site, you select a theme and template for that page.

Themes appear in the left pane of the window, while the right pane contains the templates for the selected theme. To see the themes available to you, use the pop-up menu at the top of the sheet. If you have used iWeb before, you see the pages you previously created. The rest of these steps assume you haven't used iWeb before. If you have used it, you can add new pages to your site using later steps in this chapter.

2. **Select the theme you want to use by clicking its icon on the Theme list in the left pane.** When you select a theme, the page templates available for that theme appear in the right pane. The templates are named based on the type of content they are designed to showcase. As you can probably guess, the Photos page template is designed to present photos.

3. **Select the template you want to use by clicking its icon on the right part of the sheet, and click Choose.** A new page is created from that template and appears in the left pane of the iWeb window. It is nested under the initial Web site (you can add more sites later) to show that it is part of that site.

Note

For the purpose of this chapter, it doesn't matter which template you choose for the first page on your site because you are choosing it only to meet the requirement that you create at least one page when you first launch iWeb. You can delete the page after you add pages from iPhoto to your site.

4. **Select your site by clicking the Site icon.** Site configuration tools appear in the right part of the window.

5. **Ensure MobileMe is selected on the Publish to pop-up menu as shown in Figure 10.2.**

6. **Enter the name of your site in the Site name field.** You can create and manage multiple sites in iWeb, so give your site a name that helps you recognize it and that is meaningful to visitors. If you include spaces between the words in your site name, they are replaced with underscores when you publish the site.

7. **If you want visitors to your site to contact you using an email address that is different than your MobileMe email address, type it in the Contact email field.** By default, this is your MobileMe email address, but you can use a different one if you prefer.

8. **If you want to password protect your site, select the Make my published site private check box and create the site's username and password.** Visitors to your site must be able to provide this username and password to access your site.

9. **If you use Facebook and want your Facebook profile to update when you publish your site, select the Update my Facebook profile when I publish this site check box.**

Note At the bottom of the Site window, you see the iDisk Storage gauge. As you build your site, check this to ensure that you aren't approaching the limit of your available space.

10. **Type your Facebook login information on the resulting sheet, click Finish, and follow the prompts to complete the connection to Facebook.**

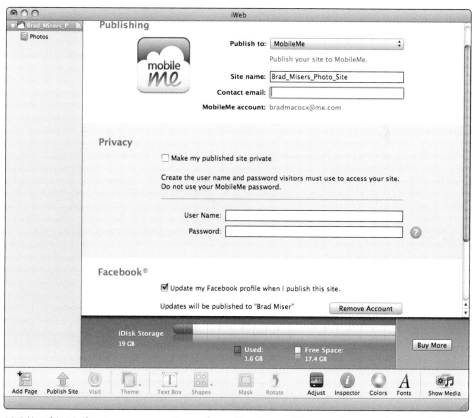

10.2 Use this window to name your site, configure its privacy settings, and connect it to your Facebook account.

Adding and designing a photo page

After you create a Web site, you're ready to start adding photo pages using iPhoto. After you create a photo page using iPhoto, you move into iWeb to design that page and configure its options.

Creating and formatting a photo page

The first step is to add the photo page to iWeb. Here's how:

1. **Select the photos you want to publish on a Web page.** The easiest way to do this is to create a photo album containing the photos you want to publish, but you can select photos individually, too.

Genius To publish all the photos in an album, just select the album in the Source pane; you don't need to select the photos within the album unless you only want to publish some of them.

2. **Choose Share ⇨ Send to iWeb ⇨ Photo Page.** iPhoto sends the photos you selected to iWeb and iWeb comes to the front. You're prompted to choose a theme for the photo page.

3. **Select the theme you want to use for the photo page and click Choose.** The page is created. The name of the page is the name of the photo album you selected or the name of the event with which some of the selected photos are associated. On the new page, you see graphic and text placeholders based on the theme you selected along with thumbnails of the photos you are publishing, as shown in Figure 10.3.

Note Because you already selected a photo page in iPhoto, you only see the Photos template for each theme.

4. **Select one of the photos on the page.** The Photo Grid dialog appears.

5. **Select the number of columns you want to appear on the page using the Columns pop-up menu.**

6. **Choose the album style you want to use by clicking the Album style menu and selecting a style.** The style determines the borders appearing around each photo.

7. **Drag the Spacing slider to the left to decrease the space between the images or to the right to increase it.**

8. **Use the Photos per page pop-up menu to select the number of photos that appear on a page when the photo album is viewed.** Your options are limited to multiples of the value you selected in Step 3. For example, if you selected 3 on the Columns pop-up menu, you can have 3, 6, 9, 12, and so on images per page.

10.3 Here, I've added a Web page based on a photo album called Scenic Photos.

9. **Use the Caption lines pop-up menu to select how many lines of caption can appear for each image, as shown in Figure 10.4.** If you don't want any captions, select 0.

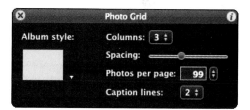

10.4 Use the Photo Grid tool to design the basic layout of a photo page.

Setting photo options

Now, use the Inspector to configure photo options to determine how users can access your page:

1. **Click the Inspector button (*i*) in the top right-hand corner of the Photo Grid dialog.** The Photos subtab of the Inspector appears, as shown in Figure 10.5.

2. **Choose a download size for photos on the Photo Download Size pop-up menu.** The options are: None (don't allow photos to be downloaded), Small, Medium, Large, or Original. Larger downloads have higher quality, but also take more bandwidth.

3. **To allow visitors to subscribe to the site so they are notified when it changes, select the Allow visitors to subscribe check box.**

4. **To enable visitors to make comments on your site, select the Allow comments check box.**

5. **If you allow comments, you can also allow viewers to add attachments to the site by selecting the Allow attachments check box.**

6. **To show the comment indicator in iWeb, select the Display comment indicator check box.** This is a blue dot that appears next to pages when someone leaves comments.

10.5 The Photos subtab allows you to configure how visitors can interact with the page you are creating.

Setting slideshow options

All photo pages have a Slideshow function so that visitors can view its photos in a slideshow. Configure the slideshow for the page with the following steps:

1. **Click the Slideshow subtab.** The Slideshow tools appear, as shown in Figure 10.6.

2. **To enable the Slideshow function, select the Enable slideshow check box.**

3. **Choose the transitions between images on the Transitions pop-up menu.**

4. **If you want images to have a reflection while they play, select the Show reflection check box.**

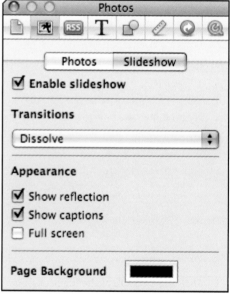

10.6 Use the Slideshow subtab to configure the slideshow options for a photo page.

5. **To display captions during the slideshow, select the Show captions check box.**

6. **If you want the slideshow to play in Full Screen mode, select the Full screen check box.**

7. **Use the Page Background menu to set the background color for the page.**

Replacing template placeholders with content

Templates include placeholders for many kinds of elements, including text, graphics, photos, and so on. You can (and should) replace a template's placeholder content with your own content. You also can delete placeholders when you don't want to use particular elements on a page.

Genius

You can delete a text placeholder by selecting it and pressing Delete. You can resize a text placeholder by selecting it and dragging its Resize handles.

Note

If you display captions for your photos, you can edit the text to be appropriate for the Web page; what appears initially is information from iPhoto — specifically, the titles.

Following are some examples showing how to replace various kinds of template elements. These examples aren't all-inclusive; however, after you learn how to replace several kinds of placeholder elements, you can use a similar approach to replace any kind of placeholder content.

Most templates include various kinds of text placeholders. Replace the text content in these placeholders using the following steps:

1. **Double-click the text you want to replace.** It becomes highlighted, indicating the text can be edited.

Genius

You can format text using the commands on the Format menu, including the Font command to open the Fonts panel, along with formatting commands such as Bold, Italic, Bigger, and so on.

2. **Type the new text, or copy and paste it.**

3. **Click the Text tab of the Inspector and open the Fonts panel (press ⌘+T) to format the text, as shown in Figure 10.7.**

Templates include graphic placeholders, such as a graphic at the top of the page. Graphic elements have a mask that determines which part of the image is displayed on the page. You can

169

control the size of the mask and the size of the image, and you can determine which part of the image appears within a mask.

10.7 Use the Text tab of the Inspector and the Fonts panel to format text on a photo page.

You can replace and format graphic elements by following these steps:

1. **Prepare the graphic you want to use.** You do this outside of iWeb, such as by using iPhoto. If you prepare the graphic in iPhoto, you can use the Media Browser to easily replace the graphic placeholder.

2. **Click the Show Media button in the iWeb toolbar.** The Media Browser appears on the right side of the iWeb window.

3. **Click the Photos tab.** The contents of your iPhoto library appear. You see similar selections as you do on the iPhoto Source pane, including all your albums. Select the source you want to use; thumbnails of the photos that source contains appear in the lower pane.

4. **Find and drag the graphic you want to use onto the placeholder, as shown in Figure 10.8.** You can find photos by browsing or searching the selected source. The graphic you drag to your iPhoto library replaces the content in the placeholder when you place the new image over the placeholder and its border turns blue.

5. **Select the new graphic.** The Edit Mask tool appears. The lines around the image represent its mask, anything inside the mask is shown on the page, and part of the image outside the mask is hidden.

10.8 Here I'm replacing the default graphic on the template with an image from my iPhoto library.

6. **Click the Edit Mask button.** The image appears at full size on the screen.

7. **Adjust the size and the part of the image that appears on the screen by performing the following actions:**

   • Drag the slider to the right to increase the size of the image or to the left to decrease it.

   • Drag the image inside the mask until the part of the image you want to be visible on the page is shown.

   • Resize the mask by dragging its Resize handles.

8. **Use the tools on the Graphic tab of the Inspector to configure the image, such as to add and format a frame or drop shadow.**

9. **When you finish, click the Edit Mask button.** Everything outside the mask is hidden, and you see the image as it will appear on the page.

Replacing page properties

You should also set some general properties of your page by performing the following steps:

1. **Click the Page tab of the Inspector, which is the first tab from the left in the Inspector window.** The Page Inspector tools appear.

2. **Click the Page subtab.**

3. **Edit the name of the page in the Page Name field, as shown in Figure 10.9.** This is the name that appears in the title bar of the Web browser when the page is visited. Just like a site name, if you use spaces in the page's name, they are replaced with underscores when the page is published.

4. **Choose how the navigation bar is configured on the page with the following options:**

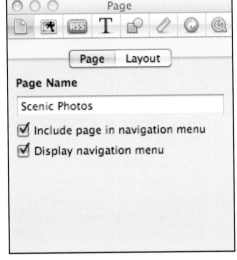

10.9 Use the Page Inspector tab to name a page and determine how it impacts the navigation menu.

   • Select the Include page in navigation menu check box if you want the page to be included in the navigation menu that appears at the top of each page; this menu contains links consisting of each page's name. You want this check box to be selected for each of the pages at the top level of your site, but want it unselected for nested pages.

Genius

Of course, these steps aren't really as linear as I present them in the sections of this chapter. You usually do them more or less simultaneously because they affect each other. For example, when you remove template elements, you probably need to replace those elements with your own content.

- Select the Display navigation menu check box to show the navigation menu on the page. You typically want this menu to appear on the pages at the top level of your site, but not on nested pages.

Testing a photo page

Now that you have designed your photo page, test it by doing the following:

- **Double-click a photo on the page.** You see the image at a large size with a thumbnail viewer on it, as shown in Figure 10.10.

10.10 The photo viewer page shows a large view of one photo and thumbnails of the rest.

- **Click the Back to Album link to return to the previous page.**
- **Browse the page to ensure it's what you want it to be and fix any problems you find.**

When you finish with these checks, you are ready to publish the page when you publish your Web site.

Adding a photo blog to a Web site

The other kind of photo page you can create using iPhoto is a photo blog page, as shown in Figure 10.11. In addition to displaying photos, this page is designed to facilitate discussion about the photos and for you to add photos to it as time passes so it is dynamic. Adding a photo blog page to a Web site is similar to adding a photo page to the site. The general steps are

Note

Blog pages are typically used for a relatively small number of photos. If you select many when you create a blog page, you see a confirmation dialog.

1. **Select the photos you want to publish on a blog page.** The easiest way to do this is to create a photo album containing the photos you want to publish, but you can select photos individually, too.

10.11 Blog photo pages are designed to have an entry for each photo where you can provide commentary on that entry's photo.

2. **Choose Share ⇨ Send to iWeb ⇨ Blog.** iPhoto sends the photos you selected to iWeb and iWeb comes to the front. You're prompted to choose a theme for the blog page.

3. **Select the theme for the blog page.** The blog is added to your Web site.

4. **Configure and format the blog page.**

Note iWeb can do a lot more than what I explain here. For example, you can add new content to pages, include music from your iTunes library, add Web widgets, and so on. You can also create multiple Web sites within iWeb for different purposes and publish them all at the same time. iWeb is a very powerful but amazingly easy-to-use tool.

Publishing an iWeb Web Site

After all the work you do to prepare a site, publishing it is a bit anticlimactic because iWeb makes it so easy. Follow these steps to publish your site:

1. **Click the Publish Site button.** iWeb begins publishing your site. Depending on the size of content in your site, this can take a few moments to several minutes. A clock icon appears next to each site's icon to give you a general idea of the progress. When the process is complete, you see a dialog telling you so, as shown in Figure 10.12.

Your site has been published to MobileMe using your personal domain.

You can visit your website anytime by typing the following into a web browser:

http://www.bradmiser.com

Your Facebook profile has been updated.

Be sure to let your visitors know your new website address. To open an email message with information about your new site, click Announce.

(Announce)   (Visit Site Now)   (OK)

10.12 When you see this message, your sites are on the Web.

Note If you enabled Facebook with your site, the first time you publish it you are prompted to link the site to your Facebook account. Just follow the on-screen instructions to complete the process.

2. **Click one of the following buttons:**

- **Announce.** This button creates an email message with a link to your site.

- **Visit Site Now.** This button opens your site in a Web browser.

- **OK.** This button closes the dialog without taking any other action.

After your site is published, you should visit it with different browsers to see how it appears in those browsers, as shown in Figure 10.13. If you see problems, return to iWeb to correct them.

10.13 Check out your Web sites in various browsers to make sure you are happy with the results.

Genius

When you move to http://web.me.com/*membername*, where *membername* is your MobileMe member name, you move to your default Web site. To choose which of your sites is the default, drag the site you want to be the default to the top of the left pane in the iWeb window. That site becomes the default site the next time you use the Publish command and will be the first stop for visitors to your Web site.

Updating an iWeb Web Site

iWeb makes it very easy to keep a Web site updated, which is critical to keeping your site current and interesting. (Visitors tend to be discouraged when they visit a site that clearly hasn't been updated for a long time.)

To make changes to your site, open iWeb and use its tools to make the needed updates. As you change a page, its icon changes from blue, indicating that the page is published, to red, indicating that there are changes to the page that haven't been published. When you're ready to update your site, click the Publish Site button and your site is updated. It really is that easy.

How Can I Use Facebook to Share Photos?

Facebook has quickly become a social phenomenon. What started as an obscure online service used mostly by college students has become a social network environment used by people of all ages. Facebook enables people to easily share information, to communicate, be entertained, and to partici- pate in activities with people designated as friends. Of course, friends can share photos with one another on their Facebook pages, and like most every- thing else having to do with photos, iPhoto can help you with this, too.

Getting Started with Facebook Photo Sharing

Of course, to share photos on Facebook, you must have a Facebook account and configure iPhoto to use it. This links iPhoto to your Facebook page so that you can share photos quickly and easily. After you have an account, you start to publish photos to your Facebook page by selecting the photos you want to share. Then you use iPhoto's Facebook tool to publish an album containing those photos to your Facebook page. After you share your photos, your Facebook friends can view them by visiting your Facebook page.

Configuring your Facebook account in iPhoto

There are two steps to complete this task. First, obtain a Facebook account if you don't have one. Second, configure that account in iPhoto.

If you don't have a Facebook account, open a Web browser and move to www.facebook.com. Complete the Sign Up form; as part of this process you type the email account that becomes your Facebook login username and a password. Once you complete this process, your Facebook page is published and is ready for you to share photos on.

To configure your Facebook account in iPhoto, follow these steps:

1. **Open the iPhoto Preferences dialog and click the Accounts tab.** On the Accounts list on the far left, you see the various types of accounts iPhoto is configured to use, such as your MobileMe and email accounts.

2. **Click the Add (+) button at the bottom of the Accounts list.**

3. **Click Facebook.**

4. **Click Add.**

5. **Type your Facebook account information (username and password), select the check box to agree to Facebook's terms, and click Login.** You return to the Accounts pane and see your Facebook account on the list with the status message saying it is enabled. You are ready to publish photos to your page.

Sharing photos in new Facebook albums

After you set up your Facebook account in iPhoto, sharing photos by creating a new album on your Facebook page is pretty simple:

1. **In your iPhoto library, select the photos you want to share on Facebook.** The easiest way to do this is to create a photo album containing the photos you want to share and then select that album on the Source pane, but you can individually select photos to share, too.

2. **Click the Share button on the toolbar.**

3. **Click the Facebook account on which you want to share the photos.**

4. **Click New Album.**

5. **Name the new album (the default name is the name of the album or event in iPhoto) and choose one of the following options on the Photos Viewable by menu, as shown in Figure 11.1:**

   - **Everyone.** Anyone who accesses Facebook can view the photos you share.

   - **Friends of Friends.** Only people who are your friends or who are friends of your friends can access the photos.

   - **Only Friends.** Only people who are your friends can view the photos.

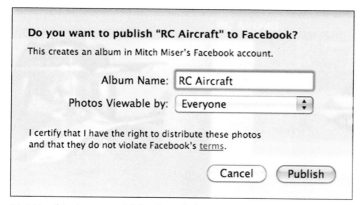

Do you want to publish "RC Aircraft" to Facebook?

This creates an album in Mitch Miser's Facebook account.

Album Name: | RC Aircraft

Photos Viewable by: | Everyone

I certify that I have the right to distribute these photos and that they do not violate Facebook's terms.

Cancel | Publish

11.1 Use this sheet to publish selected photos on your Facebook page.

Note

On Facebook, a *friend* is someone you've indicated that you have a relationship with and whom you want to be able to access your Facebook page (and photos). Friends of your friends can see limited information about you on your friends' pages, and can request to become your friend. If you accept such requests, your friend's friend becomes your friend, which is how social networks grow so quickly.

6. **Click Publish.** The photos you selected are published to your Facebook page. In the WEB section of the iPhoto Source pane, you see an icon for each of your Facebook accounts. When you select the account to which you have published photos, you see the

albums you've published. If you open an album by double-clicking its thumbnail, you see the photos it contains, as shown in Figure 11.2. When the album is being published, you see progress information in the upper-right corner of the screen. When the album has been published, you see the number of photos moved onto your Facebook page.

7. **To set a key photo for the published album, open the Info sidebar, move the pointer across the thumbnail until you see the photo you want to be that album's key photo, and click the mouse button.**

8. **To visit the album, click the right-facing arrow next to its title at the top of the iPhoto window.** Your default Web browser opens and you move to that album's page.

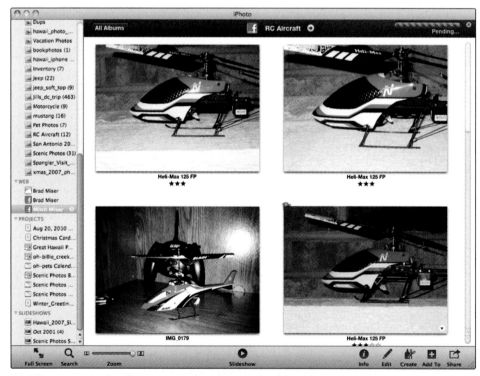

11.2 You can access the albums you've shared on Facebook by selecting the associated Facebook account on the iPhoto Source pane.

Sharing photos in existing Facebook albums

Adding photos to an existing Facebook album is even easier than creating a new album:

1. **In your iPhoto library, select the photos you want to add to an existing Facebook album.**

2. **Click the Share button on the toolbar.**

3. **Click the Facebook account on which you want to share the photos.**

4. **Click the existing album to which you want to add the selected photos.** The photos are uploaded and you see a status message in iPhoto indicating how many photos were added to the album.

Sharing photos on your Wall

You can also share an iPhoto photo on your Wall, along with your commentary:

1. **Select the photo you want to add to your Wall.**

2. **Click the Share button on the toolbar.**

3. **Click the Facebook account on which you want to share the photos.**

4. **Click Wall.** The Comment sheet appears.

5. **Type your comment about the photo.**

6. **Click Publish.** The photo and your commentary are uploaded to your Wall; you see a status message in iPhoto when the process is complete. Friends see your additions on their Facebook News Feed.

Genius

Setting your Facebook profile picture is simple with iPhoto. Select the photo you want to be your profile photo. Click the Share button, click the account for which you want to set the profile picture, and click Profile Picture. On the prompt sheet, click Set. The photo you selected is uploaded to Facebook and set to be your profile picture.

Working with Your Facebook Photos

Once published, your photos become available on your Facebook page. You can view them there starting from iPhoto or by going directly to your Facebook page. You can also invite other people to view them, which is the point of sharing photos, by sending invitations from your Facebook page or sending an email.

Using iPhoto to view your Facebook photos

Once your photos are published to Facebook, you can view them on Facebook from within iPhoto using these steps:

1. **In the WEB section of the Source pane, select the Facebook account through which you published the album you want to view.** You see all the albums published to your page.

Genius

To see all your Facebook albums published under an account, select the account and click the right-facing arrow at the top of the iPhoto window. You move to the Albums screen for your Facebook page. You can browse and view your albums from there.

2. **Open the album you want to view.** You see the photos included in that album.

3. **Click the right-facing arrow next to the album's name at the top of the window.** Your Web browser opens and you move to the album's page on Facebook, as shown in Figure 11.3. On this page, you see thumbnails of the photos you have shared along with Facebook tools you can use to work with those photos.

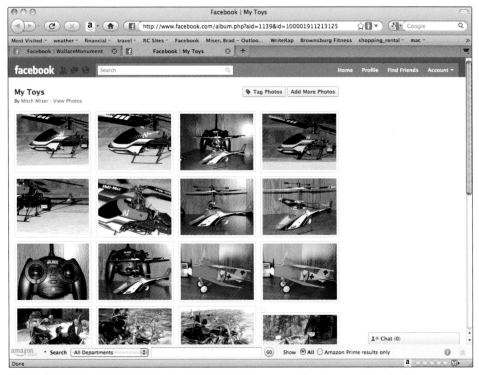

11.3 Each album you share via Facebook in iPhoto becomes an album on your Facebook page.

Note

If your Web browser and Facebook account aren't configured to automatically log in to your Facebook page, you have to log in before you can view your photos.

Using your Facebook page to view your Facebook photos

To move directly to your photos on Facebook, do the following:

1. **Open a Web browser and go to www.facebook.com.**

2. **Type your Facebook account's email address and password, and click Login.** You move to your Facebook Home page.

3. **Click your name in the upper-left corner of the window next to your profile picture.**

4. **Click the Photos tab.** You move to your Photos page, where in the Albums section you see each album you've published, as shown in Figure 11.4.

5. **To view the photos in an album, click its thumbnail.**

11.4 When you visit your Photos page, you see the albums available on your Facebook page.

Note

If you've been tagged in photos on Facebook, your Photos page has two sections. The top section, called "Photos of *You*," where *You* is your name, contains the photos in which you've been tagged. You can browse and view these photos. At the bottom of the page is the Albums section, where you see the albums you've published to your Facebook page. Figure 11.4 shows an example where the user has not been tagged in any photos.

Inviting people to view your Facebook photos

You can invite people to view your photos a couple of ways. You can invite them directly within Facebook or you can send a link via email.

Using Facebook to invite friends to share an album

To invite someone to view a photo album using Facebook, perform the following steps:

1. **Use Facebook to view the album you want to share.**

2. **Click the Share This Album link.** The Share window appears.

3. **In the To field, type any of the following:**

   - **A friend's name.** As you type, Facebook presents a list of your friends; click the friend you want to invite.

   - **The name of a friend list.**

   - **An email address.**

   As you type information, Facebook separates it appropriately, such as adding a space after you select a friend so that you can keep adding people.

4. **Repeat Step 3 until you invite everyone you want to view the photo album.**

5. **Add a message in the Message field, as shown in Figure 11.5.**

6. **Click Send Message.** When they receive your invitation, people can use it to view your album.

If you've published an album so that only friends or friends of friends can view it, make sure the people you invite fall into the security setting for the album you are sharing or they won't be able to view it.

Genius You can also share individual photos using similar steps. Just click the Send as a Message link for the photo you want to share and complete the resulting form, which is similar to sharing an album.

11.5 Use this form to invite people to view one of your albums.

Using email to invite people to view your photos

You can also use an email application to send links to your albums or to a specific photo. This is useful if you don't know whether the people with whom you want to share photos are on Facebook. Here's how:

1. **View the album or photo you want to share.**

2. **At the bottom of the page, copy the link for the album or photo.**

3. **Create a new email message.**

4. **Paste the link to the album or photo into the message.**

5. **Complete and send the message, as shown in Figure 11.6.**

Note If you aren't sure of the recipient's Facebook status, you should set the privacy setting for the albums or photos you share to be Everyone or the people with whom you share might not be able to access the photos you are sharing.

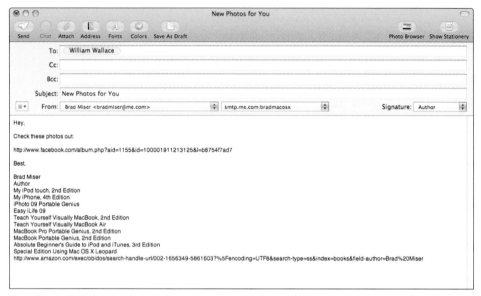

11.6 Use the links Facebook provides to create emails that enable people to view your photos.

Managing Your Facebook Albums in iPhoto

Over time, you may want to make changes to your albums. Following is a list of ways to manage your Facebook albums using iPhoto:

- If you want to reset the permission for a Facebook album, open the shared album and click the Info button. Use the Album Viewable by pop-up menu to choose a different level of security. The album is republished with the new setting.

- If you want to rename an album on Facebook, open the album and select its name at the top of the window, type the new name, and press Return.

- To add photos to a Facebook album, copy the photos, open the Facebook album to which you want to add them, and paste them in it.

- To remove photos from a Facebook album, select the photos you want to remove, press Delete, and click Delete on the resulting sheet.

- To reorganize photos, open the album and drag the photos to their new locations. The position of photos in Facebook albums in iPhoto is the same as their position on Facebook.

- To set an album's key photo, move the pointer across the album's thumbnail until the photo you want to be the key photo appears, open the contextual menu, and choose Make Key Photo.

- To remove an album from Facebook, right-click it and choose Delete Album. Click the Delete button in the resulting sheet. The album is deleted from your Facebook page.

iPhoto periodically and frequently updates your changes automatically. You can tell an update is underway by the icon that appears next to the Facebook account name on the Source pane when the update is in progress.

Genius

You can start the update process by deselecting the Facebook account and then selecting it again.

Note

Your photo pages on Facebook include tools you can use to make changes, such as adding photos, editing photos, deleting photos, and so on. Because you use iPhoto, you don't really need to use these tools. And you might be better off making changes in only one place as it can be less confusing. When you make changes in both iPhoto and Facebook, it can be unclear which changes take precedence.

Understanding How People Use Your Facebook Photos

People who view photos on your Facebook page can do quite a few things, including the following:

- **Browse your published albums.**
- **Click an album's cover to browse the photos it contains.**

Note

The specific actions someone can perform are determined by the publishing setting of the album and the person's relationship to you. For example, if you publish an album as viewable only by friends, only a person who is your friend can view it. Also, someone has to be a friend to be able to comment on your photos.

- **Click a photo to view a full-size version, and then click the Previous or Next link to move through each photo in the album.** The viewer can click the photo itself to move to the next one in the album, too.

- **Add comments to a photo.** When this happens, you are notified via email and on your Facebook Notifications page. In the email you receive, you can click the link to move to the comment that was left. Figure 11.7 shows a comment being posted.

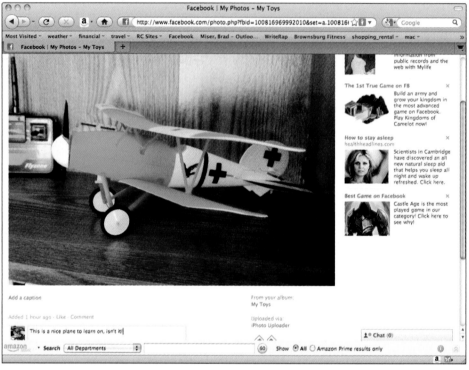

11.7 Visitors to your pages, assuming they are your Facebook friends, can leave comments about your photos.

- **Indicate they like a photo.**

- **Tag your photos (more on that in the next section).**

- **Share a photo.**

- **Share an album.**

- **Post your album or photos to their profile.**

Working with Faces and Facebook Tags

In Chapter 4, you learn how iPhoto's Faces feature can identify people in your photos. You can tag the faces in a group of photos and tell iPhoto whose face you have tagged. Then iPhoto can locate more photos that it thinks have that person in them by identifying that person's face. Over time, iPhoto learns to better recognize faces and becomes more accurate.

Including names on Facebook photos

When photos you share on Facebook are tagged with names, those names appear on the published photo when the viewer hovers over a person, as shown in Figure 11.8.

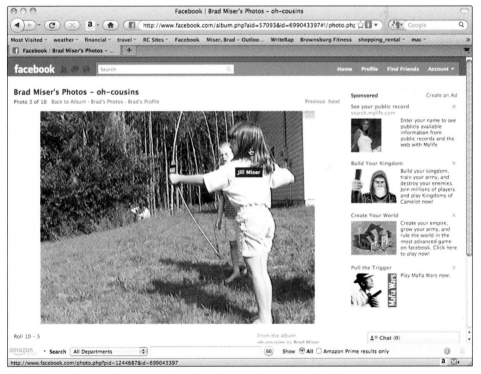

11.8 When a viewer points to a person whose face has been tagged in iPhoto, the person's name appears.

If you want people in your photos to receive notifications when you post photos of them on your Facebook page, configure the person's name and email address using iPhoto's Faces tools (see Chapter 4 for the details).

Whenever you post a photo in which the person is identified, he receives an email with a link to the photo in which he is tagged.

Working with Facebook tags in iPhoto

Visitors to your Facebook photo albums can also tag your photos by identifying people in them. The viewer clicks the Tag This Photo link and then identifies people in the photo. When a photo has been tagged, the tag remains with the photo and works just like face tags you've added in iPhoto.

The cool thing about this is that tags added in Facebook are copied from Facebook to iPhoto the next time the album is synced. So if someone tags faces on your photos in Facebook, those tags are copied to iPhoto, so the faces in iPhoto are tagged with the names from Facebook. You can then confirm the tags, which are marked with the Facebook icon to indicate they originated from Facebook. If the person isn't currently identified in iPhoto, she gets a new snapshot automatically.

This is a good way to build up face identification in iPhoto because other people actually do the work of tagging the photos for you.

Note

If the photo to which a tag is added is in one of your Facebook albums, you must approve the tag before it is applied to the photo.

How Can I Use Flickr to Share Photos?

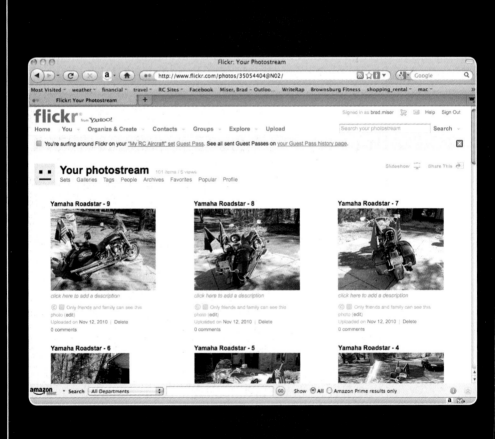

Flickr is a very popular Web site where you can share photos with other people and explore photos people around the world have shared. The site also has tools for organizing and editing photos, but because you use iPhoto, you don't need any of them. For iPhoto users, Flickr is very useful for sharing Photo photos online, so that people with Internet access anywhere in the world can view and use them. Flickr support is built in to iPhoto, making the sharing process seamless.

Getting Started with Flickr Photo Sharing

In order to share photos via Flickr, you must have a Flickr account (which is actually a Yahoo! ID). If you have an account, you can log in to that account when you share photos. If you don't already have an account, you can create one the first time you share. After that, sharing photos on Flickr requires only a few steps.

Configuring your Flickr account in iPhoto

If you don't have a Flickr account, open a Web browser and go to www.flickr.com. Click Create Your Account. If you already have a Yahoo! ID, you can just sign in to Flickr using your account's information. If you don't have a Yahoo! account, click the Create New Account button and follow the on-screen instructions to complete the process. In either case, you need your account information, namely your username and password, to be able to configure that account in iPhoto.

To configure your Flickr account in iPhoto, follow these steps:

1. **Open the iPhoto Preferences dialog and click the Accounts tab.** On the Accounts list on the far left, you see the various types of accounts iPhoto is configured to use, such as your MobileMe and email accounts.

2. **Click the Add (+) button at the bottom of the Accounts list.**

3. **Click Flickr.**

4. **Click Add.**

5. **Click Set Up.** The Password verification screen appears in your Web browser.

6. **Type your account's password and click Sign In.** You are prompted to configure the iPhoto Uploader.

7. **Click the Next button for the option "If you arrived at this page because you specifically asked iPhoto Uploader to connect to your Flickr account, click here."**

8. **Click the OK, I'LL AUTHORIZE IT button.**

9. **Close the Web browser window.**

10. **Move back into iPhoto.** After a moment, you see a message indicating iPhoto is connected to your Flickr account. You are ready to share photos via Flickr.

Sharing photos via Flickr in a new set

In Flickr, collections of photos are called *sets*; these are equivalent to albums in iPhoto or on Facebook. To share photos on Flickr, perform the following steps:

1. **In your iPhoto library, select the photos you want to share on Flickr.** The easiest way to do this is to create a photo album containing the photos you want to share and then select that album on the Source pane, but you can individually select photos to share, too.

2. **Click the Share button on the toolbar.**

3. **If you only have one account, click Flickr; if you have more than one account, click the account through which you want to share the photos.**

4. **Click New Set.** The Flickr sheet appears, as shown in Figure 12.1.

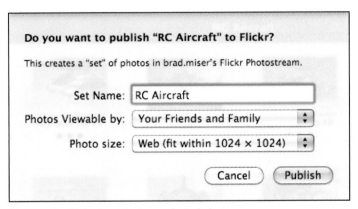

Do you want to publish "RC Aircraft" to Flickr?

This creates a "set" of photos in brad.miser's Flickr Photostream.

Set Name: RC Aircraft

Photos Viewable by: Your Friends and Family

Photo size: Web (fit within 1024 × 1024)

Cancel   Publish

12.1 Use the Flickr sheet to share selected photos.

5. **Type the name of the set.** By default, this is the name of the event or album you are sharing, but you can change the set name to something else if you prefer.

6. **On the Photos Viewable by pop-up menu, choose a setting from the following options:**

    - **Only You.** You are the only one who will be able to view the photos online.

    - **Your Friends.** People who are tagged as your friends are able to view the photos.

    - **Your Family.** People who are tagged as your family can view the photos.

    - **Your Friends and Family.** Both family and friends can view the photos.

    - **Anyone.** Everyone who visits the Flickr site can view the photos.

197

7. **On the Photo size pop-up menu, choose the size at which your photos will be uploaded to the Flickr site.** The options are Web, Half Size, and Actual Size. You can only choose the latter two options if you have upgraded your Flickr account to the Pro level.

8. **Click Publish.** In the WEB section of the iPhoto Source pane, you see an icon for each of your Flickr accounts. When you select the account to which you have published photos, you see the sets you've published. If you open a set by double-clicking its thumbnail, you see the photos it contains, as shown in Figure 12.2. When the set is being published, you see progress information in the upper-right corner of the screen. When the set has been published, you see the number of photos moved onto your Flickr site.

12.2 When a set is published to Flickr, you see the link to the Flickr page at the top of the iPhoto window next to the set's title.

9. **To set a key photo for the published set, open the Info sidebar, move the pointer across the thumbnail until you see the photo you want to be that set's key photo, and click the mouse button.**

10. **To visit the set, click the right-facing arrow next to its title at the top of the iPhoto window.** Your default Web browser opens and you move to that set's page, as shown in Figure 12.3.

12.3 When you move to a set, you see it on your Flickr site.

Sharing photos in existing Flickr sets

Adding photos to an existing Flickr set is even easier than creating a new set:

1. **In your iPhoto library, select the photos you want to add to an existing Flickr set.**

2. **Click the Share button on the toolbar.**

3. **Click the Flickr account on which you want to share the photos.**

4. **Click the existing set to which you want to add the select photos.**

5. **On the Photos Viewable by pop-up menu, choose who can view the photos.** The options are the same as when you publish photos to a new set; what you choose sets the permissions only for the photos you are uploading to the existing set.

6. **On the Photo size pop-up menu, choose the size at which your photos will be uploaded to the Flickr site.** Unless you have upgraded your account, you can only choose Web.

7. **Click Publish.** The photos are uploaded and you see a status message indicating how many photos were added to the set.

Sharing photos on your Photostream

Flickr provides a Photostream on your Flickr site in which all the photos you publish to your site appear. When you publish photos to a set, they appear in your Photostream and you can publish photos directly to your Photostream without putting them in a set. Here's how:

1. **Select the photos you want to add to your Photostream.**

2. **Click the Share button on the toolbar.**

3. **Click the Flickr account on which you want to share the photos.**

4. **Click Photostream.**

5. **On the Photos Viewable by pop-up menu, choose who can view the photos.** The options are the same as when you publish photos to a set.

6. **On the Photo size pop-up menu, choose the size at which your photos will be uploaded to the Flickr site.** Unless you have upgraded your account, you can only choose Web.

7. **Click Publish.** The photo and your commentary are uploaded to your Photostream; you see a status message when the process is complete. Friends see your additions on their Flickr pages.

Viewing your Flickr photos with iPhoto

You can easily go to your Flickr sets from within iPhoto. Here's how:

1. **In the WEB section of the Source pane, select the Flickr account through which you published the set you want to view.** You see all the sets published to your Flickr site.

Genius

To see all of your Flickr sets published under an account, select the account and click the right-facing arrow at the top of the iPhoto window. You move to the Sets screen for your Flickr page. You can browse and view your sets from there and you can click the Your Photostream link to view your Photostream.

2. **Open the set you want to view.** You see the photos included in that set.

3. **Click the right-facing arrow next to the set's name at the top of the window.** Your Web browser opens and you move to the set's page, as shown in Figure 12.4. On this page, you see thumbnails of the photos you have shared along with the Flickr tools you can use to work with those photos.

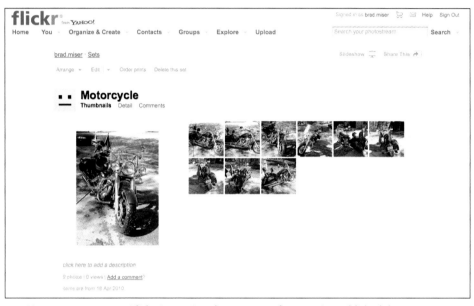

12.4 You can move to your Flickr site to view the contents of sets you've published there.

Note If your Web browser and Flickr account aren't configured to automatically log in to your Flickr site, you have to log in before you can view your photos.

Using your Flickr sets to view your Flickr photos

To move directly to your photos on Flickr, do the following:

1. **Open a Web browser and go to www.flickr.com.**

2. **Click Sign In.**

3. **Type your Flickr account's email address (if necessary) and password, and click Sign In.** You move to your Flickr Home page.

4. **Click the Your Photostream link.** You see all the photos you've published, both in sets and directly to your Photostream.

5. **You can browse the photos on your site.**

6. **To see a photo at maximum size, click its thumbnail.**

7. **To view your sets, move to your Photostream and click the Sets link.** You see thumbnails for each set you've published.

8. **To view the photos in a set, click its thumbnail.** You see thumbnails of the photos in the set, except for the currently selected thumbnail, which appears at a larger size.

Inviting people to view your Flickr photos

You can invite people to view your photos a couple of ways. You can invite them directly within Flickr or you can send a link via email. And you can invite people to view a set or an individual photo.

When you share something on Flickr, you determine its security level. If you protect what you share with the family, friends, or family and friends setting, you need to include a Guest Pass with your invitation. This option embeds the necessary security information into the resulting link so that someone can access your shared resources. If you don't include a Guest Pass when inviting someone to a secured resource, he won't be able to view it.

Using Flickr to invite friends to share a set or photo

To invite someone to view a photo set or a specific photo using Flickr, perform the following steps:

1. **Use Flickr to view the set or photo you want to share.**

2. **Click the Share This button.** The Share dialog appears, as shown in Figure 12.5.

3. **In the Enter email addresses or a contact's screen name field, type one of the following:**
   - An email address
   - A screen name

Note

After you type an email address once, Flickr remembers it. The next time you start to type it, Flickr presents it for you to select; when you do, you're prompted to type additional addresses in a new field.

4. **Repeat Step 3 until you've invited everyone you want to view the photo set or photo.** You can add multiple entries to the field by separating them with a comma.

5. **If the items you are sharing are protected (any setting except Anyone), you can provide a Guest Pass along with the message so the person can view the content regardless of her Flickr status by selecting the Friends or Family check boxes.** You should select the check box that matches the security of what you are sharing.

6. **Click Send.** The message is sent to its recipients. When they receive your invitation, people can use its information to view your set or photo. When the process is complete, you see a message saying so in the dialog.

7. **Click OK.** The dialog closes.

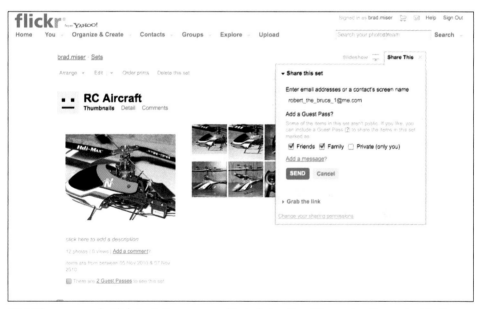

12.5 When you send a Flickr invitation, you need to include a Guest Pass unless the content isn't protected.

Using email to invite people to view your photos

You can also use an email application to send links to your sets or to a specific photo. Here's how:

1. **View the set or photo you want to share.**

2. **Click the Share This button.**

3. **Click Grab the link.** The URL to the item you are sharing appears. If the shared item can be viewed by anyone, skip to Step 5.

4. **If you've protected what you are sharing, select the Friends or Family check boxes and click the GET A GUEST PASS button.** The Guest Pass link appears in the link box.

5. **Copy the link, as shown in Figure 12.6.**

6. **Create a new email message and paste the link to what you are sharing into the message.**

7. **Complete and send the message.** When the recipient receives the message, he can use the link to view your shared content.

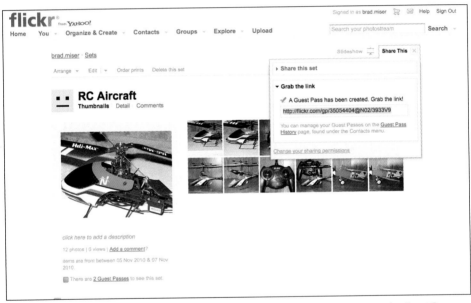

12.6 When you generate a link to an item you're going to share, make sure you get the Guest Pass version if the shared item is secured.

Managing Your Flickr Sets

Over time, you may want to make changes to your sets. Following is a list of ways to manage your Flickr sets:

- To rename a set, which changes its name in iPhoto and on Flickr, open the set, select its name at the top of the iPhoto window, type the new name, and press Return.

- To add photos to a Flickr set, copy them from the source and paste them into the set.

- To remove photos from a Flickr set, select the photos you want to remove, press Delete, and click Delete on the resulting sheet.

- To reorganize photos, open the set and drag the photos to their new locations. The position of photos in sets in iPhoto is the same as their position on Flickr.

- To set a set's key photo, view all of your sets, move the pointer across the set's thumbnail until the photo you want to be the key photo appears, open the contextual menu, and choose Make Key Photo.

- To remove a set from iPhoto, right-click on its thumbnail and choose Delete Album and click the Delete Set button in the resulting sheet. The set is deleted from iPhoto, but not from your Flickr page.

- To remove a set from iPhoto and from Flickr, right-click on its thumbnail and choose Delete Album and click the Delete Set and Photos button in the resulting sheet. The set is deleted from iPhoto and from your Flickr page.

Caution

When you delete a set, any photos that have been added to the set on Flickr but not yet imported into iPhoto are sent to the Trash. If you want to keep any photos added to the set via the Flickr Web site, select the Import photos to your library before deleting this set check box before you complete the delete task. This causes any photos uploaded via Flickr to be imported into your library before the set is selected; they will be available to you just like photos you've imported from other sources.

Note

Your photo pages on Flickr also have tools you can use to make changes, such as adding photos, editing photos, deleting photos, and so on. Because you use iPhoto, you don't really need to use these tools. And you might be better off making changes in only one place as it can be less confusing. When you make changes in both iPhoto and Flickr, it can be unclear which changes take precedence.

iPhoto periodically and frequently updates your changes automatically. You can tell an update is underway by the icon that appears next to the Flickr account name on the Source pane when the update is in progress.

Genius

You can start the update process by deselecting the Flickr account and then selecting it again. Opening a set also causes it to be updated.

Understanding How People Use Your Flickr Photos

People who view photos on your Flickr page can do quite a few things, including the following:

- Browse your published sets and photos by viewing your Photostream. Here visitors see the sets you've shared. They also see individual photos that are included in your Photostream.

- Click the Detail link to view detailed views of the photos as shown in Figure 12.7.

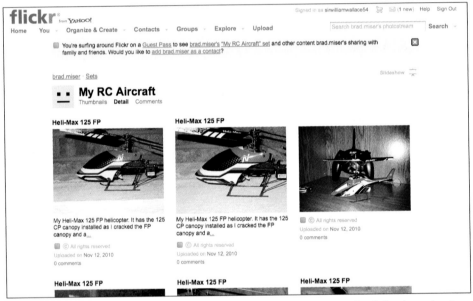

12.7 When a visitor clicks the Detail link, he sees the photos in a set in more detail than browsing it.

- Click a photo on the Detail page to view it at maximum size.

- View your photos in a slideshow by clicking the Slideshow link.

- Add comments to a photo when signed in to a Flickr account. The comments people leave appear next to the photo on your Flickr pages. If the visitor isn't signed in with a Flickr account, he can't leave comments.

- Subscribe to an RSS feed for your sets.

- Use the Send to a friend link to share a photo or set (the viewer must have a Yahoo! email account).

Performing Cool Flickr Tricks

You can use your Flickr Web site to manage your published sets, including managing the Guest Passes you have issued and creating an email address to which people can send photos to add them to your Photostream.

Managing Guest Passes

As you learned earlier, when you share a secured resource, you must provide a Guest Pass that enables someone to view that resource. You can manage the Guest Passes for a shared set by performing the following steps:

1. **Log in to your Flickr account and move to the set's page.**

2. **Click the *X* Guest Passes link, where *X* is the number of Guest Passes you have issued.** You move to the Guest Pass page, as shown in Figure 12.8. Here you see each of the Guest Passes you've issued for the set. The information for each Guest Pass includes the date on which you issued the Guest Pass, a description of the pass, how many views have been made against it, and the Expire link.

3. **To expire a Guest Pass so it no longer works, click its Expire link.** The URL for the set becomes inactive and can no longer be used to view the set online.

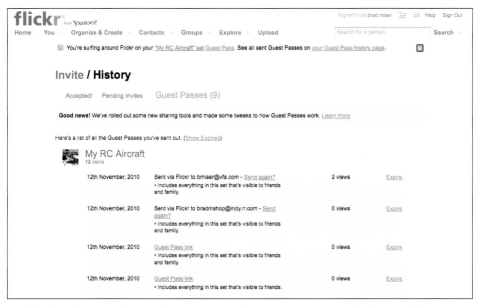

12.8 The Guest Pass page for a set shows the current Guest Passes you've provided along with their status.

Enabling people to add photos to your Photostream

You can make your Flickr site more interactive by enabling people to add their photos to your Photostream. Here's how:

1. **Log in to the Flickr Web site.**

2. **Click the link for your Flickr account name in the upper-right corner of the browser window.** You move to the Your account page.

3. **Click the Emails & Notifications tab.** You see the address to which photos can be sent to add them to your Photostream, as shown in Figure 12.9.

Upload by Email options		
Your Flickr upload email	mope73each@photos.flickr.com	edit
Your blog upload email	Before we can give you an upload-to-blog email address, you'll need to tell us a little about the blog(s) you want to upload to	
Your Flickr2Twitter upload email	Before we can give you an upload-to-blog email address, you'll need to tell us a little about the blog(s) you want to upload to	

12.9 People can send photos to Your Flickr upload email address to add pictures to your Photostream.

4. **Provide the email address to the people whom you want to be able to add photos to your site.**

When a photo is attached to an email sent to the address you created, it is automatically added to your Photostream.

Slideshows are one of the most enjoyable ways to view your photos. As you probably expect, iPhoto offers great tools you can use to create and watch slideshows; you can take advantage of iPhoto's amazing transitions, effects, and soundtracks to add even more interest and enjoyment to the viewing experience. There are three basic types of slideshows: temporary slideshows that you watch in iPhoto, project slideshows that you create and save, and slideshows in iDVD that you can burn to DVD.

Viewing Photos in a Temporary Slideshow

Viewing photos statically in the iPhoto window is good, but viewing them dynamically in a slideshow can be even better. You can view photos via a temporary slideshow; I call it temporary because the slideshow doesn't exist anywhere in iPhoto, it is really a set of options that you apply to photos to create the slideshow so you can watch it. When you stop the slideshow, it isn't saved anywhere — unlike a slideshow project, which you learn about later in this chapter.

To view a temporary slideshow, you perform two general steps. First, select the photos you want to view. Second, configure and play the slideshow.

Selecting photos for a temporary slideshow

To get started with a slideshow, you select the photos you want to view in it. There are many ways to do this, as you can see from the following list.

- Select one or more events.
- Select the Photos source and then select the specific photos you want to include in the slideshow.
- Select places or faces.
- Select one of the sources shown on the Recent list; for example, to see a slideshow of the photos you most recently imported to your Library, select the Last Import source.
- Select a photo album or folder.

After you select the photos you want to include in the slideshow, you are ready to configure and play it.

Genius

You can select many different sources of photos for a slideshow. You can always tell whether your current selection is available for a slideshow by looking at the Slideshow button on the toolbar at the bottom of the iPhoto window. If the button is enabled, you can view the selected source in a temporary slideshow. If the button is disabled, you can't.

Configuring and playing a temporary slideshow

When you play a slideshow, you configure the following slideshow elements:

- **Theme.** This determines the overall look of the slideshow, including the default transition that is used to move from slide to slide.

- **Music.** You can choose music to accompany slideshows. You can choose from theme music included with iPhoto, music you create in GarageBand, and any music stored in your iTunes Library.

- **Settings.** These enable you to control properties such as the amount of time each slide appears on the screen, captions, and so on.

To configure the slideshow, perform the following steps:

1. **Click the Slideshow button.** The iPhoto interface disappears, the first photo in the selected source is displayed in Full Screen mode, and the Configuration dialog appears, as shown in Figure 13.1. The Themes tab is selected by default.

2. **Select the theme you want to use.** Each theme has a different presentation of the slides. Try them all to see which you like best.

13.1 You use the Configuration dialog to determine how the slideshow plays.

Genius

Each tab has the Use settings as default check box. When you click the Play button, the slideshow plays with these default settings. You can play a slideshow at any time without configuring all its settings by clicking the Play button.

3. **Click the Music tab.**

4. **Enable music by selecting the Play music during slideshow check box and choosing a source of music on the Source pop-up menu.**

5. **In the bottom part of the dialog, choose the specific music you want to use from the source you selected in the previous step.** You can browse, search for, and preview music using the tools in the pane. For example, if you select iTunes as the source, you can use any music in your iTunes library for the slideshow.

6. **Click the Settings tab, shown in Figure 13.2, and configure the options you see.** The specific settings available on the Settings tab depend on the theme you select.

13.2 The Settings tab enables you to configure different aspects of a slideshow that depend on the theme you select.

Examples of the options you can set include:

- **Slide duration.** Choose to set the amount of time each slide plays (the music repeats as necessary until the show is done) or set the slideshow to fit the length of the music you've selected.

- **Transition.** Configure the transition that is used between each slide.

- **Miscellaneous options.** These include whether captions are displayed, and if so, which text is used as captions; the order of slides (random or in the order they appear in the selected source); and photo scaling.

7. **Click Play.** The slideshow begins to play, as shown in Figure 13.3.

13.3 This slideshow uses the Snapshots theme.

iPhoto remembers the most recent slideshow settings for each source. When you come back to a source you have previously viewed in a slideshow and click the Slideshow button, it plays using the previous settings. You can change the settings for the source by using the buttons on the slideshow toolbar.

When you move the pointer, the slideshow controls appear on a toolbar. From left to right on this toolbar, the controls are

- Previous slide
- Pause/Play

- Next slide

- Theme settings

- Music settings

- Settings

- Stop

- Exit slideshow

Unless you've set the slideshow to repeat, it will stop when it reaches the last slide in the show. You can stop it at any time by clicking the Stop button or by pressing Esc.

Creating and Watching Slideshows in iPhoto

In iPhoto, you can create slideshow projects that you can save within iPhoto — unlike the temporary slideshows you learned about earlier. You can also export slideshow projects outside of iPhoto.

Project slideshows can have transitions, audio tracks, and other effects similar to a temporary slideshow. You can create a slideshow from any photos in your library, including those you import from a camera or bring in from your desktop. You can organize the photos in your slideshow and then add effects and a soundtrack while controlling how the slideshow plays with the settings you choose.

Creating a slideshow

Like so many other tasks in iPhoto, you create a slideshow by selecting the photos you want it to include and then creating it as in the following steps:

Note If you don't manually select photos, iPhoto moves all the photos in the currently selected source into the slideshow when you create it. For example, if an album is selected, all its photos are included, or if you select Events and don't have a specific event selected, all the photos in your library are placed in the slideshow.

Caution At the time of this writing, you have to be in Standard mode to be able to select Slideshow on the menu that appears when you click the Create button.

1. **Select the photos you want to include in the slideshow.** You can select an album to include all its photos or you can select one or more photos directly.

2. **Click the Create button on the toolbar.** The Create menu appears.

3. **Click Slideshow.** The photos you selected are placed into a new slideshow. iPhoto does its best to name the slideshow based on the photos you select; for example, if you select an album, its name is the name of the slideshow. The slideshow's name is selected on the Source pane so you can edit it.

4. **Rename the slideshow and press Return or just press Return if the current name is what you want to use.** The Slideshow tool fills the iPhoto window, as shown in Figure 13.4. The first photo in the selected source appears with the slideshow's name in text across it. At the top of the window, you see thumbnails of all the photos in the slideshow. The photo selected on the thumbnail viewer (and highlighted with a yellow box) fills the center part of the window. At the bottom of the window, you see the Slideshow toolbar.

13.4 The thumbnail viewer at the top of the window shows all the photos in the slideshow while the toolbar at the bottom contains the tools you need to complete the show.

Note

The first slide in a slideshow is the title slide (unless you have disabled this as you learn later). When you select that slide, as in Figure 13.4, you see the first photo in the slideshow with the title text on it. If you select the second slide on the viewer, you see only the first photo without the title text.

Configuring the photos in a slideshow using the Slideshow tool

After you create the slideshow, you need to configure the photos it contains and the order in which those photos play.

Adding photos to a slideshow

You can add photos to a slideshow by performing the following steps:

1. **Find and select the photos you want to add.**

2. **Drag the photos onto the slideshow's icon in the Source pane.** When the slideshow icon is highlighted and the green circle containing the plus sign (+) appears, release the mouse button. The photos are added to the slideshow.

3. **Select the slideshow.**

4. **Scroll to the end of the thumbnail viewer.** You see the photos you added.

Removing photos from a slideshow

You can easily remove photos from a slideshow by doing the following:

1. **Use the thumbnail viewer to locate and select the photos you want to remove.**

2. **Press Delete.** The photos are removed from the slideshow.

Organizing photos in a slideshow

The order photos appear in the thumbnail viewer determines the order they appear in the slideshow from left to right. You can set the order in which the photos appear in the slideshow by dragging them to the left or right in the thumbnail viewer until they are in the order you want.

Using a standard album to build and configure the photos in a slideshow

It's easier to organize photos in a slideshow when you are working with an album than it is to use the thumbnail viewer in the Slideshow tool, mostly because the viewer is fairly small and you

218

might have to scroll a lot to move from one end to the other. Instead of configuring and organizing the photos in a slideshow in the Slideshow tool as I describe in the previous section, try this technique instead:

1. **Create a standard photo album.** You want to use a standard photo album as opposed to a Smart Album because you can manually set the order of photos in a standard album but cannot in a Smart Album.

2. **Add the photos you want to be in the slideshow to the standard album.**

3. **Organize the photos so they play in the order you want, starting with the top-left photo (which will be the first photo in the slideshow) and moving to the right until you reach the end of the first row, as shown in Figure 13.5.** The first photo in the second row will be the next photo in the slideshow. Continue ordering the photos until they are in the order in which you want them to play.

13.5 Building a slideshow is a lot easier if you start by building a standard photo album and use it to configure the photos and their playback order for the slideshow.

4. **Select the album.** Make sure you don't have any of the photos selected; only the photos you have selected get moved into the slideshow. If you have only the album selected, all its photos end up in the slideshow.

5. **Click the Create button on the toolbar.** The Create menu appears.

6. **Click Slideshow.** The slideshow is created and named based on the album you selected.

7. **Press Return to save the album name as the slideshow name.** The Slideshow tool fills the iPhoto window. The first photo in the album appears with the album's name in text across it. At the top of the window, you see thumbnails of all the photos in the slideshow. The photo selected on the thumbnail viewer (and highlighted with a yellow box) fills the center part of the window. At the bottom of the window, you see the Slideshow toolbar.

Note

After creating a slideshow based on a standard album, you must make any changes to the photos included in the slideshow or to the order in which they play using the Slideshow tool because the album and the slideshow are not linked in any way.

Designing a slideshow

Once you have the content and order of the photos set, you get to design the slideshow so it is exactly what you want it to be. There are many ways you can apply your creativity to a slideshow to make it uniquely yours.

Designing a slideshow is an iterative process. You should make changes and then preview the changes before making more changes. Sometimes, something you change affects what you had previously configured and you have to go back to make updates. You can expect to perform the design tasks described in the following sections somewhat concurrently. Also, plan on previewing your slideshow many times during the creative process.

The general order for designing the slideshow is as follows:

1. **Add the photos you want to be part of the slideshow or remove photos you don't want to include.** You should do this step before you start designing the slideshow, but you'll probably have to make a few changes to the slideshow's content as you go.

2. **Organize the slideshow in the order you want the photos to appear.** Again, it's better to do this before you start focusing on the design of the slideshow, but you'll probably have to make a few tweaks as you design it.

3. **Preview the slideshow.**

4. **Choose a theme.**

5. **Preview the slideshow.** (I've included it in the steps again for emphasis; I'm sure you get the idea that you should preview the slideshow after every major change.)

6. **Apply settings to all the slides.**

7. **Apply settings to individual slides.**

8. **Apply music.**

9. **Edit the title.**

You learned how to do Steps 1 and 2 when you learned to create a slideshow in the previous sections. In the following sections, you learn how to do the rest of them.

Previewing a slideshow

Previewing a slideshow is a somewhat repetitive and tedious task, but it is also essential. When you preview the slideshow, you see it in action, which is really the only way you can tell if the work you are doing is "right." By previewing it frequently, you immediately see the effects of changes you are making.

Slideshows default to include music. This will probably get annoying as you preview your slideshow. For now, click the Music button so the Music Settings dialog appears. Deselect the Play music during slideshow check box and close the dialog. Now you can preview the slideshow in peace and quiet. Unfortunately, you have to do this each time you select a new theme because music is enabled by default for all themes.

To preview a slideshow, do the following:

1. **Select the slideshow you are working on.**

2. **Click the Preview button, as shown in Figure 13.6.** The slideshow begins to play within the Slideshow tool. You can see the slides, their order, and the styling of the slideshow with its current theme.

3. **To stop the preview, click the Preview button again.**

Note The difference between the Preview and Play functions is that when you preview a slideshow, it remains within the iPhoto window. When you play a slideshow, the iPhoto interface disappears and you see the slideshow in Full Screen mode.

221

13.6 When you preview a slideshow, it plays within the Slideshow tool.

Choosing a slideshow's theme

A slideshow's theme determines the overall look of the slideshow along with some of its features. Some of the themes available at the time this book was written include the following:

- **Ken Burns.** This theme, made famous by its namesake, is one where photos zoom in and out and move around while on screen to provide a dynamic, but not too distracting, effect.

- **Sliding Panels.** In this theme, the photos appear to slide out of various panels on the screen (see Figure 13.7).

- **Shatter.** This theme transitions between slides using an interesting, well, shattering effect. It might be a bit much for most slideshows, but you can always try it out.

- **Scrapbook.** This theme presents the images as if they are pasted onto scrapbook pages of various configurations.

- **Snapshots.** In this theme, the slides appear on the screen as they would if they were prints being thrown down on a table.

- **Classic.** This theme lives up to its name; the photos play one after another in typical slideshow fashion with no transition effect between slides.

13.7 The Sliding Panels theme uses multiple panes to present photos on the screen.

Each theme has different options that you set by applying settings. For example, when you choose the Ken Burns theme, you set the direction and speed of the zoom function. Other themes have different settings you can apply.

Genius In a good slideshow design, the settings and music you apply should enhance the slides, not become the stars of the show. If you remember the transitions and effects in a slideshow but can't remember any of the photos, the design is probably overdone.

Applying a theme to a slideshow is simple:

1. **Click the Themes button.** The Themes sheet appears.

2. **Click the theme you want to apply and click Choose.** The theme is applied to the slideshow and the sheet closes.

Of course, you want to preview the slideshow with the new theme to see what effect it has.

Applying settings to all slides

Settings vary from theme to theme, but they all control specific aspects of how the slideshow plays and looks while it plays. You can apply settings to all the slides in a slideshow and you can apply settings to individual slides.

You use settings to control aspects of a slideshow that include the following:

- **Duration.** You can choose the playing time for the slideshow by setting the duration of each slide on the screen or you can set the slideshow to end at the same time as its music does. All themes have these settings.

- **Transitions.** These are the effects that appear when slides change.

- **Captions.** You can choose whether captions are displayed and, if they are, which text is used.

- **Title slide.** You can configure the title slide, including whether it is used.

- **Repeat.** With this setting enabled, the slideshow repeats ad infinitum.

- **Scale.** You can set the slideshow to play such that its photos fill the screen.

- **Aspect ratio.** By default, this is set to be the screen the slideshow plays on, but if you are going to export the slideshow for specific displays, you might want to select a particular aspect ratio.

The settings you apply depend on the theme you have selected. However, this example using the Ken Burns theme helps you see how to configure settings for any theme:

1. **Click the Settings button.** The Slideshow Settings dialog appears, as shown in Figure 13.8.

2. **Click the All Slides tab.** You see the settings that are applied to every slide in the slideshow.

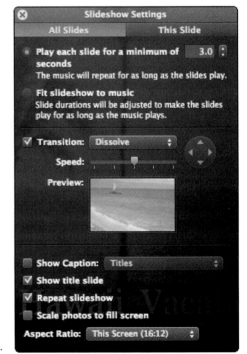

13.8 These settings are for the Ken Burns theme.

3. **Choose a duration for the slideshow by selecting one of the following options:**

   ● Select the Play each slide for a minimum of *X* seconds radio button and type the minimum duration of each slide in the box.

   ● Select the Fit slideshow to music radio button if you want the duration of the slides to be set so that the slideshow ends precisely when the music you add to it does.

4. **To apply a transition effect between the slides, select the Transition check box and choose the transition you want to use on the pop-up menu.** Use the arrow buttons to set the direction of the transition, and use the Speed slider to control how fast the transition plays (move the slider to the right to increase the speed of the effect or to the left to decrease it). Each time you make a change, you see a preview of the transition in the Preview window.

5. **To display captions, select the Show Caption check box and choose the text you want as the captions on the pop-up menu.** The options for captions are titles, descriptions, titles and descriptions, places, or dates.

Genius

You can leave the Slideshow Settings dialog open while you preview the slideshow. It floats on top so you can always see its controls. You can make a change, preview the slideshow, and then continue making changes without opening and closing the dialog.

6. **If you want the slideshow title to appear on the first slide, select the Show title slide check box.**

7. **If you want the slideshow to play until you stop it, select the Repeat slideshow check box.**

8. **To scale the slides to fill the screen, select the Scale photos to fill screen check box.** Be careful about this one. Unless your slides have the same orientation and size, scaling can cause the images to look stretched or squashed, or you might only see part of a scaled photo when it appears on the screen.

9. **Choose the aspect ratio for the slideshow on the Aspect Ratio pop-up menu.** The options are This Screen, which sets the slideshow to match the screen you are using; HDTV (16:9), TV (4:3), or iPhone (3:2). You should choose an aspect ratio that matches the device on which you intend to primarily watch the slideshow.

Applying settings to specific slides

You can also apply settings for specific slides. For example, you might want to apply a different transition every so often to keep things more interesting. The settings available for individual slides also depend upon the theme you have selected. Setting options for specific slides include the following:

- **Effects.** You can apply different effects to slides, such as Sepia, Black & White, or Antique.

- **Duration.** You can set the duration for specific slides. This is a good technique to break up a slideshow's flow or you might want to increase the duration for a very detailed slide or decrease the duration of a slide that doesn't have much content.

- **Transition.** You can override the transition setting applied to all slides.

- **Ken Burns tool.** You can control how a slide zooms and moves on the screen. The theme for the slideshow doesn't have to be Ken Burns for this to be available, though it isn't available for all themes.

As with the example of the settings you apply to all slides, an example of applying settings under a theme or two will help you understand how to apply settings to specific slides under any theme. The following steps show how you can apply settings to a specific slide using the Classic theme.

1. **In the thumbnail viewer, select the slide to which you want to apply settings.** The slide appears in the middle pane of the screen.

2. **If it isn't open already, click the Settings button to open the Slideshow Settings dialog.**

3. **Click the This Slide tab.** You see the slide settings for the theme you have applied to the slideshow, as shown in Figure 13.9.

4. **To apply an effect, click it.** You see the results on the slide in the iPhoto window. For example, if you click Sepia, the slide is converted into Sepia tone.

5. **To override the global duration setting for the slide, select the Play this slide for *X* seconds check box and type the slide's duration in the box.**

6. **To override the global transition setting, select the Transition check box and choose the transition you want to use on the pop-up menu.** Use the arrow buttons to set the direction of the transition, and use the Speed slider to control how fast the transition plays.

7. **To use the Ken Burns effect on the slide, select the Ken Burns check box and complete Steps 8 through 12.**

8. **Drag the Ken Burns slider to the Start position.**

9. **In the iPhoto window, drag the Zoom slider so the photo has the level of zoom you want it to have when it first appears and then click on the photo and drag it so the portion of the photo you want to be displayed when it comes on the screen is shown.** This sets the start of the pan and zoom effect.

10. **Drag the Ken Burns slider to End position.**

11. **In the iPhoto window, drag the Zoom slider so the photo has the level of zoom you want to have just before the slide disappears and then click on the photo and drag it so the portion of the photo you want to be displayed just before it leaves the screen is shown.** This sets the endpoint of the pan and zoom effect.

12. **Preview the slide and make adjustments until the Ken Burns effect is applied the way you want it to be.**

13. **On the thumbnail viewer, select the next slide to you want to design and use the previous steps to apply settings to it.**

13.9 When you use the This Slide tab, the settings you adjust apply only to the slide currently selected.

Note

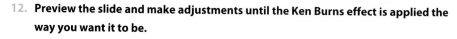
The shorter the duration for a slide with the Ken Burns effect is, the faster the effect will play on-screen.

227

Applying music to a slideshow

While music can be annoying when you are designing a slideshow, it is an important element of the design. When you think you are close to finishing your slideshow, start working with its music. Several sources of music are available within iPhoto:

- **Sample Music.** This source is provided with iLife and contains short music segments.

- **Theme Music.** This source contains some full songs, including vocals.

- **GarageBand.** You can use any music you create or manage in GarageBand for your slideshows.

- **iTunes.** Any music in your iTunes library can also be used for a slideshow.

You can apply one song as the soundtrack for your slideshow or you can create a custom playlist.

Using one song as a soundtrack

To apply music to a slideshow, perform the following steps:

1. **Click the Music button.** The Music Settings dialog appears. If you set a slideshow's duration to be a specific time, the music you apply to it repeats until the slideshow ends, unless the music is longer than the slideshow; in which case, it fades out when the slideshow ends.

2. **To play music during the slideshow, select the Play music during slideshow check box.**

3. **On the Source pop-up menu, choose the source of music you want to use.** For example, to use music in your iTunes library, choose iTunes. Under the iTunes source, you can choose your Music library or any of your playlists. When you select a source of music, its contents appear in the song list in the middle of the dialog, as shown in Figure 13.10.

4. **Find music you might want to use two ways:**

    - Browse the list of available songs in the selected source.

    - Search for music by clicking the Magnifying glass icon, choosing a search attribute (such as Artist or Song), and typing search text in the Search tool. Songs that meet your search criterion appear on the song list.

5. **Preview any song in the song list by selecting it and clicking the Play button or by double-clicking the song.** The song plays.

6. **Continue previewing music until you find the song you want to use as the slide-show's soundtrack.**

Music Settings

☑ **Play music during slideshow**

Source: iTunes

Name	Artist	Time
♫ Desolation Island	Patrick O'Brian	13:04:01
♫ Island Girl	Elton John	3:45
♫ Treasure Island	Steven Curtis Ch...	4:52
♫ 05 Desolation Island		13:04:01

Q▾ isla   ⊗   4 items

☐ **Custom Playlist for Slideshow**

Choose

13.10 You can access a variety of music to apply to a slideshow on the Music Settings dialog.

Genius The far-right column of the Music Settings dialog shows the times for the songs listed in the window. This is useful for selecting songs of the appropriate length. If you set the slideshow's duration to be the same as the music you apply, the length of the song you choose determines the time the slideshow plays.

7. **Select the song you want to use and click Choose.** The song is applied to the slide-show and will play as the slideshow does.

Using a custom playlist as a soundtrack

You can also select a combination of songs to use as the soundtrack for a slideshow. Here's how:

1. **Open the Music Settings dialog.**

229

2. **Select the Custom Playlist for Slideshow check box.** The Music Settings dialog expands so you see a playlist area at the bottom.

3. **Find the first song you want to include in the soundtrack and drag it onto the playlist.**

4. **Repeat Step 3 to add more songs to the playlist.**

5. **Drag the songs up and down the playlist to determine the order in which they should play, as shown in Figure 13.11.**

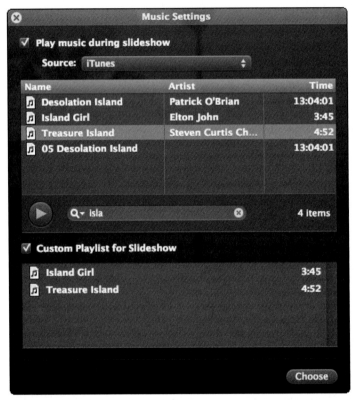

13.11 When you add songs to the custom playlist area, each song plays in the order it is listed, from top to bottom.

6. **Click Choose.** The playlist is applied to the slideshow and plays as the slideshow does.

Configuring the title slide for a slideshow

By default, the first slide in the slideshow is a title slide that contains text, which starts out as the name of the album or other object from which the photos in the slideshow come. You can enable this text slide and configure the text it contains.

Here's how:

1. **Open the Settings dialog.**

2. **Select the Show title slide check box.** Now the first slide in the thumbnail viewer is a black slide with the letter "T" in its center; this represents the title slide. However, the text is actually applied to the slide to the right of this slide.

3. **Select the Text Slide in the thumbnail viewer.** The current text appears on the first slide.

Genius

You can also enable or disable the title slide by clicking the Text Slide button on the toolbar.

4. **Select the text.**

5. **Edit the text to be what you want to appear on the slide.**

6. **Choose Edit ⇨ Font ⇨ Show Fonts.** The Fonts panel appears, as shown in Figure 13.12.

7. **Use the Fonts panel to format the text.**

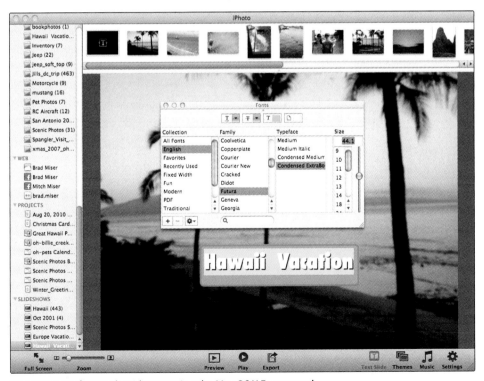

13.12 You can format the title text using the Mac OS X Fonts panel.

Genius

You can also edit the title text directly on the slide on which it appears.

Note

The position of the text on the screen depends on the theme applied to the slideshow. You can't change this; you just have to use its location as is.

Playing a slideshow within iPhoto

When you are ready to give your slideshow a spin, you can play it with the following steps:

1. **Select the slideshow you want to play.**

2. **Click the Play button.** The slideshow plays in Full Screen mode.

3. **To access controls for the slideshow, move the pointer and then click the control you want to use.** The same controls appear on the toolbar as for a temporary slideshow as shown in Figure 13.13.

13.13 When you move the pointer while a slideshow plays, you see the Slideshow toolbar.

Genius

Press the Spacebar to pause or play a slideshow.

4. **To exit the slideshow playback and return to the iPhoto window, click the Exit slideshow button or press Esc.**

Genius

If you point to the bottom of the screen during slideshow playback, you see a thumbnail browser showing you how the slideshow is progressing through the photos.

Exporting a slideshow from iPhoto

You can export a slideshow from iPhoto to use in other applications and on other devices, such as an iPhone or iPad. To do this, follow these steps:

1. **Select the slideshow you want to export.**

2. **Click the Export button.** You see the Export sheet. On this sheet, you see the various size options available to you along with the devices for which those sizes are appropriate. To get details about a format, click its Info button. In the bubble that appears, you see details, including the specific format that will be used and the resulting file size.

3. **Select the check boxes for the formats in which you want to export the slideshow.** You can choose one or all of the available formats to export at the same time, but you must choose at least one option.

4. **To move the slideshow into iTunes, select the Automatically send slideshow to iTunes check box, as shown in Figure 13.14.**

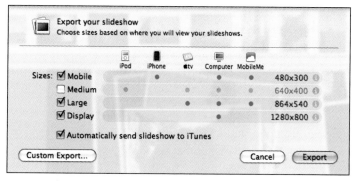

13.14 Configure the Export sheet with the formats in which you want to export a slideshow.

5. **Click Export.** The Location sheet appears.

6. **Choose a location for the exported files.** The default location is the iPhoto Slideshows folder located in your Pictures folder.

7. **Click OK.** The slideshow is exported from iPhoto. The Progress sheet appears so you can monitor the progress of the process. Depending on the number of formats you selected and the size of the slideshow, this process can take a while. When it is complete, the Progress bar closes.

8. **Move to the Finder and open the iPhoto Slideshows folder within your Pictures folder.** You see a file for each version of the slideshow that you exported. They are named so that you can tell their purpose, such as photo album name Slideshow-Mobile. m4v for the version formatted for an iPod, iPad, or iPhone. If you selected the Automatically send slideshow to iTunes option, the slideshow is in your iTunes library, where you can watch it or move it onto another device, such as an iPad or an iPhone.

Playing a slideshow in iTunes or on an iPod/iPhone/iPad

If you export a slideshow and select the Automatically send slideshow to iTunes option, the slideshow is moved into your iTunes library. From there, you can use iTunes to watch the slideshow. You can also sync the slideshow onto an iPod, iPad, or iPhone so that you can watch it on one of those devices.

Viewing an iPhoto slideshow in iTunes

You can watch a slideshow using iTunes with the following steps:

1. **Select the Movies source in the iTunes Source pane.**

2. **Browse or search for the slideshow and select it.**

3. **Click the Play button or press the Spacebar.** The slideshow begins to play in the iTunes window, as shown in Figure 13.15.

4. **Use the iTunes controls to play the slideshow.**

Note

If a slideshow is not moved into your iTunes library automatically, drag all versions of its file from the desktop to the library to add it.

13.15 You can watch your iPhoto slideshows in iTunes.

Viewing an iPhoto slideshow on an iPod/iPhone/iPad

To be able to view your slideshow on an Apple mobile device, you must sync your iTunes library with the device and include the slideshow in the sync as follows:

1. **Connect the device to the Mac.** It is mounted and appears in the iTunes Source pane.

2. **Select the device.** The Sync tools appear in the iTunes window.

3. **Click the Movies tab.**

4. **Select the Sync Movies check box.**

5. **Select the slideshow's check box.**

6. **Click Apply.** The slideshow is moved onto the device and is ready to watch.

To watch a slideshow on an iPhone, iPad, or iPod touch, perform the following steps:

1. **If you are using an iPhone, tap the iPod button; skip this step on an iPad or iPod touch.**

2. **Tap the Videos button.**

3. **Tap the slideshow.** It begins to play.

4. **Use the iPhone's on-screen controls to play the slideshow, as shown in Figure 13.16.**

13.16 Watching a slideshow you built in iPhoto on an iPhone is definitely cool.

Sending iPhoto Content to iDVD

iPhoto contains a good set of tools that you can use to create pretty amazing and entertaining slideshows. However, iPhoto slideshows require a computer or computer-related device to view them. And while iPhoto offers quite a few slideshow tricks, you deal with slideshows one by one. There's no way to create a group of slideshows for viewing or for storage.

As an alternative, you can send your photos to iDVD. In this application, you can create and design a slideshow that is delivered on a DVD that can be played in any standard DVD player. And DVDs you create in iDVD can have custom menus and other features you'd expect to see on a DVD produced by a professional movie studio.

Because this is a book on iPhoto, not iDVD, I don't cover all the details of building a DVD in iDVD. However, I can show you the process of moving iPhoto content into an iDVD project to create a slideshow there.

You can send the following content from iPhoto to iDVD:

- Photos
- Photo albums

236

- Slideshow projects
- Photo books
- Calendars
- Cards

Once this content is in an iDVD project, you can use iDVD's tools to prepare that content for delivery on a DVD.

Sending photos to iDVD

To send photos to an iDVD project, perform the following steps:

1. **Select the photos you want to send to iDVD.** You can select an album to choose all the photos it contains or you can select one or more photos directly.

2. **Choose Share ⇨ iDVD.** The selected photos are prepared and sent to iDVD. That application opens, a new DVD project is created, and you see the photos you sent on the DVD's main menu. The content is labeled with the album's name if you selected an album, or with the text Photos if you selected photos directly.

3. **To send more content to the same DVD project, repeat Steps 1 and 2.** All the content you send appears on the main menu, as shown in Figure 13.17.

13.17 Photos you move from iPhoto to iDVD appear on a new project's main menu.

Sending slideshows to iDVD

You can also send your slideshow projects from iPhoto to an iDVD project. The slideshow transfers along with all its effects and its soundtrack so that it plays on DVD as it does within the iPhoto window. Sending a slideshow to iDVD is similar to sending other content:

1. **Select the slideshow you want to send to iDVD.**

2. **Choose Share ⇨ iDVD.** If you have selected only one photo in the slideshow, which is the case when you select the slideshow in the Source pane, you see the iDVD export dialog. This gives you the option to send the selected slide or the whole slideshow.

3. **Click Send whole slideshow.** The slideshow is prepared and exported to iDVD. Depending on the size of the slideshow and the settings you applied, this process can take quite a while. When it's done, iDVD becomes active and the slideshow is added to the current project, or if a project isn't open, it is added to a new project.

To watch the slideshow in iDVD to preview it, perform the following steps:

1. **Click the Play button.** iDVD moves into preview mode. The DVD's main menu appears along with the on-screen DVD controller.

2. **Click the slideshow.** It begins to play in the iDVD window, as shown in Figure 13.18.

3. **Use the on-screen controller's tools to control the playback.**

4. **To exit the preview mode, click the Exit button on the controller.** You return to the main menu and iDVD returns to the Edit mode.

13.18 You can preview your iPhoto slideshows in iDVD to see how they will appear once you burn the iDVD project to disc.

How Can I Create Photo Books?

Photo books are a great way to enjoy your photos. iPhoto includes a wide variety of photo book designs you can use, but they are only a starting point. You can use iPhoto's powerful tools to design each individual page, unleashing your creativity on your photo book projects. And if you get your iPhoto photo books professionally printed and bound, they become a treasured keepsake you can enjoy for a long time. Photo books make great gifts, too.

Building Photo Books

Building a photo book is likely the most detailed and complicated project for which you will use iPhoto. Photo books are also one of the most rewarding because when you're done, you have created your own, professionally printed book with your photos displayed in creative and interesting ways. You should follow a process when you build photo books to make it more enjoyable and to get the best results. For this chapter, the various tasks involved are organized into the following phases:

1. **Creating a photo book.** To get started, collect the photos you want to include in the book and use iPhoto's Photo Book tools to create a book project.

2. **Designing a photo book.** When you create a photo book, you choose a theme that creates the basic design of the book. However, this is only the starting point. You apply your own style and creativity to the book, both at the book level and at the page level. Book-level design tasks include adding and removing pages, updating the theme, and so on. Page-level design is manipulating the layout, photos, and text on each page of the book.

3. **Finishing a photo book.** This is the easiest phase to skimp on because it tends to be a bit tedious, but it is arguably the most important. You should carefully review your book to look for and correct mistakes and tweak the design until the book is exactly what you want it to be.

4. **Buying a photo book.** When the project is done, you can get it professionally printed and delivered anywhere you want. You can do this easily and quickly.

As you start the process, keep the following points in mind:

- **Photo resolution.** When choosing photos for a photo book, consider the resolution of the photos you use. If you use a low-resolution image at a large size, it might not print with acceptable quality. Fortunately, iPhoto warns you in such cases so you can replace low-resolution images with higher-resolution ones or you can use the lower-resolution image at a smaller size.

- **Book length.** You can create a photo book that is from 10 to 100 pages long, depending on the style and type options you choose, and books must have an even number of pages. Each page can have many photos on it, so you'll want to have from ten to hundreds of photos collected for a book project, depending on how large the book you plan to create will be and how many photos you'll put on each page. You won't be able to tell exactly how many photos you need for a book of a specific number of pages, but as you design you change the number of pages in a book by changing the number of photos you use and how the book is designed.

- **Book price.** The cost to print a book depends on the type of book you choose and the number of pages it contains.

- **Types.** When you create a book, you also choose its type, which includes both the size of the pages and how those pages are bound in the printed book.

- **Themes.** Photo book themes include the layout of the photos on the photo book's photo pages, text elements (such as titles and descriptions), colors, and other design features.

- **Layouts.** Your books have an overall layout and each page has its own layout. The layout determines the structure. For example, a page's layout determines how many photos appear on that page.

Note

Remember that resolution is the amount of information stored in a photo, measured by the number of pixels vertically and horizontally. The more pixels a photo has (higher resolution), the more information if contains. This means it can be printed at larger sizes because there are plenty of pixels to show. If you use a low-resolution photo at a large size, iPhoto has to "spread out" its pixels, which can lead to a poor result of a blocky or blurry photo.

Creating a Photo Book

To get started, select the photos a photo book will contain and create a book project. At the end of this phase, you'll have a book containing photos designed according to the book type and theme you select. This becomes the starting point for your detailed design of the book.

Collecting photos for a book project

For faster and better results, organize the photos you are going to use in your book in an album before you create the book because it's easier and faster to add, remove, and organize photos in an album than it is in a photo book project. In the album, arrange the photos in the general order you want them to be in the photo book, from the top left for images appearing early on to the bottom right for those appearing later.

Note

You can use a standard or Smart Album to collect photos for a book. The album and book aren't linked in any way; the album is just a container for the photos you are going to use, and once you start the project, the album is no longer part of the process. So even if you use a Smart Album that changes over time as photos move in or out of it, the book in which you include photos from that album won't be affected.

You don't need to worry about getting exactly the right number, or even the right photos, at the start because you can always change the photos you use in a photo book during the design process. If you aren't sure about a photo, include it because it is easier to remove photos from a book than to add them. And having extra photos in a book project can be convenient when you change the design such that you need a couple more photos to complete a page.

Note

The details of creating and configuring albums are covered in Chapter 6.

Genius

The titles and descriptions of photos can be included in a photo book. You can also use the locations with which photos are associated to create map pages. If you haven't consistently tagged photos with this information, do so when you have created the album. This saves time and effort during the book design process because it is easier to update information for photos when they are in an album than when they are in a book. Create the album and review the information for all the photos it contains. Update this as needed. See Chapters 2 through 5 for information about tagging your photos.

Creating a book project

To create a photo book project, do the following:

1. **Select the photos you want to include in the photo book.** If you created an album for the project, select the album. You can also select photos individually.

2. **Click the Create button.**

3. **Click Book.** The photos you selected are placed into a new book, which you see in the window. The themes available for the book are shown on a rotating selector.

4. **Preview a theme by clicking it.** The theme rotates to the center and becomes in focus. You see the cover design for the book in the center window and the general layout of its pages at the bottom of the window as shown in Figure 14.1. You see cost information for the selected theme in the lower-left corner of the window with the cover options at the top of the screen.

5. **Preview themes until you find and select the one you want to use.**

Genius

You can flip through the available themes by pressing the left- or right-arrow key.

14.1 Use the rotating selector to choose a theme for the photo book.

6. **Choose a cover and binding by clicking one of the options shown at the top of the screen.** For example, to create a hardcover book, click Hardcover.

7. **Choose the size of the book by clicking one of the size buttons just above the cost information.** The options you have depend on the theme you select, such as Extra Large, Large, Medium, or Small.

Note

As you make changes, keep an eye on the cost information. Different options have different costs associated with them. The cost may influence some of your choices, such as hardcover versus softcover. In addition to the basic cost of the book, you see the cost per additional page (above the initial 10 pages included by default).

8. **Choose the color scheme for the book by clicking one of the color swatches located above the Create and Cancel buttons.**

9. **When you are pleased with your selections, click Create.** The book project is created and opens in the book designer mode. You are ready to design the book.

Designing a Photo Book

After you create a photo book, you design its pages. You use the Photo Book tool to do all the design work for a photo book. An initial design is created for you when you select a theme, so your job is to adjust that initial design until the book meets your vision for it.

The Photo Book tool is shown in Figure 14.2. This tool provides functions that you can use to design all aspects of your book from the content of pages to how those pages look. You can also add and remove pages as needed.

14.2 The Photo Book tool enables to you create sophisticated designs for your photo book projects.

Some of the tool's main features are

- **Along the top of the tool, you see the name of the project, the number of pages, and the Change Theme button.** You can click Change Theme to change the settings you selected when you created the book.

- **In the center, you see thumbnails for the covers and each page, shown in two-page spreads as they appear in the book.** To work with a specific page, you select it. It becomes highlighted in a blue box and you see the page's number in the lower-right corner of its thumbnail. You can scroll the pages using the scroll bar along the right side of the window. To change the size of the thumbnails, use the Zoom slider.

- **The Photo Book toolbar appears at the bottom of the window.** In addition to the Zoom slider, you see the Buy Book, Add Page, Design, and Photos buttons. When you click the Design button, the Design sidebar appears and you see tools to design what is currently selected, such as pages or the cover, as shown in Figure 14.3. If you click the Photos button, you see the Photos sidebar (as shown in Figure 14.4) where you see all the photos currently in the project; you use this to add photos or change the pages on which photos appear. Think of this as a storage area for the book's photos.

14.3 Use the Design sidebar to design the selected page.

14.4 The Photos sidebar shows all the photos in the project.

Note

The check mark next to a photo on the Photos sidebar indicates that the photo is currently placed in the book. If a photo doesn't have this check mark, it is available for you to place in the book, but currently isn't included in it.

Designing a book

The Photo Book tool does a lot of work for you as soon as you create a book. This includes automatically flowing the photos you select on the book pages according to the theme and style options you select. The initial design might or might not be close to what you want the book to be, but most of the time, it provides a pretty good starting point. (If not, try changing the theme and type to see if you can find a better match for what you have in mind.)

The first order of business is to design the book from the overall perspective, meaning to apply the theme you want to use, make the number of pages about what you want, and generally set the flow of the book from the front to the back cover.

Scroll through the book's pages using the Zoom slider to focus in to see details and to get a sense of how the book flows. If some pages are not what you want, don't worry about them now; page design comes later. Your purpose here is to get the foundation right. Then you can build out all the details.

Genius

You can view a photo book in a slideshow format by clicking the Slideshow button.

Changing a book's theme and type

The theme and type you choose when you create the book is only a starting point. If after reviewing the book, you aren't happy with its overall layout and look, you can change a book's theme and type at any time:

1. **Click Change Theme.** The theme and type selector appears. This is the same as when you created the book initially, except that you aren't creating a new project, but are changing an existing one instead.

2. **Use the tools to change the book's cover/binding/ theme, size, and color palette.** These work just as when you created the book, too.

3. **Click Apply.** The photo book is redesigned according to the theme and type selections you made.

Genius

When you change a book's type and theme, you are fundamentally changing the book and you might lose most, if not all, of any work you have done on individual pages. It's best to experiment with types and themes early in your design process and settle on the options you will use for each one before you invest too much time in your design work for the book itself and especially for individual pages.

Changing a book's settings

There are a couple of general settings for books. To see these, deselect any selected pages and click the Design button. In the Design sidebar, you see two check boxes. Deselect the Auto-Layout pages check box if you don't want the Photo Book tool to automatically lay out pages for you. Deselect the Include Apple logo at end of book check box if you don't want the Apple logo to appear on the back cover of the book.

Note

If you disable the Auto-Layout option, you have to manually design each page, and when you make a change that affects the flow of the book you have to make all the adjustments manually. If you want total control over the book and are willing to do the additional work involved, deselect this option. Most of the time, leaving it enabled makes the process more efficient and less tedious. You may also get better results.

Changing the order of pages in a book

You can move pages around within a book to change their order. Just drag the pages around the page browser until the pages in the book are in the order you want them to be. As you move a page around, the pages that come later in the book are reflowed.

Adding pages to a book

You can add pages to a photo book to expand its contents. When you add new pages, you select where in the book you want to add them. When you add the pages, the pages behind the pages you add slide toward the back of the book to make room for the new ones. The design of your existing pages is not affected — the new pages are empty and only have a layout applied to them. Here's how to add pages:

1. **Select the page you want new pages to follow in the book.**

2. **Click the Add Page button.** Two new pages are inserted into the book after the page you selected. The new pages are ready to be designed, as shown in Figure 14.5.

Note

Books always have an even number of pages so you have to add pages two at a time.

Removing pages from a book

You can also delete pages from a photo book. If you delete one page, the pages after it slide forward to fill the empty space. Because of this, it's better to delete two pages at a time so the layout of the remaining pages isn't affected. Remember you can't have fewer than the minimum number of pages in a book, which in most cases is 10 pages (20 sides), so you can't delete any more pages once a book is down to its minimum number of pages. To delete pages from a book, follow these steps:

1. **Move to and select the pages you want to delete.**

2. **Press Delete.**

14.5 When you add pages to a book, they don't have any photos on them.

3. **Click Yes in the confirmation sheet.** The pages are removed from the book. Any photos on the deleted pages remain in the project even though they no longer appear in the book; you can add them to other pages if you want to. You lose any text on the pages that isn't associated with a photo.

Genius

You can select multiple pages to delete at the same time by holding down the ⌘ key while you click each page you want to delete. Then press Delete.

Designing a book's pages

Once the basic layout and flow of the book are what you want, it's time to design each of the book's pages. The elements of the pages you design include:

● **Background.** This determines the background color or image over which the photos and text appear.

- **Layout.** This setting determines the number of photos on a page or if it is one of the special page types:

  - **Text.** A page that only has text on it

  - **Map.** Shows the location associated with photos on a map

  - **Spread.** Spreads a photo across two pages

  - **Blank.** Just what it sounds like

- **Photos.** You select, configure, and format the photos on each page. Photos on pages appear in frames; the number of frames on a page determines the number of photos placed there. You can change how a photo appears within its frame.

- **Text.** Some pages include text elements. You can type the text you want to appear in the book and then use the formatting tools to style that text.

There are many options in each of these areas, and there's no way to cover them all in this short chapter. However, these tools follow a pattern, so once you see this pattern, you can experiment with the tools to apply your designs to your own books.

The general steps required to design a book's pages are

1. **Double-click the page you want to design.** It appears in the editing area, as shown in Figure 14.6.

2. **Click the Design button and use the Design sidebar to configure the page's background and layout.**

3. **Configure the photos on the page by moving the existing photos around, replacing photos, or removing photos.**

4. **Select each photo on the page and set the zoom level, configure a border, and apply effects.**

5. **Type and format text on the page.**

6. **Move to the next page you want to design and repeat the previous steps until you've designed all the pages in the book.**

Note

As you work on a book, iPhoto saves your changes automatically.

14.6 When you double-click a page, it fills the window and is ready for you to design.

To move out of the edit mode, click the All Pages button in the upper-left corner of the window.

The design process is an iterative one: Things you do on one page affect the rest of the pages in the book and even affect the layout on the same page. While this chapter is laid out sequentially, you'll probably do the tasks it covers simultaneously, such as designing the layout of a page and the photos it contains at the same time. Just find a process that works for you by trying different approaches.

Following are examples of each of the general steps to show you how they work; you'll be able to apply the steps to the pages in your books.

Designing a page's background and layout

To configure a page's background and layout, perform the following steps:

1. **Double-click the page you want to design.**

2. **Click the Design button.** The Design sidebar opens. At the top of the sidebar, you see the Background options; underneath that, you see the Layout tools, as shown in Figure 14.7. The currently applied options are highlighted in blue boxes.

Genius Use the Zoom slider to make the pages an appropriate size for editing. When you zoom in such that not all the page can be displayed on the screen, the Navigation box appears. This indicates the portion of the page you are seeing on the screen in a box. You can move the box around to change the portion of the page you are viewing. You can click the left- and right-facing arrows to move between pages.

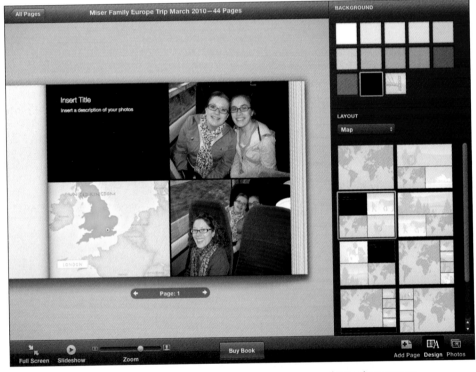

14.7 This page has a layout showing one text pane, one map pane, and two photo panes.

3. **Click the background you want to apply to the page.** You see the results on the page in the editing area.

Genius You can use a photo as the background for a page. Click the Photo tile (the only one that is not a solid color) to replace the colored background with a photo frame. You can then add a photo to the frame and configure it just like photos in the foreground.

4. **On the Layout menu, choose the page's design.** You can choose from one to sixteen photos plus four special layouts (Text Page, Map, Spread, or Blank). The layout you choose is applied to the page. When you decrease the number of photos, the photos that are removed are still available to be applied to other pages in the book. If you choose a layout with more photos, empty frames are added for each new photo; you can add photos to these (you learn how shortly).

Configuring the photos on pages

When you design the photos on a page, you can do the following tasks:

- Add photos to empty frames or replace the current photo in a frame.
- Remove photos from a frame.
- Position and zoom a photo within its frame.
- Adjust the image in a frame.

Genius

To use the mirror image of a photo, open its contextual menu (by right-clicking or Control+clicking on it) and choose Mirror Image.

To add a photo to or replace a photo in a frame, do the following:

1. **Open the page containing the frame you want to change.** You see the page in the editing area.

2. **Click the Photos button.** The Photos sidebar appears. The Show menu at the top of the sidebar determines the photos you see in the sidebar. The options are

   - **All Photos in Project.** When this is selected, you see all the photos in the project, whether or not they are placed.

   - **Placed Photos.** This shows you only the photos currently in the book.

   - **Unplaced Photos.** This shows you the photos in the project, but not in the book.

   - **Recents.** At the bottom of the menu, you see the four options in the RECENT section of the Source pane, which are: the last event you viewed, the photos you most recently imported, the photos you imported in the last X months, and flagged photos.

   When you make a selection on the menu, the thumbnails in the sidebar update accordingly. When you choose a source for photos included in the book, the placed photos are marked with a check mark. If you point to a placed photo, you see the pages on which it is placed and if you pause for a second or two, you see information about the photo, as shown in Figure 14.8.

Genius

You aren't limited to working with the photos included in the book project when you created it. To add photos to the book, find the photos you want to add and drag them onto the project's icon in the Source pane. The photos are added to the book; choose the Unplaced Photos option on the Show menu to see photos you've added (photos you add aren't placed automatically).

14.8 The Photos sidebar enables you to add photos to a book.

3. **Find the photo you want to use.**

4. **Drag the photo from the sidebar onto the frame where you want it to be placed; when the frame is highlighted, release the mouse button, as shown in Figure 14.9.**
   If the frame was empty, the new photo fills it. If there was a photo there, the new photo replaces it.

Genius

When you select a photo that is placed on a page and that photo isn't shown in the Photos sidebar, the sidebar scrolls so that you see the selected photo.

To remove a photo from a frame, do the following:

1. **Open the page containing the frame you want to empty.**

2. **Select the frame.**

3. **Press Delete.** The photo is removed from the frame and from the photo book page, but it remains in the photo book project so you can use it elsewhere.

14.9 To add a photo to a frame, drag it from the photo browser onto the frame.

Configuring individual photos on pages

To position and zoom in or out on a photo within its frame, follow these steps:

1. **Select the frame containing the photo you want to position.** Its frame is highlighted and the Zoom slider appears, as shown in Figure 14.10.

2. **Drag the slider to the left to zoom out or to the right to zoom in.**

3. **Drag the photo within the frame so the portion you want to see is shown (as you drag a photo, the pointer becomes a hand grabbing the photo you are moving).**

4. **Repeat Steps 2 and 3 until the photo appears how you want it to within the frame.**

257

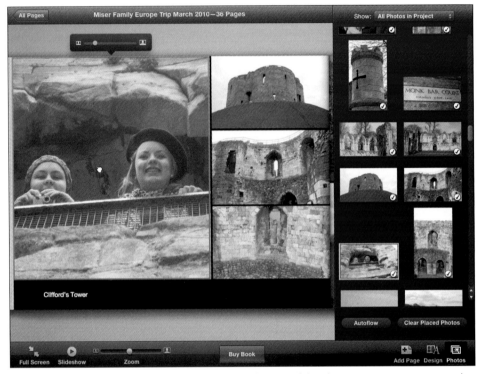

14.10 Zoom and position a photo within its frame so the part of the photo you want to appear on the photo book is shown.

You can apply effects and borders to photos as follows:

1. **Select the photo you want to apply an effect or border to.**

2. **Click the Design button.** The Design sidebar appears with tools that you use to change the photo, as shown in Figure 14.11.

Note If you click Edit Photo, you move into Edit mode and can edit the photo using iPhoto's Editing tools, which are explained in Chapter 8.

3. **Click the border you want to apply.** Most of the borders add a caption area to the photo.

4. **Click the effect you want to apply.**

14.11 You can apply borders and effects to photos in your book.

Note   Effects you apply don't actually change the image itself, just the instance of the image in the book. When you make changes by editing the photo using the Edit tools, you do change the photo everywhere it is used.

Genius   At the bottom of the Photos sidebar, you see the Autoflow button. When you have unplaced photos in the project, you can click this button to place the photos on new pages at the end of the book.

Adding maps to pages

A map is a great addition to a book because it shows the locations of the photos included in the book. You can configure a page or part of a page to have a map and then configure the content and appearance of the map.

259

Here's how:

1. **Select a page and use the Layout menu to make it a Map page.** You can have the entire page as a map or choose to include a map pane.

2. **Select the map and open the Design sidebar.** You see the map configuration tools, as shown in Figure 14.12.

14.12 Adding maps to a photo book is a great way to make the book more interesting and provide information about the photos it contains.

3. **Apply a style to the map by clicking a Style button.**

4. **Choose the locations shown on the map by selecting or deselecting their check boxes.** The available locations are those with which the related photos are associated.

5. **If there are multiple locations on the map, use the Line menu to choose if and how those places are connected on the map.**

6. **Use the Show check boxes to determine if elements are shown or hidden.**

7. **Use the Zoom slider and drag the map to set which part of the map is shown in the frame.**

Configuring text on pages

Most of the photo book themes include pages with text frames for various kinds of text you might want to include in a book. They include captions, titles, and larger text areas. To configure the text in a photo book, perform the following steps:

1. **Open a page containing a text frame.**

Genius

You should typically not work on text until you are happy with the photo book's layout and how the photos appear on each page because the text is usually dependent on those other elements.

2. **Select a text frame.** It becomes outlined with a blue line and the text it contains is selected.

3. **Open the Design sidebar.** You see the text formatting tools, as shown in Figure 14.13.

14.13 Add text to and format text in text frames on your photo book's pages.

4. **Type the text you want to include.** By default, iPhoto checks your spelling as you type. You can use iPhoto's text-editing tools to work with text just as they work in other Apple applications.

5. **Format the text using the font, style, size, spacing, and other tools in the Design sidebar.**

Genius

You can write text in another application, such as a word processor, and then copy and paste that text into frames on a photo book's pages.

Finishing a Photo Book

After you design each page in the book, you're almost finished, but some of the most important work remains. Now is the time to polish your book to make sure you'll be completely happy with it when it is printed. You need to proof your book to find and fix mistakes or to make improvements. If some of the photos in your book have a resolution that is too low to print well, you need to correct those problems before ordering the book.

Proofing a book

After you design a photo book, you should preview and edit it before you order a copy. First, create a PDF version of the document so you can preview it electronically:

1. **Open the Print dialog.**

2. **Open the PDF menu and choose Save as PDF.**

Note

Make sure you use a page size that is at least as large as the pages in your book or some of the pages may be cut off and not useful for proofing.

Genius

An easier way to create a preview is to view the book, right-click, and choose Preview Book.

3. **Choose a location and save the file.** A PDF version of the photo book is created.

4. **Open the PDF version.** It appears in the Preview application, or whichever application you use as your default PDF reader, as shown in Figure 14.14.

5. **View the photo book.** If you find problems or want to make improvements, go back to iPhoto and make changes. Then create a new PDF and repeat the process until you are satisfied.

Once you are happy with the PDF version, you might want to print a version as a draft with your desktop printer. This often exposes issues that aren't apparent when you view a photo book on-screen. Review the printed version carefully, and use iPhoto to fix any mistakes you find.

Genius

Don't skimp on the proofing process. If you print a photo book that has mistakes, you don't get a refund. It's up to you to make sure the photo book is worth the cost to get it printed professionally.

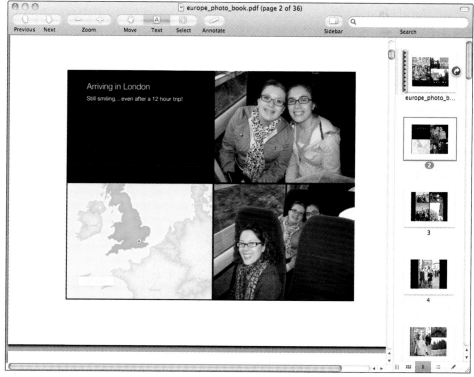

14.14 Previewing a photo book via PDF before printing it saves time and money.

Dealing with resolution problems in a photo book

When iPhoto encounters a photo that might have a printing problem because of its resolution, the photo is marked with the Warning icon, which you see in both the page browser and when a problem photo appears on a page in the editing area. You should fix resolution problems before you order a photo book, as this might indicate that the photo will not print very well in the final product. Here are some suggestions to do so:

- **Zoom out so more of the photo is included within its frame.** This increases the amount of information displayed on the page and improves the quality of the printed version.

- **Use the image in a smaller frame.** You can move the image to a smaller frame or add more photos to the page so its current frame becomes smaller.

- **If the image has been cropped, remove the cropping.** Edit the image and choose Photos ⇨ Revert to Original. The image is restored to full size, which means more information is in the frame.

- **Edit the photo to distort it.** You can apply effects to a photo, such as converting it to Sepia Tone or adjusting the saturation way up, to disguise a lower-quality image. This doesn't correct the resolution issue, but might artistically hide the problem.

If none of these approaches solves the issue and the image is important to you, you can print the book with the image as it is. It might not look as good as other photos in the photo book, but if the photo is important enough to you, it might be worth the risk.

Buying a Photo Book

To order a professionally printed and bound version of the photo book, do the following:

1. **Select the photo book you want to order.**

2. **Click Buy Book.** iPhoto checks the photo book and reports any problems it finds, including missing photos, empty text frames, and so on. Fix those problems before proceeding. When iPhoto doesn't find any issues, you see the Your Order screen, as shown in Figure 14.15.

3. **Configure the purchase and delivery options in the Order Book dialog.** You use an Apple ID to order books and other printed material from Apple.

4. **Click Check Out and follow the on-screen instructions to complete the purchase.** The printed photo books will be delivered to the location you configure.

14.15 Use the Order Book screen to set the quantity you want to buy along with where the photo book will be shipped.

Note

To delete a photo book, select it in the Source pane and press Delete. After you confirm your action, the photo book is removed from the Source pane. Before you get rid of a book, know that once you delete it, it's gone forever (well, it might still be available in a backup as you see in Chapter 18).

How Can I Create Cards?

Almost everyone likes to give and receive cards for holidays and special occasions, or, even better, just for fun. Generally, the more personalized a card is, the more meaningful it is. With iPhoto, you can create cards that include your photos and text; you can't get any more personalized than that! After you create your cards, you can have Apple print them, which makes them a great combination of personalization and outstanding quality.

Creating a Card

As with other projects in iPhoto, you start a card by selecting the photos you want to use on the card and creating it. When you create a card, you choose its type, theme, and other attributes that determine the card's overall appearance.

To start a card project, perform the following steps:

1. **Select the photos you want to include in the card.** You can create a photo album for the card, add the photos you want to use, and select the album from your library. You can also select photos directly. Because cards use a relatively small number of photos, usually selecting them directly is more efficient. The specific number of photos you need depends on the theme you select. You should select one to ten photos, closer to one if you have a pretty good idea of what you want to do with the card, and more toward ten if you aren't so sure. You don't need to worry about getting exactly the right number, or even the right photos, at the start because you can always change the photos you use during the design process.

Genius

Flags are a great tool to use for card projects. As you browse your photos, flag those that you want to use in a card. When you create the card, select the Flagged source and then select the specific photos you want to use.

2. **Click the Create button.**

3. **Click Card.** The photos you selected are placed into a new card project, which you see in the Card tool. The themes available for the currently selected type of card are shown on a rotating selector.

Note

If you have Apple print your cards, which is usually the case, you need to be aware of the resolution and quality of the photos you are using. iPhoto monitors this and warns you if you use a photo that might not be of sufficient quality to print well.

4. **Click the type of card you want to create by clicking one of the following buttons, which are located at the top of the window:**

   - **Letterpress.** Letterpress cards contain design elements that are pressed into the paper so that they are raised, making a nice look and feel for the card. Like traditional cards, letterpress cards are made from a single sheet of paper that is folded to create four sides.

- **Folded.** This is the more traditional card type, which consists of one sheet that is folded to create four sides.

- **Flat.** A flat card is like a postcard; it has two sides with no fold.

When you choose a card type, you see the themes available for that type.

5. **If you select a Folded or Flat card, click the left or right category arrows just under the Type buttons to browse the various kinds of categories available, such as All to view all categories of cards, Holidays to see holiday-inspired cards, and so on.** When you make a selection, the themes available for that category appear.

6. **Preview a theme by clicking it.** The theme rotates to the center and comes into focus. You see the cover design for the card in the center window and the general layout of its sides at the bottom of the window, as shown in Figure 15.1. You see cost information for the selected theme in the lower-left corner of the window. This includes a single card price for all card types and the price per card for Flat and Folded cards you buy in groups.

7. **Preview themes until you find and select the one you want to use.**

15.1 Use the rotating selector to choose a theme for the card.

Genius

You can flip through the available themes by pressing the left- or right-arrow key.

Note

When you select the Letterpress type, you can click the Play button at the bottom of the window to see a video about this type.

8. **If you are creating a Flat or Folded card, choose the orientation of the card by clicking either the Landscape or Portrait button located just above the cost information.**

9. **If you are creating a Flat or Folded card, choose the background color for the card by clicking one of the color swatches located above the Create and Cancel buttons, as shown in Figure 15.2.**

10. **When you are pleased with your selections, click Create.** The card project is created and opens in the Card tool, and you are ready to design the card.

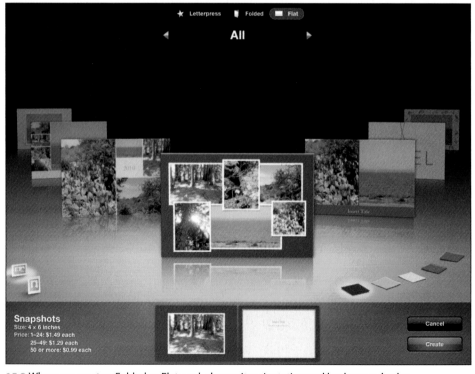

15.2 When you create a Folded or Flat card, choose its orientation and background color.

Note As you make changes, keep an eye on the cost information. Different options have different costs associated with them, and the cost may influence some of your choices. In addition to the basic cost of the card, consider the cost per card for multiple copies of the card.

Designing a Card

After you've created a card, you design it. To do this, you use iPhoto's Card tool. You lay out the card's photos and configure its text. You can also configure settings for a card and adjust its photos until the card is what you want it to be.

Working with the Card tool

The Card tool is shown in Figure 15.3. This tool provides functions that you can use to design all aspects of your card, including the photos and text it includes.

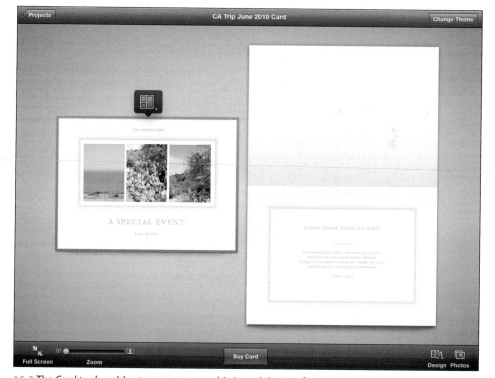

15.3 The Card tool enables to you create sophisticated designs for your card projects.

Genius

When you create a new card project, iPhoto automatically names it based upon the photos you selected. You can change the project's name by selecting the current name, shown at the top of the Card tool window, typing a new name, and pressing Return. You should use a name that will help you identify the card project in case you want to return to it in the future.

Some of the tool's main features are

- **Along the top of the tool, you see the name of the card project and the Change Theme button.** You can click Change Theme to change the settings you selected when you created the card.

- **In the center, you see thumbnails for each side of the card on which you can place content; for example, for a letterpress card, you have two sides to work with.** To work with a specific side, you select it. It becomes highlighted in a blue box. To change the size of the thumbnails, use the Zoom slider.

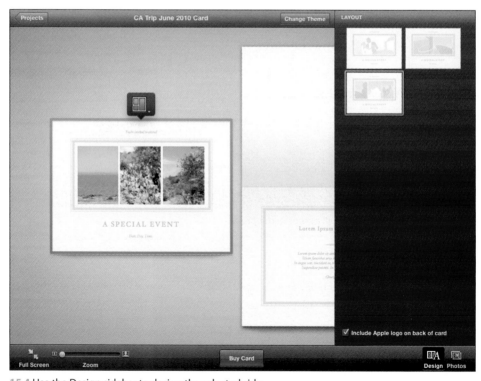

15.4 Use the Design sidebar to design the selected side.

◉ **The Card toolbar appears at the bottom of the window.** In addition to the Zoom slider, you see the Buy Card, Design, and Photo buttons. When you click the Design button, the Design sidebar appears and you see tools to design the side that is currently selected, as shown in Figure 15.4. When you click the Photos button, you see the Photos sidebar (as shown in Figure 15.5) where you see all the photos currently in the project; you use this to add photos or change the photos that appear on the card; think of this as a holding area for the card's photos.

15.5 The Photos sidebar shows all photos in the project.

Note The check mark next to a photo on the Photos sidebar indicates that the photo is currently placed in the card. If a photo doesn't have this check mark, it is available for you to place in the card, but currently isn't included in it.

Changing a card's overall design

You can change a card's type, theme, orientation, or background color at any time to restyle the card into a completely different project as follows:

1. **Click Change Theme.** The theme and type selector appears. This is the same as when you created the card initially, except that you aren't creating a new project, but are changing an existing one instead.

2. **Use the tools to change the card's type, theme, orientation, and background color.** These tools work just as when you created the card, too.

3. **Click Apply.** The card is redesigned according to the type, theme, and other selections you made.

Genius

When you change a card's type or theme, you are fundamentally changing the card and you might lose most, if not all, of any design work you have done. It's best to experiment with types, orientations, and themes early in the design process and settle on the options you will use for each before you invest too much time in designing the card.

Designing a side's background and layout

To configure a side's background and layout, perform the following steps:

1. **Select the side you want to design.**

Note

The theme and type you select for a card present different options on the Design sidebar. However, if you use these steps as general guidelines, you'll be able to quickly design any card type and theme because the basic process and tools are consistent across all types and themes.

2. **Click the Design button.** The Design sidebar opens. At the top of the sidebar, shown in Figure 15.6, you see the Background options; underneath that, you see the Layout tools. The currently applied options are highlighted in blue boxes.

3. **Click the background color you want to apply to the side.** You see the results on the side in the editing area.

4. **Use the orientation menu to choose Horizontal (Landscape) or Vertical (Portrait).**

Genius

Use the Zoom slider to make the side an appropriate size for editing. When you zoom in such that not all the side can be displayed on the screen, the Navigation box appears. This indicates the portion of the side you are seeing on the screen in a box. You can move the box around to change the portion of the side you are viewing.

15.6 This side has a horizontal orientation (landscape) and four photo frames, one of which is currently empty.

Genius

If you change a card's orientation, you need to consider the orientation of the photos included on it, especially if you have cropped any of them. When you change the card's orientation, you can affect its photos in ways you might not expect. Of course, you'll catch any issues when you proof the card later, but it's better to settle on these major types of design decisions earlier in the process.

5. **Choose the number of photo frames you want to appear on the side; or choose Text Page to include only a text block on the side.**

Genius

If you want to include a lot of text in a card, use the Horizontal orientation, make a side a Text Page, and choose the layout option that spreads the text across two sides.

6. **Click the layout option for the number of photos you selected.** The side's design is updated according to your selections. When you decrease the number of photos, the photos that are removed are still available to be applied to other sides. If you choose a layout with more photos, empty frames are added for each new photo; you can add photos to these (you learn how shortly).

7. **If you don't want the Apple logo to appear on the back of the card, deselect the check box.**

Genius

Some card designs have a side that contains only text. You can add photos to these sides by choosing the number of photos you want to include. The resulting layout options include both text and photo frames.

Designing the photos on a card

When you design the photos on a card, you can do the following tasks:

- Add photos to empty frames or replace the current photo in a frame.
- Remove photos from a frame.
- Position and zoom a photo within its frame.
- Apply effects to photos.

The tools you use to design photos in card projects are very similar as those you use to work with photos on pages of a photo book. The detailed steps to accomplish each of the photo design tasks in the previous list are provided in Chapter 14.

Configuring a card's text

Cards include text blocks in various places that you can fill with your own text and then format to match the look and feel you are going for. To configure a card's text, perform the following steps:

1. **Open a side containing a text frame.**

2. **Select a text frame.** It becomes outlined with a blue line and the text it contains is selected.

3. **Open the Design sidebar.** You see the text formatting tools, as shown in Figure 15.7.

Genius You should typically not work on text until you are happy with the card's layout and how the photos appear on each page because the text is usually dependent on those other elements.

15.7 Add text to and format text in text frames on your card.

4. **Type the text you want to include.** You can use iPhoto's text-editing tools to work with text just as they work in other Apple applications.

Genius You can write text in another application, such as a word processor, and then copy and paste that text into frames on a card. This is especially useful for cards with large text blocks.

5. **Format the text using the font, style, size, spacing, and other tools in the Design sidebar.**

Genius

To have iPhoto check your spelling as you type, choose Edit ⇨ Spelling ⇨ Check Spelling While Typing.

Proofing a Card

After you design a card, you should preview and edit it before you place an order for your custom cards.

Proofing with a PDF

First, create a PDF version of the document so you can preview it electronically:

1. **Open the Print dialog, open the PDF menu, and choose Save as PDF.**

2. **Choose a location and save the file.** A PDF version of the card is created.

3. **Open the PDF version.** It appears in the Preview application by default, as shown in Figure 15.8.

15.8 Be disciplined: Preview your card via PDF before you buy it.

4. **View the card.** If you find problems or want to make improvements, go back to the Design mode and make changes. Then create a new PDF and repeat the process until you are satisfied.

Note

Make sure you use a page size that is at least as large as the card or some of the card may be cut off and not useful for proofing.

Proofing with paper

When you are satisfied with your electronic review, commit the card to paper:

1. **Open the Print dialog, as shown in Figure 15.9.**

2. **Print the card.** Ideally, you can print the card on one sheet of paper.

3. **Fold the card.** If you printed the card on two sheets of paper, match them up back to back and then fold them to simulate a card.

4. **Review the printed card.** If you find problems or want to make improvements, go back to the card project and make changes. Then print a new copy and repeat the process until you are satisfied.

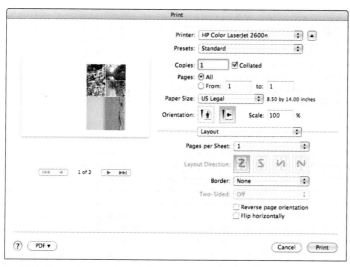

15.9 Printing a draft card can help you catch mistakes that you might miss looking at a PDF.

Identifying and solving photo resolution problems

When a photo is marked with the Caution icon (exclamation point within a yellow triangle), it might have a printing problem because of its resolution. You should fix photos with this problem before you order a card. If you don't, you might not be too happy with the card that is printed.

I address solving photo resolution problems in Chapter 14.

Note All projects, including cards, photo books, and so on, are stored in the PROJECTS section of the Source pane. You can return to a project at any time by selecting it on the Source pane.

Buying a Card

To order professionally printed cards, do the following:

1. **Select the card you want to order.**

2. **Click Buy Card.** iPhoto checks the card and reports any problems it finds, including missing photos or text and resolution problems. Fix those problems before proceeding. You can choose to ignore iPhoto's warnings, but I don't recommend this unless you are quite sure the problem being reported isn't really a problem. When there are no issues or you choose to continue anyway, you see the Your Order screen.

Caution If you buy a card that has mistakes, you don't get a refund. Take a few moments to check out the card completely before you click Buy Card.

3. **Type the number of cards you want to buy and the ZIP code where the cards will be shipped, and select the shipping method.** You see the estimated cost of the order, as shown in Figure 15.10.

4. **Click Check Out and follow the on-screen instructions to complete the purchase.** The printed cards will be delivered to the location you configure.

Note One of the great things about buying cards you create from Apple is that you get matching envelopes with the cards.

15.10 Ordering cards is easy, and they are delivered to any address you choose (move over Hallmark!).

Note   To delete a card, select it in the Source pane and press Delete. After you confirm your action, the card is removed from the PROJECTS section of the Source pane. Before you get rid of a card project, know that once you delete it, it's gone forever (well, it might still be available in a backup, as you see in Chapter 18).

How Can I Create Calendars?

Although many people use electronic calendars, there's still something nice about a paper calendar that hangs on a wall — it's even better if that calendar contains your own photos. While it might not be quite as practical and useful as an iCal calendar, many people enjoy the look and feel of these "old-fashioned" calendars. With iPhoto, you can design custom calendars and you can order professional prints of them so they are "wall worthy." Of course, iPhoto calendars make great gifts, but you might even want one for yourself.

Creating a Calendar

The first task in creating a calendar is to select the photos it contains and choose its theme. You can use any of your photos in a calendar. However, keep in mind the resolution of the photos you use. If you use a low-resolution image at a large size, it might print poorly. Fortunately, iPhoto warns you so you can replace low-resolution images with higher-resolution ones or you can use the lower-resolution image at a smaller size.

You can create a calendar that includes from 12 to 24 months. iPhoto's calendars typically have more than one picture per photo page, so you should plan on about 20 to 30 photos for a 12-month calendar, and add 3 or 4 more photos per additional month. As I'm sure you can guess, longer calendars are more expensive.

Calendar themes address the photo layout on the calendar's photo pages; text elements (such as titles and descriptions); and the style of the dates shown on the date pages, colors, and other design features.

Here's what you need to do to get started:

1. **Select the photos you want to include in the calendar.** The easiest way is to create a photo album for the calendar, add the photos you want to use to the album, and select the album. You can also select photos directly. The specific number of photos you need depends on the layout you select. You don't need to worry about getting exactly the right number, or even the right photos, at the start because you can always change the photos you use in a calendar during the design process.

Genius   You'll be able to design a calendar faster, with better results, if you organize its photos in an album first. It's easier to add, remove, and organize photos in an album than it is in a calendar project. In the album, arrange the photos in the general order you want them to appear in the calendar, from the top left for images appearing early on to the bottom right for those appearing later. Then select the album and create the calendar.

2. **Click Create.**

3. **Click Calendar on the resulting menu.** The photos you select are placed into a new calendar, which you see in the window. The themes available for the calendar are shown on the rotating carousel.

4. **Preview a theme by clicking it.** The theme rotates to the center and comes into focus. You see the cover design for the calendar in the center window and the general layout of its pages at the bottom of the window, as shown in Figure 16.1. You also see cost information for the selected theme in the lower-left corner of the window.

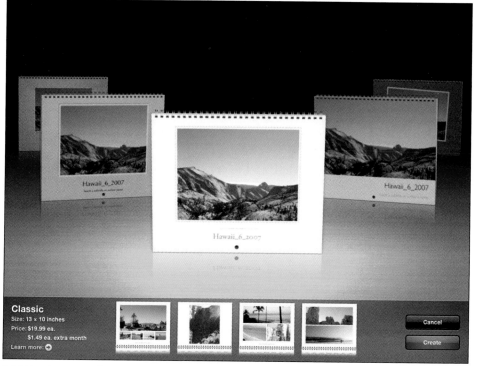

16.1 Use the carousel to choose a theme for the calendar.

Genius

You can flip through the available themes by pressing the left- or right-arrow key.

Note

As you make changes, keep an eye on the cost information. Different options have different costs associated with them; cost may influence some of your choices. In addition to the basic cost of the calendar, you see the cost per additional month (above the initial 12 months included by default).

285

5. **Preview themes until you find and select the one you want to use.**

6. **Click Create.** The Calendar configuration dialog appears, as shown in Figure 16.2.

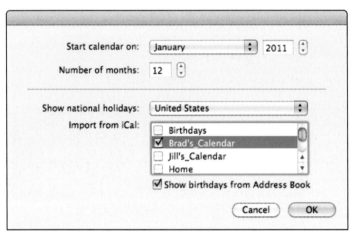

16.2 This dialog enables you to set the time frame for the calendar and add date information from your iCal calendars.

7. **Select the month and year in the Start calendar on pop-up menu and year field to configure the first month in the calendar.** You can start a calendar in any month and year (talk about personalized — how about a calendar that starts in February?).

8. **Select the number of months for the calendar you are creating in the Months box.** This can be up to 24 months.

9. **If you want national holidays to appear on the calendar, open the Show national holidays pop-up menu and choose the country whose national holidays you want to show.**

10. **If you want to include events on calendars you manage in iCal, select the check box for each iCal calendar you want to include.** When you include an iCal calendar, events on that calendar are shown on the event dates on the iPhoto calendar you are creating.

11. **If you want birthdays for your contacts in the Address Book application to be included on the calendar, select the Show birthdays from Address Book check box.**

12. **Click OK.** The calendar project is created. The photos you selected are automatically placed on the calendar's pages and the project appears in the Calendar tool.

Designing a Calendar

After you create a calendar, you design its pages. An initial design is created for you when you select a theme, so your job is to adjust that initial design until the calendar is what you want it to be.

Working with the Calendar tool

When you design a calendar, you use the Calendar tool, as shown in Figure 16.3.

16.3 The Calendar tool enables you to design the content and format of each page.

Some of the tool's main features are

⊙ **Along the top of the tool, you see the name of the project, the number of months, and the Change Theme button.**

⊙ **In the center, you see thumbnails for the covers, and each month shown in two-page spreads as they appear in the calendar.** To work with a specific page, you select it. It becomes highlighted in a blue box. You can scroll the pages using the scroll bar along the right side of the window. To change the size of the thumbnails, use the Zoom slider.

287

16.4 Use the Design sidebar to design the selected cover, photo page, or date page.

⊙ **The Calendar toolbar appears at the bottom of the window.** In addition to the Zoom slider, you see the Buy Calendar, Design, and Photos buttons. When you click the Design button, the Design sidebar appears and you see tools to design what is currently selected, such as the photo page or the date page, as shown in Figure 16.4. If you click the Photos button, you see the Photos sidebar (shown in Figure 16.5) where you see all the photos currently in the project; you use this to add photos or change the pages on which photos appear. Think of this as a storage area for the calendar's photos, both for photos used (placed) in the calendar and those in the project, but not included (unplaced) in the calendar.

Note

The check mark next to a photo on the Photos sidebar indicates that the photo is currently placed in the calendar. If a photo doesn't have this check mark, it is available for you to place in the calendar, but currently isn't included in it.

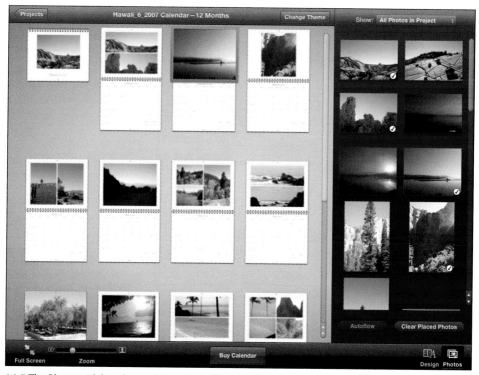

16.5 The Photos sidebar shows all the photos in the project.

Designing the overall look of a calendar

The Calendar tool does a lot of work for you as soon as you create a calendar. This includes automatically flowing the photos you selected on the pages of the calendar according to the theme you selected. The initial design might not be close to what you want the calendar to be, but most of the time, it provides a pretty good starting point. (If not, try changing the theme to see if you can find a better match for what you have in mind.)

The first order of business is to make sure the theme of the calendar is correct.

Scroll through the calendar's pages using the Zoom slider to focus in to see details, to get a sense of how the calendar flows. If some pages are not what you want, don't worry about them now; page design comes later. Your purpose here is to get the foundation right. Then you can smooth out all the details.

Changing a calendar's theme

The theme you chose when you created the calendar is only a starting point. If after reviewing the calendar, you aren't happy with its overall layout and look, you can change a calendar's theme at any time:

1. **Click Change Theme.** The theme selector appears. This is the same as when you created the calendar initially, except that you aren't creating a new project, but are changing an existing one instead.

2. **Select a new theme for the project.**

3. **Click Apply.** The calendar is redesigned according to the theme selection you made.

Genius

When you change a calendar's theme, you are fundamentally changing the calendar and you might lose most, if not all, of any work you have done on individual pages. It's best to experiment with themes early in your design process and settle on the theme before you invest too much time in your design work for individual pages.

Changing a calendar's settings

You can also change a calendar's settings; most of which are the same as when you created the calendar. To see these, deselect any selected pages and click the Design button. In the Design sidebar, you see three setting areas: MONTH SETTINGS, DAY SETTINGS, and STYLES.

Use the controls in the MONTH SETTINGS and DAY SETTINGS areas to change the number of months in the calendar, its start date, which events are imported from iCal, and so on. These are exactly the same as when you create a new calendar.

Genius

Like changing the theme, when you change the number of months included in a calendar, the calendar is redesigned to match the number of months you select. So, settle on these settings before moving into designing individual pages or you may end up reworking those pages.

Note

If you disable the Auto-Layout option, you have to manually design each page, and when you make a change that affects the flow of the calendar you have to make all the adjustments manually. If you want total control over the calendar and are willing to do the additional work involved, deselect this option. Most of the time, leaving it enabled makes the process more efficient and less tedious. You may also get better results.

Deselect the Auto-Layout pages check box if you don't want the Calendar tool to automatically lay out pages for you. Deselect the Include Apple logo at end of calendar check box if you don't want the Apple logo to appear on the back cover of the calendar.

Changing the order of pages in a calendar

You can move photo pages around within a calendar to change their order. Just drag the pages around the page browser until the photo pages in the calendar are in the order you want them to be; you are moving only the photo pages because the calendar pages remain in the order of their months.

To add pages to or remove them from a calendar, you change the calendar's time frame by adjusting its settings.

Note

Designing a calendar's pages

Once the basic layout and flow of the calendar is what you want, it's time to design each of the calendar's pages. The elements of the pages you design include:

- **Background.** This determines the background color or image over which the photos and text appear.

- **Layout.** This setting determines the number of photos on a page and how those photos are arranged on the page.

- **Photos.** You select, configure, and format the photos on each page. Photos in pages appear in frames; the number of frames on a page determines the number of photos placed there. You can change how a photo appears within its frame.

- **Text and dates.** You can type the text you want to appear in the calendar and then use its formatting tools to style that text. You can also enter or format date information on the calendar pages.

There are many options in each of these areas, and there's no way to cover them all in this short chapter. However, these tools follow a pattern, so once you see this pattern you can experiment with the tools to apply your designs to your own calendars.

The general steps required to design a calendar's pages are

1. **Double-click the page you want to design.** It appears in the editing area, as shown in Figure 16.6.

16.6 When you double-click a page, it fills the window and is ready for you to design.

2. **Click the Design button and use the Design sidebar to configure the page's background and layout (only photo pages have the LAYOUT tools; calendar pages don't have this option).**

3. **Configure the photos on the page by moving the existing photos around, replacing photos, or removing photos.**

4. **Select each photo on the page, position it in its frame, set the zoom level, and apply effects.**

5. **Type and format text and date information (calendar pages only).**

6. **Move to the next page you want to design and repeat the previous steps until you've designed all the pages in the calendar.**

As you work on a calendar, iPhoto saves your changes automatically.

Note

To move out of the edit mode, click the All Pages button in the upper-left corner of the window.

Following are examples of each of the general steps to show you how they work; you'll be able to apply the steps to the pages in your calendars.

Designing a page's background and layout

To configure a page's background and layout, perform the following steps:

1. **Double-click the page you want to design.**

2. **Click the Design button.** The Design sidebar opens. At the top of the sidebar, you see the Background options; underneath that, you see the layout tools as shown in Figure 16.6 when you select a photo page. When you select a calendar page, as shown in Figure 16.7, you only see the Background options. The currently applied options are highlighted in blue boxes.

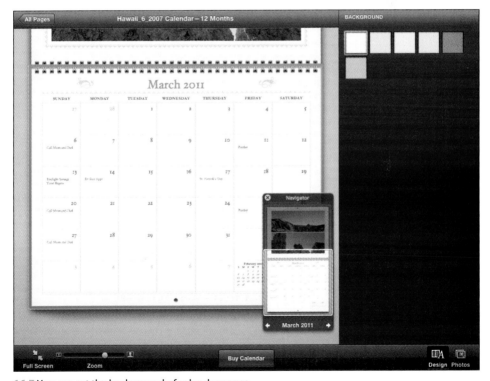

16.7 You can set the background of calendar pages.

3. **Click the background you want to apply to the page.** You see the results on the page in the editing area.

Genius

Use the Zoom slider to make the pages an appropriate size for editing. When you zoom in such that not all the page can be displayed on the screen, the Navigator box appears. This indicates the portion of the page you are seeing on the screen in a box. You can move the box around to change the portion of the page you are viewing. You can click the left- and right-facing arrows to move between months.

4. **When you design a photo page, on the Layout menu, choose the page's design by selecting the number of photos you want to appear on the page and the layout of the frames on the page.** You can choose from one to five photos. The layout you choose is applied to the page. When you decrease the number of photos, the photos that are removed are still available to be applied to other pages in the calendar. If you choose a layout with more photos, empty frames are added for each new photo; you can add photos to these (you learn how shortly).

Genius

If you select a photo page to edit, but Layout tools don't appear, close and open the Design sidebar to refresh the tools.

Configuring the photos on photo pages

When you design the photos on a photo page, you can do the following tasks:

- Add photos to empty frames or replace the current photo in a frame.
- Remove photos from a frame.
- Position and zoom a photo within its frame.
- Apply effects to photos.

Genius

To use the mirror image of a photo, open its contextual menu (by right-clicking or Control+clicking on it) and choose Mirror Image.

To add a photo to or replace a photo in a frame, do the following:

1. **Open the page containing the frame you want to change.** You see the page in the editing area.

2. **Click the Photos button.** The Photos sidebar appears. The Show menu at the top of the sidebar determines the photos you see in the sidebar. The options are

- **All Photos in Project.** When this is selected, you see all the photos in the project, whether or not they are placed.

- **Placed Photos.** This shows you only the photos currently in the calendar.

- **Unplaced Photos.** This shows you the photos in the project, but not in the calendar.

- **Recents.** At the bottom of the menu, you see the four options in the RECENT section of the Source pane, which are: the last event you viewed, the photos you most recently imported, the photos you imported in the last *X* months, and flagged photos.

When you make a selection on the menu, the thumbnails in the sidebar update accordingly. When you choose a source for photos included in the calendar, the placed photos are marked with a check mark. If you point to a placed photo, you see the pages on which it is placed and if you pause for a second or two, you see information about the photo, as shown in Figure 16.8.

16.8 The Photos sidebar enables you to add photos to a calendar.

You aren't limited to working with the photos included in the calendar project when you created it. To add photos to the calendar, find the photo you want to add and drag it onto the project's icon in the Source pane. The photo is added to the calendar; choose the Unplaced Photos option on the Show menu to see photos you've added (photos you add aren't placed automatically).

3. **Find the photo you want to use.**

4. **Drag the photo from the sidebar onto the frame where you want it to be placed; when the frame is highlighted, release the mouse button, as shown in Figure 16.9.**
If the frame was empty, the new photo fills it. If there was a photo there, the new photo replaces it.

16.9 To add a photo to a frame, drag it from the photo browser onto the frame.

When you select a photo on a page, it appears on the Photos sidebar even if the sidebar has to scroll to show it.

Genius

296

To remove a photo from a frame, do the following:

1. **Open the page containing the frame you want to empty.**

2. **Select the frame.**

3. **Press Delete.** The photo is removed from the frame and from the calendar page, but it remains in the calendar project so you can use it elsewhere.

Configuring individual photos on pages

To position and zoom in or out on a photo within its frame, do these steps:

1. **Select the frame containing the photo you want to position.** Its frame is highlighted and the Zoom slider appears, as shown in Figure 16.10.

2. **Drag the slider to the left to zoom out or to the right to zoom in.**

16.10 Zoom in or out and position a photo within its frame so the part of the photo you want to appear on the calendar is shown.

3. **Drag the photo within the frame so the portion you want to see is shown.**

4. **Repeat Steps 2 and 3 until the photo appears as you want it to within the frame.**

You can apply effects to photos as follows:

1. **Select the photo to which you want to apply an effect.**

2. **Click the Design button.** The Design sidebar appears with tools that you use to change the photo, as shown in Figure 16.11.

16.11 You can apply effects to photos in your calendar.

Note

If you click the Edit Photo button, you move into Edit mode and can edit the photo using iPhoto's Editing tools, which are explained in Chapter 8.

3. **Click the effect you want to apply.**

Note

Effects you apply don't actually change the image itself, just the instance of the image in the calendar. When you make changes by editing the photo using the Edit tools, you do change the photo everywhere it is used.

Adding text to or changing text in date boxes

If you included iCal calendars, national holidays, or birthdays from Address Book in your calendar, the text associated with those items is placed on the related dates automatically. You can manually add text to any date box, such as to note an event that isn't on one of the iCal calendars you included. You can also format text in the date boxes, whether it was imported from iCal or you typed it. Here's how:

1. **Move to and click the date box to which you want to add or format text.** It opens in a text box and you see any existing text, such as text that was imported from iCal.

2. **Open the Design sidebar.** You see the text formatting tools, as shown in Figure 16.12.

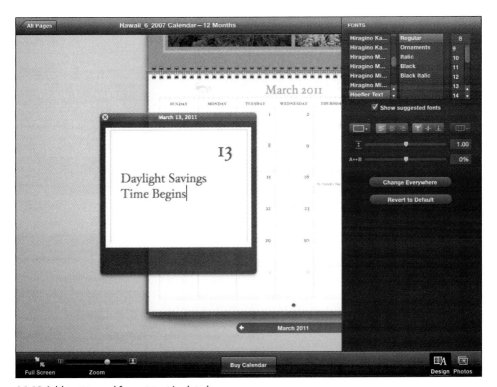

16.12 Add text to and format text in date boxes.

Genius

You can return to the default formatting for the text's type by clicking Revert to Default.

3. **Select text you want to format.**

4. **Use the formatting tools in the Design sidebar to change the font, spacing, alignment, and other formatting elements.**

5. **To apply that formatting to all the text in the calendar of the same type, click Change Everywhere.** For example, if you select text imported from an iCal calendar, you can change the formatting for that kind of text throughout the calendar.

6. **Type more text and format it, as shown in Figure 16.13.**

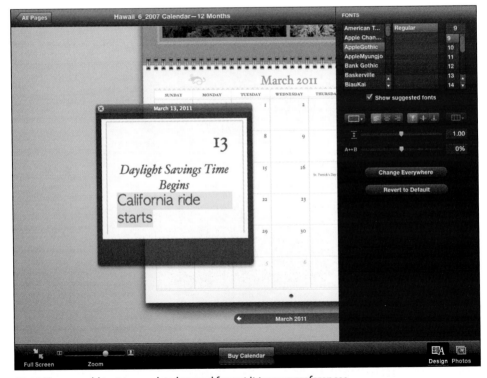

16.13 You can add text to any date box and format it to your preferences.

Note

If you format or add text such that it doesn't fit in the date box, iPhoto flags it with a caution icon. You need to fix these issues before ordering a calendar.

7. Move through the calendar and make the text in its date boxes what you want.

You can write text in another application, such as a word processor, and then copy and paste that text into frames on a calendar's pages. You can also use the Mac's standard text editing tools such as the Spell Check on the calendar's text.

Configuring the text on the calendar's cover

Calendars have text on their covers, and by default, iPhoto names the project based on the photos you selected, such as the name of the album. This might not be what you want the title of the calendar to be. To configure the text on the calendar's cover, edit the cover and select the text. Type the calendar's title in the text box and format it using the pop-up formatting tools, as shown in Figure 16.14 or open the Design sidebar to use its formatting tools.

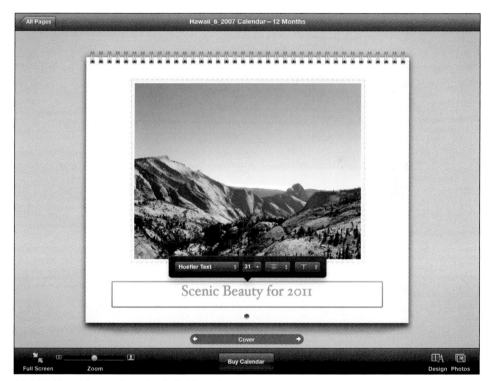

16.14 Add and format the calendar's title on its cover.

Genius The calendar's title is not related to the name of the calendar project. If you want to change the project's name, select it at the top of the iPhoto window and edit it.

Finishing a Calendar

After you design each page in the calendar, you're almost finished, but some of the most important work remains. Now is the time to polish your calendar to make sure you'll be completely happy with it when you it's printed. You need to proof your calendar to find and fix mistakes or to make improvements. If some of the photos in your calendar have a resolution that's too low to print well, you need to correct those problems before ordering the calendar. You should also check for text issues.

Proofing a calendar

After you design a calendar, you should preview and edit it before you order a copy. First, create a PDF version of the document so you can preview it electronically:

1. **Open the Print dialog.**

2. **Open the PDF menu and choose Save as PDF.**

Note

Make sure you use a page size that is at least as large as the pages in your calendar or some of the pages may be cut off and not useful for proofing.

3. **Choose a location and save the file.** A PDF version of the calendar is created.

4. **Open the PDF version.** It appears in the Preview application, or whichever application you use as your default PDF reader, as shown in Figure 16.15.

5. **View the calendar.** If you find problems or want to make improvements, go back to iPhoto and make changes. Then create a new PDF and repeat the process until you are satisfied.

When you are happy with the PDF version, you might want to print a version as a draft with your desktop printer. This often exposes issues that aren't apparent when you view a calendar on-screen. Review the printed version carefully, and use iPhoto to fix any mistakes you find.

Genius

Don't skimp on the proofing process. If you print a calendar that has mistakes, you don't get a refund. It's up to you to make sure the calendar is worth the cost to get it printed professionally.

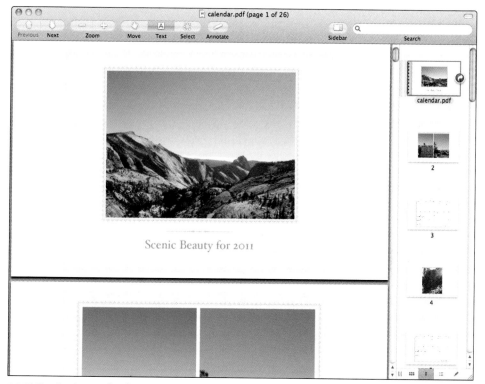

16.15 Previewing a calendar via PDF before printing it saves time and money.

Fixing photo resolution problems

When iPhoto encounters a photo that might have a printing problem because of its resolution, the photo is marked with the Caution icon. You should explore and fix such problems before you order a calendar as this might indicate that the photo will not print very well in the final product. You can correct such issues with one or more of the following techniques:

- **Zoom out so more of the photo is included within its placeholder.** This increases the amount of information displayed on the page and improves the quality of the printed version.

- **Use the image in a smaller placeholder.** You can move the image to a smaller place-holder or add more photos to the page so its current placeholder becomes smaller.

- **If the image has been cropped, remove the cropping.** Edit the image and choose Photos ⇨ Revert to Original. The image is restored to full size, which means more information is in the placeholder.

- **Apply effects to or adjust the image to distort it.** You can apply effects to a photo, such as converting it to Sepia Tone or use the editing tools to turn the saturation way up, to disguise a lower-quality image. This doesn't correct the resolution issue, but might artistically hide the problem.

If none of these approaches solves the issue and the image is important to you, you can print the calendar with the image as it is. It might not look as good as other photos on the calendar, but if you feel the photo is essential to your calendar project, it might be worth the risk.

Fixing text problems

When the text in a date box doesn't fit, iPhoto flags it with the Caution icon. You can address this problem several ways:

- **Edit the text in the box.** When you remove enough text so that the remaining text fits, the Caution icon disappears. This technique is most useful for occasional text problems.

- **Change the text format.** Use the text formatting tools to adjust the format so it fits into its box.

- **Remove iCal information.** Use the calendar settings to remove iCal calendars or other information. The previous text is replaced using the new settings. If you reduce the included iCal information sufficiently, some of the text cautions may be cleared.

Buying a Calendar

To buy a professionally printed and bound version of the calendar, do the following:

1. **Select the calendar you want to order.**
2. **Click Buy Calendar.** iPhoto checks the calendar and reports any problems it finds, including missing photos, text issues, and so on. Fix those problems before proceeding. When iPhoto doesn't find any issues, you see the Your Order screen, as shown in Figure 16.16.

Note
The ZIP code you type on the Your Order screen is only to estimate shipping charges. You can set a delivery address in a different ZIP code later in the purchase process.

3. **Configure the purchase and delivery options on the Your Order screen.**

4. **Click Check Out and follow the on-screen instructions to complete the purchase.**
   This includes typing your existing Apple ID or creating a new Apple ID to order calendars and configuring other options, such as where the calendar will be shipped. The printed calendars will be delivered accordingly.

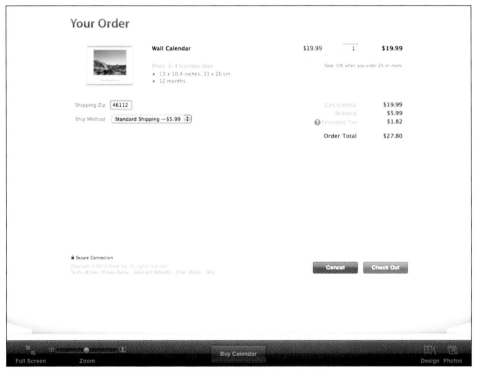

16.16 Use the Your Order screen to set the quantity you want to buy along with the ZIP code where the calendar will be shipped.

Note

To delete a calendar, select it in the Source pane and press Delete. After you confirm your action, the calendar is removed from the Source pane. Before you get rid of a calendar project, know that once you delete it, it's gone forever (well, it might still be available in a backup as you see in Chapter 18). Of course, the photos it contains are not affected.

What Else Can I Do with Photos?

f you use it for any length of time, I'm sure you agree that iPhoto is an amazing application. It enables you to do many fun and creative projects with your photos along with more mundane, but equally important, things such as keeping your photos organized. In this chapter, you find a number of useful iPhoto tasks that help you squeeze even more value out of the application.

Sharing Photos on a Local Network

If you have more than one Mac on a local network, and who doesn't these days, you can share the photos in your iPhoto library with any of the people on the network and vice versa. Sharing includes viewing each other's photos and photo albums, as well as copying photos between libraries.

Sharing your photos on a local network

To enable other people to access your photos, you need to share them on the network. To configure iPhoto to share your photos on the network, follow these steps:

1. **Press ⌘+, (comma).** The iPhoto Preferences dialog opens.

2. **Click the Sharing tab.**

3. **Select the Share my photos check box.**

4. **Configure the photos you want to share with one of the following options:**

   - **Share entire library.** Select this radio button to share all the photos in your library on the network.

   - **Share selected albums.** Select this radio button and then select the check boxes next to the photo albums you want to share on the network to limit access to only the photos in those photo albums.

Note

Your current sharing status appears at the bottom of the Sharing tab.

5. **Type in the source name that people sharing your photos will select to view them in the Shared name field.** The name you type appears in the SHARED section of the iPhoto Source pane on the other computers running iPhoto.

6. **To require others to use a password to access your photos, select the Require Password check box and type the password in the Require password field, as shown in Figure 17.1.** If you require a password, don't forget to tell people whom you want to be able to access your photos what the password is!

7. **Close the Preferences dialog.** iPhoto begins sharing your photos according to the settings you entered.

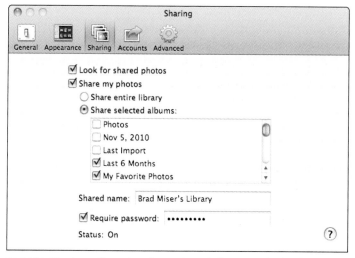

○ ○ ○   Sharing

General Appearance Sharing Accounts Advanced

☑ Look for shared photos
☑ Share my photos
　　○ Share entire library
　　● Share selected albums:
　　　☐ Photos
　　　☐ Nov 5, 2010
　　　☐ Last Import
　　　☑ Last 6 Months
　　　☑ My Favorite Photos

Shared name: Brad Miser's Library
☑ Require password: •••••••••
Status: On   ⑦

17.1 This Mac is configured to share selected albums on the local network, but viewers need a password to access photos.

Accessing photos being shared with you on a local network

Accessing photos being shared with you is a two-part process. First, configure your Mac to look for shared photos. Second, access those shared photos.

To configure your Mac to look for shared iPhoto libraries, do the following:

1. **Press ⌘+, (comma).** The iPhoto Preferences dialog opens.

Note

A Mac has to be running (not asleep), connected to the network, and iPhoto has to be open for its shared photos to be available.

2. **Click the Sharing tab.**

3. **Select the Look for shared photos check box.**

4. **Close the Preferences dialog.** iPhoto mounts any shared libraries under the SHARED section in the Source pane.

To access photos being shared with you, do this:

1. **Expand the SHARED section of the Source pane if it is collapsed.** If a single iPhoto library is being shared with you, it appears directly under the SHARED section. If more than one library is available to you, you see the Shared Photos source.

2. **Expand the Shared Photos source.** You see icons for each computer sharing photos. If an icon includes a lock, that means the library is shared with a password, which you have to have to be able to view its contents.

Note   If you fail to type the correct password for a shared source three times in a row, the shared source disappears from your Source pane. Restart iPhoto to see the source again.

3. **Select the library whose photos you want to view.** If it is password protected, you are prompted to type its password. If not, skip to Step 5.

4. **Type the source's password and click OK.** If you type the password correctly, the shared source is enabled. If not, you're prompted to type it again.

5. **If a shared source has photo albums, click its expansion triangle to see them.** The shared source opens and you see the albums it is sharing underneath its icon.

6. **Select the album whose photos you want to view.** The photos appear, as shown in Figure 17.2.

When you work with a shared source, keep the following points in mind:

- **You can view a shared source's photos just like you view the photos in your library.** For example, you can select an album and click the Slideshow button to view those photos in a slideshow.

- **You can drag photos from the shared source to your library to copy them onto your computer.** The photos you drag are imported into your library similarly to how they are imported from other sources.

- **You can't view projects, such as slideshows, greeting cards, and so on, on your computer.** However, you can view the photos in those projects on your computer.

- **You can mount between one and five shared sources at the same time.** You can work with a specific shared source by selecting it.

- **You can remove a shared source from your Source pane by clicking its Eject button.** The shared source disappears from your Source pane. If you don't change your sharing settings, the shared source comes back the next time you restart iPhoto. You typically would only need to do this if you want to share more than five sources; if you already have five shared sources, you have to eject one of the current ones to add another.

17.2 Photos stored on a different computer on the same network appear just like photos stored in your iPhoto Library.

Printing Photos

It should be no surprise that you can print photos from iPhoto. You can do it two ways: You can print them directly from iPhoto to a printer to which you have access, or you can order prints from Apple.

Each method has its benefits. Printing photos on your printer is fast and convenient, and you can probably get pretty high-quality photos. Having Apple print photos will likely yield higher-quality results at less cost than printing them yourself. And you can have photos that Apple prints for you shipped to any location.

Each method also has its downsides. Printing them yourself can be a hassle because you will probably need to experiment with combinations of print settings and paper to get the best results. And printing photos yourself is likely to be more expensive than having Apple print them. The downside of having Apple print them is that you have to wait from the time you order the prints until you have them in your hands.

Printing photos using your own printer

Most modern printers, whether they are ink jet or color laser, can print very good-quality photos.

To print your photos quickly, perform the following steps:

1. **Select the photos you want to print.** You can select an album to print all its photos or you can select photos directly.

2. **Press ⌘+P.** The Print sheet appears, as shown in Figure 17.3. In the left pane, you see the styles of prints that iPhoto provides. For example, Standard prints one photo per page, Contact Sheet prints multiple small versions of the photos on one page, and so on.

17.3 Use the Print sheet to configure how you want selected photos to print.

3. **Select the style of prints you want.** An example of the style you selected appears in the right pane of the sheet. You also see how many pages will be printed.

4. **Configure your printer's settings using the controls at the bottom of the sheet.** Your options depend on the specific kind of printer you use.

5. **Click Print.**

You can tackle more complex print projects by using the Custom print option. Here's how:

1. **Select the photos you want to print.**

2. **Press ⌘+P.** The Print sheet appears.

3. **Click Customize.** A new print project is created and the Printing source in the RECENT section of the Source pane appears, and you see the tools that you can use to completely configure and print your photos, as shown in Figure 17.4. At the top of the window, you see the browser. It has two tabs: the Photos tab (lower), which enables you to browse the photos included in the print job, and the Pages tab (upper), which enables you to browse the pages of the print job (which are the photos plus any settings and effects you've applied). You see the current page selected in the Page browser at the top of the window. Here, you can edit the design of the print page. At the bottom, you see the Print toolbar.

4. **Use the features of the Print project tool to configure and print the print job.**

The Print project tool works similarly to the photo book, calendar, and greeting card tools. For space reasons, I won't go into the details of using each option. So refer to Chapters 14, 15, and 16 to learn the details of how those tools work. For a summary of the Print project tools, read on:

- **Print Settings.** Click this button to open the Print sheet.

- **Themes.** This button/menu enables you to choose the type of printing you want to do. The same options are in the Print sheet, and include Contact Sheet, Standard, and so on.

- **Background.** This menu enables you to apply backgrounds to the photos.

- **Borders.** This menu enables you to choose the borders that surround each photo you print.

Note

Unlike other projects, you can only have one print project at a time, so you need to complete one before you can start another.

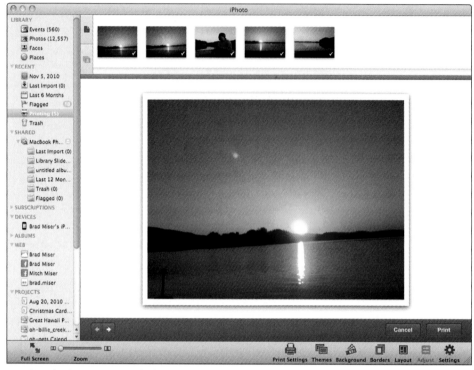

17.4 Use the Print project tool when you want to go beyond simple photo printing.

- **Layout.** This menu gives you different options for the number and layout of photos depending on the theme you select.

- **Adjust.** This tool enables you to adjust various properties of the photos you print, such as contrast, exposure, and so on.

- **Settings.** This tool enables you to set the fonts for titles, choose the number of photos per page, and other options.

- **Print.** This button sends the print project to the printer.

Ordering prints of photos from Apple

Buying prints from Apple is inexpensive and easy, and you'll probably get better quality than you can by printing them yourself. Here's how to order prints:

1. **Select the photos you want to print.**

2. **Choose File ⇨ Order Prints.** The Order Prints screen appears, as shown in Figure 17.5.

Caution If a size option is marked with the Caution icon (an exclamation point within a yellow triangle), the photo doesn't have a high enough resolution to print well at that size. You can still order the print, but you might not be pleased with the results.

3. **Choose the quantity of each size of each photo you want to print.** As you configure the order, the total cost is shown in the lower-right corner of the dialog.

4. **Click Buy now.** You move to the Your Order screen.

5. **To get an estimate of the shipping cost, type the ZIP code to which you are going to ship the prints (this is optional) and click Check Out.**

6. **Follow the on-screen instructions to complete the order process.** You sign into your Apple Store account using an Apple ID and provide shipping and payment instructions to complete the order. The prints are delivered directly to the address you indicate on your order.

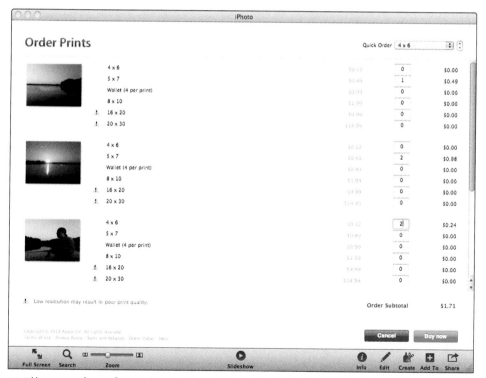

17.5 You can order professional prints of your iPhoto photos via Apple's Print Service.

Emailing Photos

Email is a great way to share your photos with other people. With iPhoto's built-in email function, it's also very simple.

Configuring email accounts in iPhoto

To send emails using iPhoto, configure the email accounts through which you want to email by performing the following steps:

Note If you use Apple Mail, iPhoto picks up your email accounts from that application. Just verify that the account you want to use is configured correctly.

1. **Open the Preferences dialog.**
2. **Click the Accounts tab.** If the email account you want to use already appears on the accounts list, you are ready to use iPhoto to send email through it. If not, continue these steps.
3. **Click the Add (+) button at the bottom of the accounts list.**
4. **Click Email.**

Note If MobileMe is configured on your Mac, you shouldn't need to add its account as iPhoto should pick it up automatically. If not, click MobileMe and type the member name and password for the account or just choose MobileMe in Step 6 and follow the rest of these steps.

5. **Click Add.**
6. **Click the type of email account you want to add, such as Gmail.** A sheet with fields applicable to the kind of account you select appears.
7. **Complete the fields on the sheet and click OK.** You need to type the same information that you would in an email application, and it depends on the type of account you are adding and your specific information. When the account appears on the accounts list, you can use it to send email from iPhoto.

Genius If you are already using the account in an email application, you can copy the information you need from its account configuration screens.

Emailing photos with iPhoto

Here's how to send your photos quickly and easily:

1. **Select the photos you want to email.**

2. **Click the Share button.**

3. **Choose Email on the resulting menu.** The photos you selected are pasted onto a new email message. In the right pane of the window, you see the themes you can choose for the message.

4. **Click the theme you want to use.** The message is reformatted accordingly.

5. **Complete any text fields that appear in the message.** Each theme has a set of text placeholders that you should fill with your text. See Figure 17.6 for an example.

17.6 When you select a template for an email message, iPhoto adds text placeholders that you fill with your text.

6. **On the Photo Size menu, choose Optimized to resize the photos for optimal email transmission or Actual to leave them at their native size.**

317

7. **Address the message, update the subject (if needed), and choose the account from which you want to send the message on the From menu (if you have more than one email account configured).**

8. **Click Send.** The email message and photos are sent. When the process is a complete, you see a status message indicating the number of photos that were emailed.

Genius

Most email gateways limit the file sizes attached to email messages. In many cases, this limit is 5MB, but almost all systems limit email messages to 10MB or less. You can see the size of the photos you have added to an email message at the bottom of the message window. If you want to share photos that are larger than these limits when they're combined, use another technique, such as sharing via MobileMe or in an iWeb Web site.

Emailing photos with other applications

You can email photos with any email application that supports attachments, and of course, all of them do. The general steps to do this are

1. **Export the photos you want to send (refer to the next section).**

2. **Create a new email message in the application you want to use.**

3. **Use that application's tools to attach the exported figure files to the message.** In most cases, you can drag the files from the location where you exported them into the new message window.

4. **Complete and send the message.**

Like emailing photos with iPhoto, you need to be aware of the file size limitations many email systems place on attachments. Generally, you should keep the total file size to 5MB or less, but some email systems will accept up to 10MB of file attachments.

Exporting Photos as Files

There are some instances where you will want to export photos from iPhoto to your desktop. For example, you might want to use a photo in a document. To do this, you export the photo from iPhoto and it becomes a file on your desktop. Then you can import it into another application. To export photos as files, follow these steps:

1. **Select the photos you want to export.**

2. **Choose File ⇨ Export.** The Export Photos dialog appears.

3. **Click the File Export tab, as shown in Figure 17.7.**

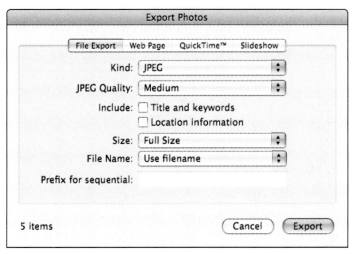

17.7 The Export Photos dialog enables you to select the type of files you create and to configure their quality.

4. **Set the type of file you want to export using the Kind pop-up menu.** The options are Original, Current, JPEG, TIFF, or PNG. The Quality pop-up menu updates to reflect the type of file you selected in the previous step.

5. **Choose the level of quality for the files you are exporting on the Quality pop-up menu.** The options on the menu depend on the file format you've selected. As always, you trade off image quality for file size. The higher the quality of the files, the larger the file sizes will be.

6. **Select the Title and keywords and Location information check boxes if you want that information associated with the exported files.**

7. **Choose the size of the images you want to export using the Size pop-up menu.** The options are Small, Medium, Large, Full Size, or Custom. If you select Custom, the Export Photos dialog expands so you can set a specific size.

8. **Choose how you want the files to be named using the File Name pop-up menu.** The options are Use title, Use filename, Sequential, or Album name with number.

9. **If you select Sequential file names, type the prefix for the sequence in the Prefix for sequential field.**

10. **Click Export.** The Save sheet appears.

11. **Choose a save location for the files and click OK.** The photos are exported as files to the location you selected.

Using Photos on Your Desktop

Your Mac desktop has a desktop photo that serves as the background for your work. You can use your iPhoto photos as your desktop photo. You can set the desktop photo from within iPhoto or you can set more advanced options in the System Preferences application.

Setting a desktop photo using iPhoto

To set a desktop photo from within iPhoto, do the following:

1. **Select the photo you want to use as your desktop picture.**

2. **On the iPhoto menu bar, choose Share ⇨ Set Desktop.** The photo you selected becomes your desktop photo on your primary display.

Note

If you have two displays, you must use the System Preferences application to set the desktop picture on the second display. So there's really no reason to use the iPhoto function when you have more than one display.

Setting desktop photos using the System Preferences application

To use the System Preferences application to set your desktop pictures, perform the following steps:

1. **Open the System Preferences application and click the Desktop & Screen Saver icon.** The Desktop & Screen Saver pane appears.

2. **Click the Desktop tab.** The Desktop picture tools appear, as shown in Figure 17.8. You can select pictures for your desktop from the sources of images that appear on the left.

3. **Expand the iPhoto source.** At the top of the list are events from your iPhoto library followed by albums, so that you can choose any images in your iPhoto library to use as desktop pictures. You can also select the Photos item to see all the photos in your iPhoto library.

4. **Select a source of images in the left pane of the window, such as an iPhoto photo album.** Thumbnails of the images in that source appear in the right pane of the window. At the top of the window, the current desktop in the small image well appears (unless you have the Change picture option selected). At the bottom of the pane are the controls you use to fine-tune your desktop pictures.

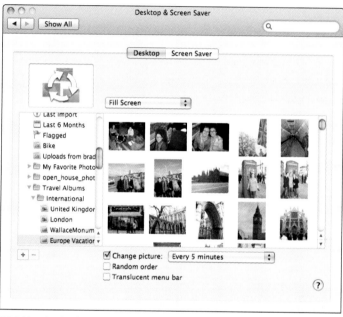

17.8 Use the Desktop tab of the Desktop & Screen Saver pane of the System Preferences application to configure your desktop photos.

5. **Click the image that you want to apply to the desktop.** The image fills the desktop and you see it in the image well at the top of the Desktop pane.

6. **Use the pop-up menu at the top of the window to choose how you want photos to be scaled to the desktop.** Choose Fit to Screen to have photos scaled down so that they fit the screen. Choose Fill Screen to have photos scaled to fill the screen, Stretch to Fill Screen to make the photo fill the desktop, Center to center the image on the desktop, or Tile to have images that are smaller than the desktop fill the desktop space as tiles.

7. **If the image doesn't fill the screen, click the Color button that appears to the right of the menu when it can be used (it is enabled only when the options selected allow it).**

8. **When it appears, use the Color Picker to choose the background color that appears behind photos when they don't fill the desktop.**

9. **To have the image change automatically, select the Change picture check box.** The image in the image well is replaced by the recycle symbol.

10. **On the Change picture pop-up menu, choose how often you want the picture to change.** Select one of the following options: when logging in (a new picture is selected each time you log in to your user account), when waking from sleep, every 5 seconds, every minute, every 5 minutes, every 15 minutes, every 30 minutes, every hour, or every day.

11. **If you want images to be selected randomly instead of in the order they appear in the source, select the Random order check box.** A new image from the selected source becomes your desktop photo according to the timing you selected.

12. **To make the menu bar translucent, so you can see the desktop picture behind it, select the Translucent Menu Bar check box.** With this option deselected, the menu bar becomes a solid color.

If you have multiple displays, you see a Desktop pane for each display, as shown in Figure 17.9. They can be configured separately so each display has its own desktop picture settings.

17.9 When you have multiple displays, each display has its own Desktop Picture pane.

Subscribing to Photo Feeds

Many photo Web sites and other sources provide photo feeds that inform you about and provide updates in iPhoto based on events that occur at the source, such as when the photos on a site are updated. You can subscribe to these feeds in iPhoto so you can work with the photos they provide.

To subscribe to a photo feed, you need the URL for the photo feed to which you are going to subscribe. You have to get this at the source. Most sites provide a URL for this purpose.

Once you have the URL you need, subscribe to the feed as follows:

1. **Copy the feed's URL.**

2. **Choose File ➪ Subscribe to Photo Feed or press ⌘+U.** The Subscribe sheet appears, as shown in Figure 17.10.

    Enter photo feed address (URL) to subscribe to:

    Cancel   Subscribe

    17.10 You can subscribe to a photo feed by pasting its URL into this sheet.

3. **Paste the URL into the field.**

4. **Click Subscribe.** The feed to which you subscribed is added to the Subscriptions section of the Source pane. You can select the feed to see the photos it contains. As the source changes, the feed will update the subscribed source in iPhoto.

Note Some sites, such as Flickr, offer a Subscribe to link that you can use to add a subscription to iPhoto.

What Can I Do to Protect My Photos?

It's said that a picture is worth a thousand words, but the photos in your iPhoto library are literally priceless. That's because they can't be re-created at any price. If they get lost or damaged, they are gone forever, with no hope of recovery. Kind of a scary thought, isn't it! Fortunately, with a few simple and relatively painless tasks, you can protect your photos so that you don't ever have to face this irrevocable loss.

Understanding Options for Protecting Your Photos

There are a number of ways to safeguard your photos, and you should use at least a couple of them; using all of them is an even better idea. Because of their value to you, you shouldn't rely on just one method to protect your photos. Each method you learn about in this chapter has its own benefits, as well as requirements you need to meet to use them.

When you consider how you'll protect your photos, the easier the options are to implement and the less you have to do, the better. That's because doing the kind of tasks you learn about in this chapter isn't particularly fun and not necessarily what you allot time for in your day. However, you don't want to let these tasks slip down your priority list, unaddressed until that very bad day when you discover your photos are permanently gone. The less hassle a method is, the more likely you will do it consistently, so that even your most recent photos are protected.

Following is an overview of the protection methods covered in this chapter:

- **Protecting your Mac.** Because your iPhoto library is stored on your Mac, taking care of your Mac is an important part of safeguarding your photos.

- **Using Time Machine.** With Mac OS X's Time Machine, you can automate the backup process so that it occurs without your having to even think about it, as shown in Figure 18.1. When your iPhoto library is included in your backups, you can easily recover your entire iPhoto library or even individual photos should you accidentally delete them.

- **Using iPhoto DVDs.** You can burn your iPhoto photos onto DVDs for safekeeping. This method has a number of benefits that make it one to consider using, especially if you can store your backup DVDs away from your computer.

- **Using iDVD DVDs.** When you put iPhoto slideshows onto iDVD projects, you can save all the figure files onto the DVD, from which they can be restored when needed.

- **Using photo books and prints.** Hard copies of your photos, in photo books or in prints, can be a fail-safe method for at least some of your photos. (It's unlikely that you will print every photo you have.) While this method is better than not having any kind of backup, it has a number of problems, the most of important of which is that the backed-up photos are not digital.

- **Using other options.** Some other options are worth considering though there isn't room in this chapter to provide details about them.

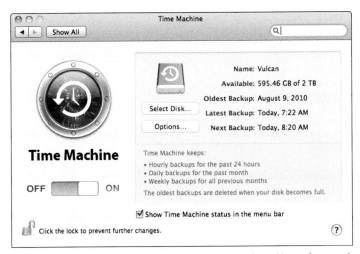

18.1 It's wise to use Time Machine to back up your iPhoto library frequently.

Protecting Your Mac

Your iPhoto photos live on your Mac and you use your computer to access them. Part of protecting your photos, therefore, is to protect your Mac. In the following sections, you learn about some of the most important things you can do to guard your Mac, and thus the iPhoto library stored there.

Keeping Apple software current

Mac OS X itself is the most important software you need to keep current because it determines how well your Mac runs, and to a large extent, how secure its data is. The good news is that Mac OS X includes the Software Update tool, which makes keeping both Mac OS X and your Apple applications, such as iPhoto, current simple and easy. You can configure Software Update so that it checks for and downloads updates automatically by performing the following steps:

1. **Open the System Preferences application.**

2. **Click Software Update.** The Software Update pane appears, as shown in Figure 18.2.

3. **Click the Scheduled Check tab if it isn't selected already.**

4. **Select the Check for updates check box.**

5. **On the Check for updates pop-up menu, choose how frequently your Mac checks for updates by selecting one of the options:**

   - Daily

   - Weekly

   - Monthly

327

I don't recommend selecting Monthly. Choose Daily or Weekly to ensure your Mac's software is updated frequently.

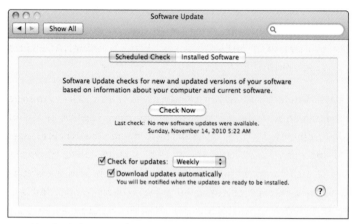

18.2 Use the Software Update pane to configure your Mac to update its Apple software automatically.

6. **If you want updates to be downloaded automatically, select the Download updates automatically check box.** Updates include those that affect your system and have the most impact on its security. I recommend that you select this check box so these updates are downloaded as soon as they are found. If you don't select this check box, you're prompted to download updates when they are available.

7. **Quit the System Preferences application.** When the specified amount of time passes, Software Update checks for new software. When it finds new versions, it downloads them automatically and then prompts you to allow them to be installed, or to be downloaded and then installed.

Protecting your Mac from Internet attacks

The largest and most significant computer threat is attacks from the Internet. These attacks can take many forms, including using your computer to launch other attacks, attempts to steal your information and your identity, and attempts to damage your data for no other reason than to wreak havoc. However, with some basic precautions, you can defend yourself from these attacks fairly easily.

When you are using your home network, you should shield your Mac from Internet attacks through an AirPort Base Station. When you are using networks outside of your control, such as one available in public places, you should use the Mac OS X firewall to prevent unauthorized access to your computer.

Using a base station to shield your Mac

You can protect the computers on your local network from attack by placing a barrier between them and the public Internet. You can then use a Dynamic Host Configuration Protocol (DHCP) server that provides network address translation (NAT) protection for your network, or you can add or use a hub that contains a more sophisticated firewall to ensure that your network can't be violated. A benefit to these devices is that you can also use them to share a single Internet connection.

One of the easiest and best ways to protect machines on a local network from attack and to share an Internet connection is to install an AirPort Extreme Base Station, Time Capsule, or AirPort Express Base Station. These devices provide NAT protection for any computers that obtain Internet service through them, and for most users, this is an adequate level of protection from hacking. That's because the addresses of each computer on the network are hidden from the outside Internet. The only address exposed is the one that is assigned to the base station by the cable or Digital Subscriber Line (DSL) modem. This address is useless to hackers because there isn't any data or functionality exposed to the Internet from the base station.

Note   For help configuring an AirPort Base Station, see *MacBook Pro Portable Genius, 2nd Edition* (Wiley, 2009).

Using the Mac OS X firewall to shield your Mac

You can also configure the Mac OS X firewall to protect your Mac from Internet attack. You can use this in conjunction with a base station, but it is especially important when you are using your Mac outside of your network, such as when you travel and connect to various networks in public places, hotel rooms, and so on. In most cases, these networks are configured to limit access to your computer (similar to how a base station shields it), but you can't and shouldn't count on this. Instead, protect your Mac with its firewall by performing the following steps:

1. **Open the System Preferences application.**
2. **Click the Security icon.** The Security pane opens.

Note   If the Lock icon at the bottom of the window is locked, you need to click it and authenticate yourself as an administrator to be able to change the firewall settings.

3. **Click the Firewall tab.**
4. **Click Start to activate the firewall.** The firewall begins running with default settings.

329

Note

As soon as you turn the firewall on, you may start getting prompts asking if applications should accept incoming connections. Carefully review these prompts, and if you recognize and are using the application allow the connection. If not, deny it.

5. **To further configure the firewall, click the Advanced button.** The Advanced sheet appears, as shown in Figure 18.3.

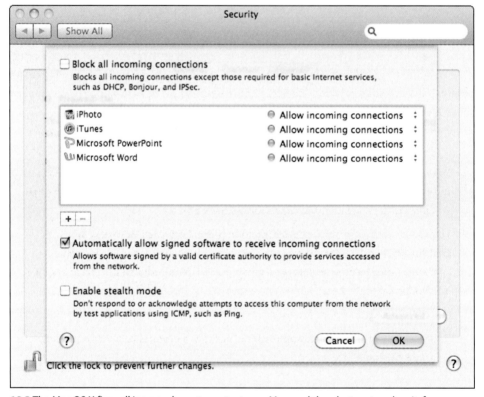

18.3 The Mac OS X firewall is a good way to protect your Mac, and the photos stored on it, from Internet attacks.

6. **To block all incoming connections, select the Block all incoming connections check box.** If you select this, no applications will accept incoming connections, and some of those might not work correctly. Use this option when you want to "tighten down" your Mac as much as possible.

7. **To configure how specific applications interact with incoming connections, do one of the following actions:**

   ○ **Add an application to the list.** Click the Add button (+) and select the application you want to add to the list. Use the application's menu to configure its firewall settings.

   ○ **Configure an application's connection permissions.** Each application on the list has a menu that you use to set incoming connection permissions for the application. The options are Allow incoming connections or Block incoming connections. If you block incoming connections, some applications might not work correctly.

Note

When you allow an application to accept incoming connections at the prompt described previously, it is added to the list.

   ○ **Remove an application from the list.** To apply default firewall settings to an application, select it on the list and click the Remove button (-).

8. **To allow applications that have been verified through the "signature" process to receive incoming connections automatically, select the Automatically allow signed software to receive incoming connections check box.**

9. **To prevent your Mac from responding to requests from the network, select the Enable stealth mode check box.** Your Mac will not respond to requests it receives. Some functionality might not work correctly with this feature enabled, but it does apply an additional layer of security for your computer.

10. **Click OK.** The Advanced sheet closes.

11. **Quit the System Preferences application.** The firewall protects your Mac in accordance with your configuration.

Protecting your Mac from viruses

Due to the extensive media hype about viruses, you are likely to be keenly aware of them. Although many viruses are relatively harmless, some can damage your machine and potentially your photos as well. In the past, the Mac OS was used by such a small percentage of overall computers, the Mac platform was a less desirable target for virus creators and was relatively immune from serious virus threats. As its market share has increased over the past several years, viruses could become a larger threat. Even so, you are much more likely to be attacked and suffer greater damage from an Internet-based attack than you are a virus. However, you still need to be aware of them and protect your Mac accordingly.

When it comes to viruses, the old cliché "an ounce of prevention is worth a pound of cure" applies. The main way to avoid viruses is to avoid files that are likely to have viruses in them. Following are some practices you should follow to limit the chances that your Mac will become infected:

● **Find and use a good antivirus software program; keep the virus definitions for that application up to date.**

● **Be wary when you download files from any source, particularly email.** Even if an email is apparently from someone you know, it doesn't mean the attachments it contains are safe. Some users will unknowingly transmit infected files to you (especially beginning users). Some viruses can use an email application to replicate themselves. Before you open any attachment, be sure it makes sense given who the sender appears to be and that the attached files appear to be something you would expect to receive from the sender.

● **When you download files, download them from reputable sites, such as magazine sites or directly from a software publisher's site.** These sites scan files for viruses before making them available so your chances of getting an infected file are lower.

● **After you download a file, run your antivirus software on it to ensure that it isn't infected.** Most programs let you designate the folder into which you download files and automatically check files in this folder.

Using Time Machine to Protect Your Photos

You can use Mac OS X's Time Machine to back up your iPhoto library (and other important files) with minimal effort on your part; in fact, once you set it up, the process is automatic. And Time Machine makes recovering files you've lost easy and intuitive.

The Time Machine software is built into Mac OS X. The only thing you need to add to your system to make backing up with Time Machine a reality is an external hard drive.

Time Machine uses this hard drive to back up your data for as long as it can until the backup hard drive is full. It stores hourly backups for the past 24 hours. It stores daily backups for the past month. It stores weekly backups until the backup drive is full. Once the drive is full, it deletes the oldest backups to make room for new backups. To protect yourself as long as possible, use the largest hard drive you can and exclude files that you don't need to back up (such as System files if you have the Mac OS X installation DVD) to save space on the backup drive.

To use Time Machine, you need to gain access to an external hard drive and then configure Time Machine. You should also know how to use Time Machine to restore files should you need to.

Obtaining and installing an external hard drive

To use Time Machine, you need to be able to store data on an external drive. You can accomplish this with the following options:

- **Time Capsule.** This Apple device is a combination AirPort Extreme Base Station and hard drive, as shown in Figure 18.4. With capacity options of 1TB and 2TB, you can gain a lot of backup storage space. Additionally, a Time Capsule is also a fully featured AirPort Base Station, so it makes an ideal backup drive for any computer connected to the AirPort network it provides. The downside of Time Capsule is that it is more expensive than a standard hard drive, but if you don't already have a modern AirPort Base Station, it is slightly less expensive than buying a base station and hard drive separately. When you use a hard drive for Time Machine, its icon on the desktop and in Finder windows becomes the Time Machine icon.

18.4 Apple's Time Capsule is useful as a backup drive for your Mac, and it is also an AirPort Base Station.

Genius

It's best if you don't use a backup hard drive for any purpose beyond backing up your data. You want to keep as much space available for your backups as possible. You can share a backup drive among multiple computers, but if you do this, make sure it is a very large drive.

Note

Ideally, your entire Home folder is included in your backup so that your most important data, including iPhoto photos, iTunes content, and your documents, are protected.

- **A hard drive connected through USB (Universal Serial Bus), FireWire, or FireWire 800.** You can use a hard drive directly connected to your Mac as a backup drive. This provides the fastest performance of any option, and hard drives are inexpensive and easy to configure.

- **A shared hard drive.** You can back up to a hard drive that you can access via File Sharing over a local network. This is the least desirable option because it's likely the hard drive will be used for other purposes, too.

You can connect a Mac to a Time Capsule wirelessly as part of an AirPort network or you can connect the two with an Ethernet connection. For help with this task, see *MacBook Pro Portable Genius, 2nd Edition* (Wiley, 2009).

To use an external hard drive, simply connect the drive to your Mac and power it up. In most cases, you're prompted to configure Time Machine with the new drive.

Note

At this time, Time Machine doesn't support backing up to a hard drive connected to an AirPort Extreme Base Station, which would be a very convenient option. Hopefully, a future software update will provide this capability. You can't use Time Machine to back up to an iPod, either.

Configuring Time Machine to back up your photos

After you gain access to a backup hard drive, you can configure Time Machine to back up your data. In an ideal world, your backup hard drive is large enough so that you can copy the entire drive onto the backup so you can restore any file on your machine. However, unless you have a relatively small amount of data on your computer or a very large hard drive, making a complete backup will limit the time for which backup data is stored. So you might want to exclude certain files, such as system software files that are on the installation DVD, to make your backups smaller so that they can be stored longer.

To configure Time Machine, perform the following steps:

1. **Choose Apple menu ⇨ System Preferences.**

2. **Click the Time Machine icon.** The Time Machine pane opens.

3. **Drag the slider to the On position.** Time Machine activates and the Select drive sheet appears.

4. **Select the drive on which you want to store the backed-up information.** If you've connected an external hard drive to your Mac, select it. If you're connected to a Time Capsule, select that.

5. **Click Use for Backup.** The sheet closes and you return to the Time Machine page. The drive you selected appears at the top of the pane and the timer starts the backup process, which you see next to the Next Backup text.

6. **Click the Stop button (X) next to the Next Backup text.** This stops the backup process so you can configure it more specifically.

7. **Click Options.** The Do not back up sheet appears. This sheet enables you to exclude files from the backup process. You can exclude files you have saved in other ways to conserve space on the backup drive. For example, you can exclude the System Files and Applications as long as you have the Mac OS X installation DVD and the installers for your applications. If you have a large backup drive, don't exclude any files so you have a complete backup. This is the ideal case, and if it is your situation, you can skip to Step 13.

   However you configure the options, make sure that you are including the Pictures folder within your Home folder because that is where the iPhoto files reside.

8. **Click the Add button (+).** The select sheet appears.

9. **Move to and select the folders or files you want to exclude from the backup.**

10. **Click Exclude.**

11. **If you selected system files, click Exclude System Folder Only to exclude only files in the System folder or Exclude All System Files to exclude system files no matter where they are stored.** If you exclude system files, you should exclude them anywhere they are stored.

12. **Repeat Steps 8 through 11 until you've excluded all the files you don't want to be part of your backup.**

13. **If you want be warned as old backups are removed from the backup, select the Warn when old backups are deleted check box.** This is a good idea because it lets you know when your backup drive fills up.

14. **Click Done.** You return to the Time Machine pane. The timer starts and when it expires, the first backup is created. You can see the progress of the process in the progress bar. From then on, Time Machine automatically backs up your data to the selected hard drive. New backups are created every hour. You can see the status of your backups in the top-right corner of the Time Machine pane, as shown in Figure 18.5.

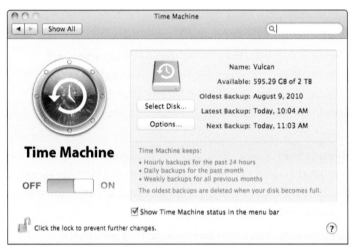

18.5 You see information about your Time Machine status on the Time Machine pane of the System Preferences application.

15. **Select the Show Time Machine status in the menu bar check box.** This puts the Time Machine menu on the Finder menu bar, making managing your backups easier and more convenient.

16. **Quit the System Preferences application.**

Caution

Is Time Machine perfect? It's close, but there are some things you need to be aware of. Hard drives can fail, and if your backup drive fails, it is no longer protecting your photos. If you don't discover this until you need to restore them, you'll be out of luck. That's why you shouldn't rely on Time Machine as your only protection against the loss of your photos.

Managing your Time Machine backups

Time Machine backups happen automatically, but to ensure things are working properly, consider a few simple suggestions:

- **Open the Time Machine pane of the System Preferences application.** You see information about the status of your backups. Keeping an eye on drive space helps you know how far back in time you'll be able to go, and the date of the oldest backup tells you exactly how far back in time you've gone.

- **As the backup drive gets full, you see warnings when old backups are deleted.** You need to make sure that there aren't files in the old backups that you might need at some point. This can happen if you delete a document or folder from your Mac but don't restore it for a long time. Eventually, the only copy left might be in the oldest backup that gets deleted when the hard drive gets full.

- **When your backup system has worked for a while, check the status of the hard drive you are using.** If it is filling up rapidly, consider removing some of the system and application files that might be part of it to reduce the space required. The most important files to protect over a long period of time are those you've created, changed, or have purchased, not the least of which are your photos.

- **If there are files you want to keep, but don't use any more, consider moving them onto a DVD or CD for archival purposes.** Then delete them from your Mac's hard drive, and over time they'll be removed from the backups or you can exclude them from Time Machine to reduce the amount of drive space required.

- **Test your backups periodically to make sure things are working properly by attempting to restore some files (explained in the next section).** If you don't discover a problem until you need to restore important files, it is too late, so make sure your backup system is working properly. Create a couple of test files and let them exist long enough to get into your backups (at least one hour assuming you are connected to your backup drive). Delete some of the files and empty the Trash. Make and save changes to some of the test files. Then, try to restore both the deleted files and the original versions of the files you changed. If you are able to restore the files, your data is protected. If not, you have a problem and need to resolve it so that your data isn't at risk.

- **Use the Time Machine menu on the Finder menu bar to quickly access commands and information.** At the top of the menu, you see the date and time of the most recent backup. You can use the Back Up Now command to start a backup at any time, such as immediately after you import new photos into iPhoto. Select Enter Time Machine to restore files. Select Open Time Machine preferences to move to the Time Machine pane of the System Preferences application.

Using Time Machine to restore your photos

If you only have to use the information in this section to test your backups, it's a good thing. However, there may come a day when you need to use this information "for real" to recover your photos. You might have accidentally deleted a photo or realized you wanted a previous version. Or something might have gone haywire on your Mac and you lost some photos.

The reason this function is called Time Machine is that you can use it to "go back in time" to restore files that are included in your backups. You can restore files and folders from the Finder and you can recover your photos from within iPhoto.

Use the following steps to recover photos in iPhoto:

1. **Open iPhoto.**

2. **Launch the Time Machine application by doing one of the following:**

   - Clicking its icon (the clock with the arrow showing time moving backward) on the Dock

   - Double-clicking its icon in the Applications folder

   - Choosing Time Machine menu ⇨ Enter Time Machine

   The desktop disappears and the Time Machine window fills the entire screen. In the center of the window is the iPhoto window, as shown in Figure 18.6. Behind it are all the versions of that window that are stored in your backup, from the current version as far back in time as the backups go. Along the right side of the window is the timeline for your backups starting with the current day and moving back in time as you move up the screen. At the bottom of the screen is the Time Machine toolbar. In the center of the toolbar is the time of the window that is currently in front. At each end are controls you use to exit Time Machine (Cancel) and the Restore button (which is active only when you have selected a file or folder that can be restored).

3. **Move back in time by:**

   - **Clicking the time or date on the timeline when the photos you want to restore were available.** The higher on the timeline you click, the farther back in time you go. As you point to lines on the timeline, you see the date and time the backup was saved. When you click a time and date, the iPhoto windows roll back to the time and date you selected.

- **Clicking the back arrow (pointing away from you) located just to the left of the timeline.** Each time you click, you move back one backup. Click the forward arrow (pointing toward you) to move to more recent backups.

- **Clicking an iPhoto window behind the front one.** You move back to the window as it was at that time.

As you move back in time, you see the versions of the window that are saved in the backup you are viewing and the date and time of the backup in the center of the toolbar.

4. **Use the iPhoto controls to move to the photos you want to restore.**

5. **Select the photos you want to restore.**

6. **Click Restore.** The photos are returned to iPhoto and you can use them as if they'd never been lost.

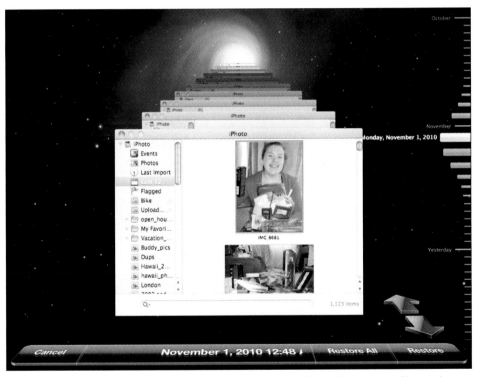

18.6 Using Time Machine, you can go back to the version of your iPhoto library where files you have lost were available.

To restore all the files in the front window, click Restore All.

Restoring files from the Finder isn't that much different than restoring files from within iPhoto. You launch the Time Machine application and move to the version of the Finder window that contains the files you want to restore. Select the files and click the Restore button. They are returned to their original location.

Using DVDs to Protect Your Photos

Using a backup application such as Time Machine is the way to go because it automates the process for you. This means that your backups are more likely to be current. (An outdated backup is not much better than no backup at all.)

However, you can burn your iPhoto photos to DVD as another way to back up your photos. This method is good because you can store the DVDs away from your Mac; this way, if something happens to your Mac, your backups won't be harmed. It is also inexpensive because all you need is the DVD media you'll use to store the files on. Even though you might need quite a few DVDs, it won't cost you a lot.

However, this method has a couple of significant downsides. The most important is that it is a manual process, which means you have to rely on yourself to remember to update your backups as you make changes in iPhoto. This reduces the chances that your backups will be current at all times. The second downside is that if you have a large iPhoto library (and eventually you will), you have to burn parts of your library to different DVDs.

Nevertheless, I recommend burning your iPhoto library to DVD to supplement your backups (rather than using it as a primary backup method).

Preparing a large iPhoto library for DVD

Single-layer DVDs hold only about 4.7GB of data while dual-layer DVDs hold about twice as much. It is likely that your iPhoto library will be larger than that at some point if it isn't already. In this case, you need to organize your library into segments that fit onto a single DVD. Because photos are always associated with time frames, using the years with which photos are associated is a good way to segment your library into chunks that will fit on a DVD. Create a Smart Album for each period you want to put on DVD. Here's how:

1. **Create a Smart Album with the conditions set to be a few years at a time, as shown in Figure 18.7.** (For help with Smart Albums, see Chapter 6.) After the Smart Album is created, all the photos in that time frame are contained in it.

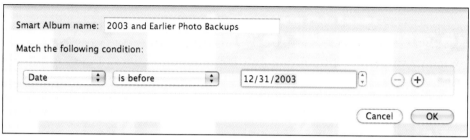

18.7 A Smart Album based on date is a good way to segment your iPhoto library so each segment fits on a DVD.

2. **Test the segment by attempting to burn the DVD.** (See the section on burning your iPhoto library to DVD for the details.)

3. **If the segment is too large, edit the Smart Album so it spans less time and so has fewer photos.**

4. **Repeat Steps 1 through 3 until you have a set of Smart Albums that include all the photos in your iPhoto library, as shown in Figure 18.8.**

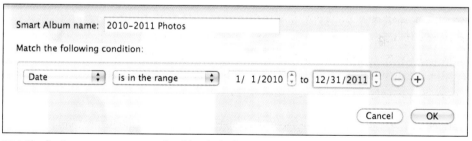

18.8 The final segment you create should include the current time period and one some distance into the future.

Burning your iPhoto library to DVD

Putting your iPhoto library on DVD doesn't take a lot of thought, but it can take a lot of time:

1. **Select the source you want to back up on the Source pane, as shown in Figure 18.9.** If you had to segment your library, select the first segment you need to back up.

18.9 Here, I've selected the last segment of my library, which is called "2010-2011 Photos."

2. **Choose Share ⇨ Burn.** The Burn sheet appears. You are warned that the DVD you burn is only useable in iPhoto. Because you use iPhoto, that should be fine with you. You're also prompted to insert a DVD.

3. **Insert a blank DVD and click OK.** iPhoto moves into Burn mode and you see the burn tools above the iPhoto toolbar. If you have more photos than will fit on a DVD, you see a disc full message, in which case you need to adjust the source so it fits on a DVD.

4. **Type a name for the DVD.** Use the same name as the source, as shown in Figure 18.10.

5. **Click Burn.** The Burn Disc dialog appears.

6. **Click Burn.** The burn process starts and you see progress messages in the iPhoto window. When the process is complete, the DVD is ejected.

7. **Repeat Steps 1 through 6 until you've burned all the segments of your library onto DVDs.**

8. **Label the DVDs and put them in a safe place.**

18.10 The Burn toolbar, which appears just above the iPhoto toolbar, shows the selected photo album fits onto a DVD.

Updating your iPhoto library on DVD

You need to keep your backups current. This means each time you make significant changes to your library, you need to back it up again. If you've segmented your library based on date, you need to burn the photo album for the current time period each time you add photos or make other changes to your library.

Restoring your photos from DVD

If the day comes when you need to restore photos, you simply import the photos from your backup DVDs:

1. **Insert the backup DVD into your Mac's drive.** The DVD is mounted on the desktop.

2. **Choose File ➪ Import to Library.** The Import Photos dialog appears.

3. **Select the iPhoto Library on the DVD, as shown in Figure 18.11.**

343

18.11 To restore files from your backups, import them from an iPhoto DVD.

4. **Click Import.** The files are moved into your iPhoto library.

5. **Repeat Steps 1 through 4 until you have restored all the photos from your backup.**

Genius

When you insert a DVD burned with iPhoto, it is mounted and appears on the Source pane. You can move photos from the DVD into your library by selecting the disc, pressing ⌘+A to select all the photos it contains, and then dragging the photos onto the Photos source. This copies the photos from the DVD into your library.

Using iDVD DVDs to Protect Your Photos

If you use iDVD to create DVDs with iPhoto content on them, they also serve as a backup for your photos. Make sure you enable the data files to be written to DVDs you create so that you can get back to the original files along with the slideshows themselves.

Backing up photo files on an iDVD DVD

Follow these steps to back up files on an iDVD DVD:

1. **Create the slideshow in iPhoto.**

Note

For help creating slideshows, see Chapter 13.

2. **Select the slideshow.**

3. **Choose Share ➪ Send to iDVD.** The slideshow is sent to iDVD, where it is added to a new project, as shown in Figure 18.12.

4. **Double-click the slideshow.** Its configuration menu opens.

5. **Click the Settings button.** The Settings sheet appears, as shown in Figure 18.13.

6. **Select the Add image files to DVD-ROM check box.**

7. **Click OK.**

8. **Burn the DVD.**

18.12 When you add a slideshow to an iDVD project, it appears on the DVD's main menu.

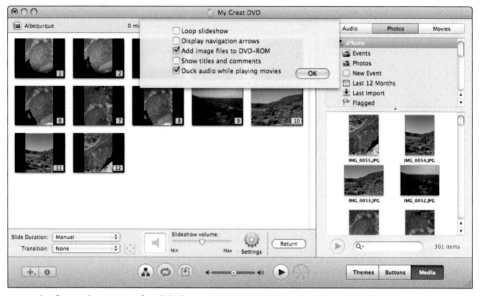

18.13 Configure the settings for slideshows on an iDVD DVD so that the image files are saved on the DVD.

Restoring photo files from an iDVD DVD

To recover files from an iDVD DVD, do the following:

1. **Insert the iDVD DVD into your Mac's drive.** The DVD is mounted on the desktop.

2. **Choose File ⇨ Import to Library.** The Import Photos dialog appears.

3. **Move to the folder for the slideshow on the DVD.**

4. **Select all the files in the image folder.**

5. **Click Import.** The files are restored to your iPhoto library.

Using Photo Books and Prints to Protect Your Photos

Earlier in this book, you learned how to print photos, photo books, calendars, and other projects, as shown in Figure 18.14. While I don't recommend relying on printed versions of photos and projects as true backups, they do provide some level of protection in case of a catastrophic loss of your Mac and other backups.

18.14 Ordering a photo book is one way to back up photos.

The benefit of paper backups is that you probably create them for other purposes, such as to enjoy your photos, so there's no additional work or expense to use them as backups. Another benefit can be if you've sent hard copies of your projects to other people; these are sort of like an off-site backup.

There are many downsides to paper as a backup. The biggest is that your backups aren't digital; you lose the benefits digital photos bring. Another is that you are unlikely to print all your photos, so it is not a complete backup.

Understanding Other Options for Protecting Your Photos

A couple of other backup options are worth mentioning as potential components of your backup system.

Using Apple Backup

If you are a member of MobileMe, you can download and use Apple Backup at no additional cost. This application enables you to configure backups in a more sophisticated way than you can with Time Machine, and you have many more options for storing your backups, including hard drives, online disk space, DVD, and so on. You can use multiple methods at the same time with scheduling so that you can mix and match methods to ensure you always have your files protected. For example, you can schedule frequent primary backups to a hard drive and less frequent backups to DVD. Both can be on a schedule so they either happen automatically or you are at least prompted to make sure they get done.

If you are a member of MobileMe, you can download the Backup application by opening the Software folder on your iDisk.

Genius

If you are a member of MobileMe, you can use Backup to back up files to your online iDisk storage. This protects your data because it is stored away from your Mac and you can automate the process — both of these are major advantages for this option. The limitation to this that your iDisk has a relatively small amount of disk space (20GB by default, up to 60GB with upgrades) for backup purposes. But you can choose to protect critical files, such as your photos, on this space even if you can't store all your backups there.

Using online backup services

You can use a number of online backup services to back up your data to remote servers. This keeps your backups away from your Mac, which means they are protected even if something happens catastrophically with your Mac and backups. Generally, you open an account with these services, install the software that manages the backup process for you, and configure that software. The backups happen automatically after that, which is a very good thing.

The downside of these services is that you have to pay a fee to use them, though that annual fee is usually only a few dollars per month. Backing up using these services is very slow because you are copying the data over the Internet. Because the process happens in the background, it won't stop you from doing what you want, but it can dramatically slow down the performance of your network. The other downside is that to recover your files, you usually have to request the files on DVD, which means there could be a several-day lag before you can restore your files.

If you aren't able to routinely store backups in another location, consider using a backup service because storing the backups in a second location substantially improves your level of protection.

Index